Advance Praise for

Ten Dollars in My Pocket

"This memoir offers a captivating portrait of U.S. society in the early postwar years through the perspective of a sensitive and keenly perceptive young woman survivor of the Holocaust. The intertwining of a story of personal maturing with a difficult and humorously told acculturation process unfolds in a riveting way. Ample quotations from diaries and letters of that time give the remembered story an extraordinary immediacy."

Walter H. Sokel, Commonwealth Professor Emeritus,
University of Virginia

"The reader enters the author's archives of personal letters and diaries, travelogues, published first impressions of America, and highly relevant documents for a life starting anew. Interspersed with retrospective reflections, as intimate as self-critical, they show a courageous young woman conquering a bewildering but ultimately welcoming new world. Sharply drawn portraits of a most diverse cast of characters, from fellow immigrants and the working world of New York City to such distinguished teachers as Vladimir Nabokov and René Wellek, make this a memoir of irresistible vitality."

Sigrid Bauschinger, Professor Emeritus,
University of Massachusetts

Ten Dollars in My Pocket

PETER LANG
New York • Washington, D.C./Baltimore • Bern
Frankfurt am Main • Berlin • Brussels • Vienna • Oxford

Elizabeth Welt Trahan

Ten Dollars in My Pocket

The American Education of a Holocaust Survivor

A Memoir in Documents

PETER LANG
New York • Washington, D.C./Baltimore • Bern
Frankfurt am Main • Berlin • Brussels • Vienna • Oxford

Library of Congress Cataloging-in-Publication Data

Trahan, Elizabeth Welt.
Ten dollars in my pocket: the American education of a Holocaust
survivor: a memoir in documents / Elizabeth Welt Trahan.
p. cm.
Includes bibliographical references.
1. Trahan, Elizabeth Welt. 2. Jews—United States—Biography.
3. Holocaust survivors—United States—Biography.
4. Jews, Austrian—United States—Biography. I. Title.
E184.37.T737A3   940.53'18092—dc22   [B]   2006023023
ISBN 0-8204-8693-0

Bibliographic information published by **Die Deutsche Bibliothek**.
Die Deutsche Bibliothek lists this publication in the "Deutsche
Nationalbibliografie"; detailed bibliographic data is available
on the Internet at http://dnb.ddb.de/.

Cover design by Sophie Boorsch Appel

The paper in this book meets the guidelines for permanence and durability
of the Committee on Production Guidelines for Book Longevity
of the Council of Library Resources.

© 2006 Peter Lang Publishing, Inc., New York
29 Broadway, New York, NY 10006
www.peterlang.com

All rights reserved.
Reprint or reproduction, even partially, in all forms such as microfilm,
xerography, microfiche, microcard, and offset strictly prohibited.

Printed in Germany

Dedicated to the memory of the many friends and mentors who appear on those pages but are no longer with us. All of them, even those who crossed my path only briefly, have left a valuable imprint, and I thank them for it.

Table of Contents

Acknowledgments ix

Part One: New York (1947–1949) 1

Part Two: Sarah Lawrence (1949–1951) 93

Part Three: Cornell (1952–1953) 155

Part Four: Yale (1953–1956) 229

Acknowledgments

My special appreciation goes to Eva Schiffer who most generously provided advice and assistance for my project, to Paula Horowitz whose enthusiasm for its conception encouraged me to persevere, and to Walter Sokel and Sigrid Bauschinger for their thoughtful and constructive criticism. I would also like to express my gratitude to Dr. Heidi Burns for expressing her confidence in my writing ability even before seeing the entire manuscript.

Since this autobiographical account draws not only on diary entries, letters, publications and documents, but also on personal memories and reflections, some references to or descriptions of events and locales may be approximations. However, all persons appearing in the account are real, even though some names were changed.

Marine Marlin, 1947
Photograph by Hans Graf, Hamburg

PART ONE

New York
(1947–1949)

1.

    Friday evening—

        Listen to the wind
        wafting and blowing
        forward and on.

        The ship's hull is heavy and full,
        the wind breaks against its walls,
        blows through your hair,
        sweeps your eyes clean,
        softens the cheeks' fear—
        and inexorably pushes you on.

        On into what is all movement,
        on into what is pure will,
        where there's no looking back
        and where one cannot stand still.

        Hold on to the ship,
        hold on to its walls,
        look back my eyes,
        keep shoulders tall.

        This wind, do you feel the wind?
        The land, do you see it drift?
        The sea, in its eternal shift—
        never will it stand still!

        There is no spot that's my own,
        no thing to cling to any more,
        no word to welcome me home.

        How can one find oneself in this flux,
        how can one ever find a firm shore?"

It isn't much of a poem nor do I recall writing it, but the handwriting is definitely mine, and I knew immediately when and where I must have composed it: in July 1947, the American troopship SS Marine Marlin *was taking us displaced persons or "D.P.s" as we were classified and, after initial reluctance, called ourselves as well,* ins Land der unbegrenzten Möglichkeiten—*to the land of unlimited opportunities. I was, in American terms, twenty-two years old, and "almost twenty-three" by European count. Though bruised and disoriented by the hardships and nightmares of the immediate past, I was still unusually immature—a belated teenager brimming over with the excitement and dreams of high adventure and success.*

Perhaps not entirely. The poem seems to reveal traces of anxiety, perhaps also a touch of guilt: here I was escaping the hardships and hatred of a war-torn country through no merit of my own, but through a quirk, for having been born in Germany, a "good quota country"; meanwhile those of my friends, who had likewise survived the war, and who had suffered at least as much as I, were now stuck in Vienna, with bad quotas and little hope of emigrating. Or was it not even a matter of quotas but simply luck, the result of an arbitrary or unfathomable selection process? The thought never occurred to me, and now it is too late to find out.

But why am I returning to that poem now, fifty-five years later? I was looking for a ghost from the past—the picture of a classmate from grade school. I had run into her on a spring evening in 1948, when both of us were taking the entrance examination at Hunter College. I felt eyes on me without recognizing the face. But the eyes were persistent, and I had to force myself to concentrate on my essay. When, on the way out, their owner stopped me and uttered my name followed by a question mark, her name suddenly surfaced, in a shock of recognition.

My emotions were mixed. In Ostrau, Lilli had been a wild tomboy, while I was a shrinking violet, at least physically. She would make fun of me whenever she could, and I tried to give her as wide a berth as possible.

"You are much prettier than you were as a child," she said during that encounter sixteen years later. Her remark discomforted me even more since I did not feel I could return the compliment. Nor was I sure it was one.

We briefly compared notes on how and where each of us had survived the war. She mentioned a classmate who was still (or again?) living in Czechoslovakia, but whom I remembered only vaguely. Then we parted. Only now that I am able to dismiss the mischievous, needling memory imps of my early childhood with a shrug or a laugh, do I regret not having asked Lilli for her phone number or address.

Very recently—more than half a century later—I seemed to be given a second chance. During a visit to New York City (I now live in Massachusetts) I saw someone who resembled Lilli walking ahead of me in Times Square. I hurried to catch up with her, but the woman turned out to be a stranger. Nonetheless, this near-encounter awakened in me the urge, for the first time in years, to return to the past and look for tools that might open its doors.

I didn't find the class picture. Instead, the poem surfaced. It was penciled on yellowed onionskin, the kind of paper we would, long before copying machines and printers, place under a sheet of sumptuously glossy deep blue carbon paper, in order to preserve our creative efforts for posterity—or to prop up our memory. Except that the sheet before me was not a carbon copy but an original.

The memories which crowded around me as I was now reading the poem evoked a number of questions: what had I been like fifty-five years ago, how had I seen the world and myself? And had my past shaped me consistently, predictably, or had I streamlined it in retrospect, allowing a selective memory to compose a relatively uncomplicated, successful life?

I have been a hoarder from way back, more than likely conditioned by the war. Thus it was easy to take up the challenge. Stored on a top shelf were two large, dusty boxes not opened in decades, and I soon found myself sitting on the floor, surrounded by newspaper clippings saved for one reason or another, by diaries, loose sheets of paper, a few file cards with hand-scribbled notes, a box of snapshots, an envelope with school transcripts and other documents (among them my embarkation card for the SS Marine Marlin, *dated July 8, 1947), another envelope bulging with cancelled postage stamps, three copies of* Weltenwende *which contained articles I had sent to my father for the journal he was publishing in Vienna from 1947 to 1949, finally, a great many letters, both to and from me. Some of them seemed to be originals, others drafts or carbon copies.*

As I began to read and reread, align and realign, I became increasingly puzzled. Was this really me who, I had always thought, knew upon her arrival in the States exactly what she wanted, and achieved it without great hardship—namely, a proper education to make up for the many years of schooling lost under Hitler, a doctorate, and a good teaching career? Not necessarily planned but happily accepted were marriage, a talented and successful daughter, an equally appreciated son-in-law, and two promising grandchildren. "A real success story"—I would now and then be introduced publicly.

Now I discovered, much to my consternation, that the persona emerging from the trail of evidence before me was very different, even though the facts were accurate. The voices in which she spoke diverged widely, as if belonging to a Dr. Jekyll and several Mr. Hydes. The three eye-witness accounts, published in Weltenwende, *seemed mature, eloquent and level-headed. So were many of the letters. However, the diary entries were not only highly emotional, but at times disjointed, repetitious, embarrassingly melodramatic. Even so, most reflected a genuine striving for insight and a personal voice.*

Something else struck me: after the first shock of recognition and bewilderment, I found myself scrutinizing this assortment of documents with the detachment of an uninvolved by-

stander—as if I were reading someone else's case study. And now a new question arose: who or what had shaped that path and that character? Shifting moods and desires, genes, the challenges and opportunities of a new environment? Or had it all been mere chance, luck, a host of coincidences—unless one believed in providence? Finally, were these the typical stages of a teenager's maturation, however belated, or the outcome of a very special combination of a happy European childhood scarred by a nightmarish Holocaust adolescence, then repeatedly sidetracked but eventually reoriented toward the opportunities available in a new and hospitable country?

I decided to retrace the events recorded on those pages, and to supplement them with whatever thoughts and memories have stayed with me or might surface in the process. I can't tell whether it will be a fruitful undertaking, but perhaps a pattern will emerge and make sense, even if it is not a familiar pattern, nor the expected sense.

* * *

I was surprised to find that quite a few of the earliest diary entries were written in English. Theirs is a strange English—quite literate and yet peculiarly convoluted, at times outright jarring. In the hope that the stylistic and grammatical eccentricities of these texts will entertain rather than annoy the reader, I shall present them exactly as written. On the other hand, letters and diary entries originally in German will be translated only as literally as correct English permits, except that I may provide some of the more unusual German expressions in both languages—for the amusement of the multi-lingual reader.

The first entry was written before my departure. I will nonetheless include it since it reflects the state of mind of a twenty-two year old going on fourteen! It was written in English.

Vienna, May 7

It is strange that love, this much talked of marvel, should be something so earthly, so human and so easily to be understood if you omit all false pretenses. I cannot help thinking that what we call "love" is mere bodily correspondance, attachment, let us say, attraction which either vanishes when habit made fade the attraction of novelty, or which persists if mental correspondance and mutual understanding join in. I cannot believe in the "great unique love" which, crossed, leaves an eternal wound, as I cannot help thinking 2/3 of this great feeling fictitious. I may be reproached that I never experienced it myself. But I can very well imagine what such a great love is like. It combines the joy I feel for Walter when he kisses me with the admiration which I feel for some screen hero and with the thrill I felt whenever, still in Ostrau, I saw my *Gymnasium* math professor.

NEW YORK (1947–1949)

I might have loved Walter, as I might have loved Harry before, had I not kept telling myself, that it is only a passing infatuation, that the two of us have not enough in common for a longer union, that his faults would annoy me some time in the future *usw.* [*etc.*] I noticed that I could work myself up into a state of nearly complete indifference, same as I might have (and to my evil did sometimes) persuaded myself to love and yearn and long—till I had reached a state of absolute unhappiness, distress, Weltschmerz, tiredness of a life alone—within short what we call "love." For as soon as the phone rings, this state changes into one of unhealthy insanity, nervousnes and expectation mixed with fear of disappointment, to be continued—the moment it turns out that it is *him*—by a happiness, unbearable alone, therefore excessing into [followed by an illegible word], singing, dansing and similar madness. All of which, as any expert will tell you, makes in its total again so-called "love."

So it depends only on you, what you make of love and how much you allow yourself to be ruled by it! As long as you consider the pros and cons, you speak of a flirtation; the moment you feel so much involved that you are too tired or happy to consider anything any more (before it is too late), but with some silly bliss allow yourself to be submerged in happiness (= passion) and fate (= mostly the will of the other party), you speak of a great love. The result is always pretty much the same, only that it is easier to awake from a short half-conscious nape than to find one's feet after a long conscienceless giddiness.

Oscar Wilde said somewhere—or was it somebody else—that of two lovers the more loving part is happier and unhappier at the same time. I do not know whether I should want myself to be thus. I am afraid of such a total submerging as I know how hard I find back then. But on the other hand, dont you spoil many fine hours by too much musing and pondering, instead of enjoying them thoughtlessly? But I cannot help my nature and probably it has made up for that grief by many griefs I avoided by this very slowness and reconsidering of every action.

It is strange, how easy all that looks if handed down—and how confusing it becomes when put to the test. I remember, with 16 I was so self-assured and calm and reasonable and convinced to make an ideal woman and wife—and now? But any way, I have not too bad a time at present, am rather well and in balance, as the prospect of the pending voyage to the States makes me excited and keeps my vitality up. But no more now, it is 24 00 hours, I am dead tired. So long.

A few editorial comments: Harry was my first boyfriend and partner in a great but unconsummated romance during the war. It lasted three wonderful months but ended from one day to the next, when he was deported. After Harry returned from Theresienstadt at the end of the war, half-hearted attempts on both sides to resume the relationship petered out soon. He, too, eventually emigrated to the States, married, and became a physician. By now he has a large family. We have met a few times over the years, he phones now and then, and we exchange birthday letters. It is still a very special relationship: whenever we are together, it is as if we were nineteen again, and whenever he phones, his voice flirts, caresses and arouses me. Yet, when we hang up, I have no regrets—and doubt that he has any—only gratitude for being able to bring back those unique memories for a few moments, and relive them.

Walter, originally Viennese but by then in a British uniform, participated in an innocent flirtation during the final months before my departure for the United States. His name will crop up in this account now and then, but his person won't.

* * *

[*translated*] June 25, 1947

In Munich—indeed! There is much to tell and, as always, when I turn to you, diary, it means that I have lost my equilibrium. But let's begin at the beginning.

I still can't grasp that I am now on my way to America, in the midst of a new experience, en route to a future totally unknown and detached from the past. Until three days ago, I relished the adventure with body and soul. And now? I am unhappy, idiotically infatuated! To talk myself out of it, I will write it all down.

On Tuesday, the 12th, at 4 o'clock in the afternoon, the historic moment had arrived. To the last second, what with errands, packing and farewell visits, I didn't have time to reflect on what was really happening. Shortly before departure, Harry came to say good-bye. For the sake of a harmonious conclusion, I flirted once more, for the last time, but without regrets about leaving. Walter came and we were alone for a half hour, but we parted without even a farewell kiss. Vienna with all its ties was suddenly not important enough to be taken seriously. Only one moment, that of saying goodbye to Trude, felt—*als wär's ein Stück von mir* [*"as if it were a piece of me"*—a line from a popular German song, describing the death of a comrade-in-arms].

Only in the car when, after much rushing during the final moments, we drove to the station, did it hit me that I was now tearing myself away from all that was dear to me, from every inch of familiar soil, and that I was doing so of my own free will and responsibility. I haven't regretted it yet, though I have already experienced a few disappointments.

In the chaos at the station, I recovered my objectivity as our transport began to move. I saw my father's waving figure recede and shrink and, despite my relief at getting away from him, I had to swallow a few times. Then it was over, and I settled on my suitcase.

Hilde, a young girl whom I had met the week before—we had taken to each other—now disappointed me. Though nice and helpful, she kept bragging all the time and turned out to be spoiled, vain, and a real complainer. But some of the other women were rather nice, and so I was soon again cheerful and able to joke, which helped make the uncomfortable ride, at least at first, quite pleasant. A disgusting lack of organization though—our train stood at the Vienna transfer station for six hours without our being allowed to leave the car, then it stopped several times en route. However, the historic moment of leaving the Russian zone, usually endless and often full of unpleasant surprises, went smoothly and took only an hour.

We arrived in Linz at 4 o'clock on Wednesday afternoon, were in Salzburg at eleven, and arrived in Munich on Thursday at noon.

When four hours later the trucks from the camp came to pick us up, I was jubilant, for now the hardship would be over. Oh really? When we entered the gate which they had opened for us, I felt a cold shiver travel down my spine: it was like entering a concentration camp. Was I to get a taste of it still now that the war was over?

The registration was endless, the treatment rough: "Pants off—belly bared—fit—next!" [*I now wonder what that belly inspection might have been for—to eliminate pregnant women? Would they be sent back?*] Filthy barracks, sirens calling to meals (which are awful), barked commands by the Ukrainian anti-Semitic block leader, an argument with him for treating us like prisoners, some improvement since then but passes needed to leave the barracks. It seems you can get used to anything: since we are allowed to leave during the day and explore Munich, we try to ignore the hours in camp as much as we can. Ammersee, Dachau—an adorable, sparklingly clean German town which makes the horrible concentration camp only three miles away quite unimaginable. I saw Berchtesgaden, was on the Obersalzberg and inside its mine, at the Chiemsee and in the Herrenchiemsee Castle which is one of the most impressive castles in Germany, not at all destroyed so that its splendor almost suffocated me, and of course all over Munich.

Our trip to Garmisch and the Zugspitze had to be dropped because of bad weather, and now there is not enough time left for it. However horrified I was initially at the indefinite period to be spent in Munich, now I almost regret that our departure is scheduled for the first of the month. In a way, that is good for I have succeeded in falling for someone in our group, and I fear that, if I am not in New York soon, I will lose my common sense. He sleeps next door, and yesterday, instead of pulling myself together, I did something outright stupid. But I don't want to talk about that, not even to you, diary. I make all the mistakes one can make. Even though I know that he is a jerk, he tempts and attracts me. Won't I ever grow up?

Just now the two of us had a serious argument and I am noticeably cooled off. It is essential that I end this relationship because I have been the more active participant, and that is definitely wrong.

Jewish survivors who had no relatives in the United States willing to provide "affidavits of support" for prospective immigrants often turned for help to the American Joint Distribution Committee, a Jewish service organization. It sponsored and financed the emigration of those displaced and/or subjected to persecution. I applied to the JOINT right after the war ended, and had just about given up hope when I received, in quick succession, notification of my acceptance, and assignment to a group transport. That explains at least partially the confused emotional state described earlier in this diary entry.

* * *

[translated] June 26—still in Munich

Yesterday I caught a bit of a sunburn, which is why I am lying in the shade today, determined to study. I brought my shorthand book along so I could practice. The business with Jackie is total nonsense. Even though I am not yet entirely sensible in his presence, I am definitely cooled off and not likely to do anything stupid again. It is shocking how something like that can throw you so completely. I am no longer myself—my whole being longs to be near him. Perhaps my sunburned state contributed to that, but now it is much better. I must regain my equilibrium. Tomorrow we want to try for the Zugspitze again since luggage inspection is only on Monday.

I am almost afraid of myself, for I never suspected that I could let go so completely. And to my own feelings and nothing else, for except for a few playful attempts by Jackie and some lewd remarks which I knew were directed at anyone who would listen, all encouragement came from me. I must reason myself out of my yearning. Of course, I would prefer if our paths separated right now and I would not have to travel with him all the way to New York.

[*Entry continues in English.*]

Lady Chatterley's Lover keeps coming back into my thoughts. I had finally succeeded in borrowing the book from Walter. I refused to read it two years ago and then was hunting for it for half a year. It was probably because of the begun and not accomplished intimacy that I was now keen on a book of which I had heard only the worst reports. To my shame I must confess that after the first shock I read with real interest and curiosity. I felt like being in school and there listening to a medical lecture—and, to stick to the truth, a bit of a thrill. It was like playing with yourself, not quite the right thing. I dared not to tell to the others my impressions of the book as they were so strange.

It is true, I had a certain feeling of dissatisfaction because here the dirty linen was being washed so openly in public, but this feeling was lost in the background. The chief impressions were that the doctrine attributed to L. that he wants to show the importance of physical attraction above all, is not proved by this book. Though Lady Ch. finds her satisfaction in her game keeper, a simple, even common man, that proves nothing, as she is a very supercilious woman, hardly interested in any brainwork. So, as her husband is disabled, she runs to the first man coming her way. And as she is a pretty womanly woman, there is not much wonder about the gamekeeper's feelings towards her. So besides a very open description of sexual life, the book has nothing to say and is therefore—and not because of its shocking openness—not worth reading.

* * *

"Lisa Mondo:

A D.P. Sees America

It is not easy to describe what takes hold of all of us now that a strip of land has appeared on the horizon. That strip stands for far more than land and the soothing proximity of terra firma, after days of solitude with only water, sky and one's agitated expectations!

A thousand people on an emigrant ship, collected from all corners of the globe, with different languages, different customs and habits, yet all sharing a common bond that draws them to one another: the suffering during the time of terror which they have overcome, and the timid, uncertain hope for a new beginning, a better future. And because the past still sits so heavily on their limbs, and because the uncertainty and fear of everything unknown and of possible new disappointments so frequently overshadows the joy of expectation, the feeling that seizes them at this first glimpse of American soil reflects a combination of confused, happy excitement and anxiety. They are reflected on every one of the thousand faces lined up at the railing—as if no one dared be alone at this moment—and questioning eyes stare at the strip of sunbathed land that is opening up before them.

I am uneasy, infected by the widespread restlessness, but I am not afraid. When you have survived seven years of persecution in Hitler Germany, you become indifferent. And yet, there was a moment, and not too long ago, when a vague fear took hold of me and could not be dispelled. As I now stand at the railing while the land patiently watches our slow approach, while the decks are being swept clean and the cooks are preparing the final meal, while the stewards smooth out the snow-white bed sheets and neatly fold the many dark blue blankets, I remember Munich...

A Viennese transport of about fifty people, compressed into three dirty cattle cars and freezing for three nights on hard suitcases, we were waiting for Munich as one waits for paradise. And then—entry into an army camp through a high iron gate, endless registering, dirty rooms with torn straw mattresses on rusty iron bedsteads, no sheets, no pillows, only two ill-smelling, gray-brown blankets per person, no electric light, indescribably neglected washrooms and toilets, and in each door curious or hostile glances, some of them focusing on our luggage with unmistakable greed. German nationals from all parts of Europe, Ukrainians and White Russians, Poles and Jews, Mexicans and South Americans, thousands of people who, uprooted and homeless, were now waiting, often not knowing for what or for whom, and who, intimidated or hardened by suffering and deprivation, had become either resigned or ruthless. And we are suddenly part of this medley, we who have American visas and our passage paid for in American dollars, we who had already considered ourselves free and equal human beings.

Our papers have been taken from us upon arrival, and when we ask if we will move on to Bremen the next day as was promised in Vienna, the reply is only a condescending smile. And each day we trudge to the blackboard at the camp entrance which announces the next transport and its destination, and each day we return to our barrack a little more distraught and disheartened because there is no word about our Bremen departure.

Three times daily a shrill siren calls us to the kitchen barrack, where we line up with dull gray aluminum bowls in hand, and wait for an indefinable, thin soup and a slice of white bread. We learn to accept all that. We even submit silently to the command to clean hallways, washrooms and toilets once a week, and to peel smelly, moldy potatoes in the kitchen for eight hours at a time. But when the block leader, a boxer-like Ukrainian, doesn't allow us a moment of peace but throws the door open at any hour of the day or night for a roll call, when he withholds the candle we have been allotted and orders us to do the cleaning every third day instead of once a week, we decide to complain to the higher authority, the American officer in charge. We are indignant but still believe that all this is an incredible mistake which those in charge are totally unaware of. As the best English speaker in the group, I head the three-person delegation.

The officer listens to me quietly; then he declares very politely that he will give us a half hour to come to an agreement with the block leader. If within that time span things are not straightened out, he will not return our visas to us, and then we can see how far we get. For two years he has had no problems here and he won't for our sake question his capable assistants, let alone initiate an investigation.

At that moment something in me collapsed—a hope, an expectation—and a burning fear spread within me. Not because he might implement his threat—the representative of the committee, whom we approached in our dismay, assured us that that could not happen—but because the emissary of a country on which I had placed such high expectations was disregarding the law ...

And now the shore is spread out before me, and as the harbor patrol approaches our side and begins to fasten the gangplank, a few thin, vertical lines emerge behind the green bank, grow, stretch upward, and turn into buildings, tall buildings—our first skyscrapers!

I can't help thinking of Bremen, and of the streetcar ride through miles and miles of rubble fields and ruins, without a single intact building. The barracks were once again outside the town and totally isolated. Even so, we heaved a sigh of relief. The proximity of the water, of ships—one of them was, after all, expecting us—and the monotonous yet sensible routine of the camp calmed our tense nerves. This time our rooms were clean and bright, and they had bedding and pillows. Food was served on real dishes and, though not very varied, was fresh and filling. And our papers were returned to us so that we no longer felt helpless and ostracized, but were able to relax.

Soon the day arrived when we were given our boarding cards, except that once again we faced an unpleasant surprise: not all of us were on the boarding list! What in reality may have meant only a slight delay of a few days, renewed our fears of being left behind, of being once again rejected, condemned to an enervating, indefinite wait. This time I was no longer shocked when I found out that people with connections managed to secure tickets. In fact, I was hardly surprised. I shook off my disappointment, set my jaw, and decided to fight for my boarding pass. Somehow, it seemed to me that if I wanted to assert myself in America, I had to succeed now.

And here I am and, after nine wonderfully carefree days at sea, America is within reach. How will it show itself, this new world, what will its message to us be? Courage, hope and success, or struggle, disappointments and resignation?

The Statue of Liberty sparkles in the brilliant sunshine, and behind it soars Manhattan's imposing "skyline"—slim skyscrapers, bunched together, their narrow shapes reflected in the water. As we approach and the harbor traffic begins to churn up the water, these giants take on individuality, are of different shapes—one narrow and pointed, another one heavy and blunt, and far back, barely visible, the thin, graceful finger of what I am told is the Empire State Building, at one hundred and two stories the tallest building in the world.

The call comes to line up for passport control, and I return from excited admiration to prosaic reality. Back down into the narrow hallways where the air is hot and heavy, but after endless hours of waiting which sucks up the last remnants of my enthusiasm and expectation, I am outside, in a now dark but illuminated New York. Its lights seem cold and alien, and I move with a heavy heart along the metal gangplank which hands me over, unconditionally, to this new country. I know that no one is waiting for me, for I have no relatives or close friends in New York, and the ten dollars the committee gave to each of us and which seemed so precious in Germany, are now insignificant and weightless. I hesitate, come to a stop—but the lady from the service organization recognizes me by the tag I am wearing. Yes, my name is on her list. My suitcase is carried off after a cursory customs inspection; I am taken by the hand and pointed toward a bus; inside I find, much to my relief, familiar faces. America is bidding me a friendly welcome.

We travel on and on, through endless streets which are not lit nearly as brightly as I had expected, and with innumerable right and left turns; but now I no longer feel lost or lonely. From my cozy corner I watch with curiosity the bursts of light which reveal New York for moments at a time. And then I am in the hotel, am received, given instructions, recognize my suitcase, struggle to drag it to the elevator, am told by a smiling black man to "take it easy," watch how, with one grasp, he transports my entire possessions into the elevator, find myself in a small hot room on the sixth floor and, while from below subdued street noise reaches me, I realize with amazement that I have arrived, that I am now really in America.   (To be continued.)"

The above is, in translation, the first of several reports I sent to my father for inclusion in the journal he was publishing in Vienna at the time. It was called WELTENWENDE zu Vernunft und Menschlichkeit. Unabhängige Zeitschrift [*World's Turning toward Common Sense and Humanity. An Independent Journal*]. *The essay appeared in the October 1948 issue.*

*　　　　　　　　　　* * * *

Trude and I had met in Vienna during the war, when both of us were studying English at Frau Kautezky's language school. Trude was not Jewish, but when she mentioned that her father had been fired from his teaching position because he refused to join the Party, I opened up toward her, and we soon became close friends. Her English was probably as good as mine, but our correspondence was carried out entirely in German and is therefore translated.

My dearest Trudi,　　　　　　　　　　　　　　　　　　　　July 13, 1947

Here is my first report, written aboard the *SS Marine Marlin*. I will mail it the moment we arrive so that you know I am thinking of you.

The ship seems enormous, even though it is probably considered small. Very impressive, like a big hotel. I say to myself over and over: I am on my way to America, to a new life, to real life! The excitement of this new beginning swept over me as I stepped onto the gangplank in Bremerhaven, and it has been with me from the moment I wake up to when I climb into my bunk at night. Now and then a wave of anxiety about the future hits me, especially just before I go to sleep, but I usually mange to shake it off right away. I still cannot quite believe that I am sailing—or rather steaming—toward America, by myself, with one suitcase and ten dollars in my pocket, like a true pioneer. "Don't worry," the refugee committee had said, "we will help you find work and a place to live." I certainly don't worry since I speak English and also because, in addition to their promise, I have several addresses and phone numbers from my father and his friends that I can contact for advice or help.

I was actually assigned a lower bunk, but Frau Farkas asked me to trade with her since she might have to use the toilet at night. I have no problem sleeping through the night, and besides, climbing up and down is fun—like climbing a mountain, with a safe shelter on top to slide into. Of course, now I no longer need a shelter since no bombs are falling, no SS-men lying in wait ...

Frau Farkas is a very interesting woman, and I am learning a lot from her. I met her shortly before we left Vienna, in line at the embassy. Later we were in the same freight car, and that was very comforting. You would never guess that she has survived two camps; she is always cheerful and enterprising. Despite a few wrinkles, mainly on the neck and around her eyes, she is very attractive, has short, reddish-blond, wavy hair, a good figure, small, regular teeth, and black eyes that always seem to be laughing. She is really quite sexy, despite her age.

Once I watched her put on make-up, and I was amazed at the transformation. After she washed her face, it looked very bland and showed its wrinkles. But she massaged her cheeks with a cream, in a rotating movement up- and outward, slapped them lightly for a minute or two, added another cream which made her skin look tanned, and rubbed a fingertip of red lipstick lightly onto her cheeks. Now I know why she always has such good color. I would love to try one of her creams! And you know what she told me? That she tries to smile a lot because that straightens out the wrinkles at the corners of one's mouth!

She is also amazingly resourceful. She smiles at people and says something nice or funny to them—and she gets what she wants. Of course she didn't have to flatter me for that lower berth. But she manages to "organize" things like cigarettes or chocolates from the crew or the officers, even though her English is rather poor. During the war, *organisieren* meant buying things on the black market, but Mrs. F. not only organizes things but gets them for free! I don't smoke and so am not interested in her cigarettes (some people here are ready to kill for a cigarette!), but if she gives me a piece of chocolate, I am delighted. The sailors are also very generous with chewing gum. It comes in thin slices, each looking like a wrapped-up flat noodle, about 8 cm long. Everyone seems wild about these noodles except for me. Why would anyone chew (you mustn't swallow it) just for the sake of chewing? I am sure it's bad for your teeth. The children make a game of it, blowing it into bubbles in front of their lips. It looks like a cow foaming at the mouth. The weather hasn't made me sick, but watching them almost does.

Frau Farkas has a sister in Los Angeles who is married to an American and has secured a job for her, as a housekeeper in Beverly Hills. That is a suburb of Los Angeles. The man is a widower, she told me, and very rich, with a big cotton plantation in Texas. "Who knows what the future will bring," she said and winked at me as if we were co-conspirators. I have tried to wink like that into the mirror and smile as sexily as she does, but it looks ridiculous, and I feel like a hypocrite.

Her German has a Hungarian tinge but she also speaks Yiddish, and that was a blessing when we were stuck in the Munich barracks. She was able to bargain with the Jewish refugees in the D.P. camp next door, and brought back treasures—good soap and real toilet paper. What a pleasure it was not to have to use those rough newspaper squares speared on a nail in the wall, especially since it was usually too dark there to read them first. It's not that these refugees would not have understood my German, but anyone speaking German was hated, Jewish or not. Czech was no good either, and the few words of Polish I know were not adequate.

Those D.P.s (most of them from Eastern Europe) were an odd group. When we tried to explain that we were on our way to America, they shrugged as if to say—believe that, and you'll go to heaven! [*"Wer's glaubt, wird selig"—a popular German saying, based on the bible.*] They had apparently been told the same thing months ago, and were still waiting. I was horrified. Fortunately, they were wrong. After three unpleasant weeks in the Munich barracks we were sent on to Bremerhaven and embarkation, and I was finally on my way to America and freedom. However, after those awful days, first in the cattle car, then with the D.P.s in Munich, and finally an encounter with an arrogant American officer who was in charge of the camp and treated us like dirt, I was beginning to have real doubts about the freedom aspect.

But now I am so excited I can hardly stand still, in spite of the danger of running into Jackie—or do I still want to run into him? I hope not! I will tell you about him later for now it's time for dinner. More tomorrow.

* * *

New York, July 30, 1947

I am awfully sorry, Trude, that in the excitement of my arrival I forgot to mail my letter to you. By now you must think that the ocean has swallowed me up! No, on the contrary, all is going well, and I am getting Americanized rapidly. I work in an office, live in my own room, and have already acquired a radio to keep me informed about what's happening in this country and the rest of the world. But let me first continue my report about the voyage.

The *SS Marine Marlin* was a real Tower of Babel, except that the German group was very small because so few have survived. Also, the weather was not at all congenial. High waves and almost every day a mean wind which pushed the horizon up and down and turned the ship into a swing. But I quickly learned to trick it by always facing forward or backward, and ignoring the sides.

Quite a few passengers were sick. They were lying outside on the top deck looking chalky and miserable. I felt sorry for them because they could not eat, when there was finally food, so much food that I could not imagine where it had come from after all those years of shortages. The few of us who were able to eat lined up three times a day at the enormously long counter in the dining hall where behind a partition were large steaming platters. One only had to point at a dish for the waiter to put the food on a plate, and the plate on a tray for you. Everything you could wish for was there—goulash, Schnitzel, chicken, spaghetti, rice, potatoes, several vegetables, even fresh lettuce and tomatoes! And you could come back as often as you wanted.

Breakfast was especially sumptuous. On an enormous platter, with hot water underneath to keep them warm, sat stacks of scrambled eggs—real eggs, if you can believe it. Also fried potatoes, cut into narrow, rectangular sticks, each 5-10 cm long and very crisp; and strips of what they call bacon, although it is very different from our *Speck*. I always hated that white fat, no matter how thinly it was sliced, and how much paprika grandma put on top to disguise the taste. She considered it a delicacy, but I much preferred *Extrawurst* [*a kind of bologna*] on my bread. The American bacon is very different: thin, crinkled strips of smoked meat, hot and very crisp, a little like *Grammeln* [*crisply fried squares of goose skin*] but less fatty. And the orange juice, although it comes out of a huge glass container, tastes like real oranges. Except that it is pale, almost yellow, not red like the blood oranges from before the war.

The only bad food is the bread, and it is really terrible! Soft like a sponge and white like chalk. no color or taste, and no crust to bite into. Perhaps it is meant for toothless old people, but everyone is eating it, young and old, and they don't seem to mind. You can get it toasted; then it tastes a little better but still not like bread, more like the dry *Zwieback* we children would get when we were sick. They spread butter on it to give it a little taste, but that doesn't help much because the butter is salted, if you can imagine that!

I usually don't touch the bread and wouldn't, even if it tasted better. Not after having had nothing else for years than that crumbling mixture of corn and who knows what else, which used to be called bread. But now I think that even that was better. And what is worse, unless you say right away—"No bread, please!" they automatically put a plate with two slices on your tray, and if you then say that you didn't want any bread, they simply empty the plate into the trash! I couldn't believe my eyes when the waiter on the ship did that. When I told him that I had not touched the bread and tried to explain that people in Europe were still starving, and it was a sin to waste food, he just shrugged and grinned at me as if I were peculiar.

There is also something called French Toast, which is that same bread but fried, after it has been dipped in milk and food color. You are supposed to pour sugar syrup over it—but who wants dessert for breakfast? So I stick to orange juice, eggs, bacon and those fried potato sticks. (They are called "French fries" —how do the French deserve this?) Although I love soft-boiled eggs and, before the war, ate one every morning, here they are served without the shell and in a cup. That way they don't taste nearly as good. So I prefer to order them fried and have learned to say "sunny side up"; otherwise, they come looking like an omelet. "Sunny side up," if translated literally, means *Sonnenseite nach oben*—a funny name but probably not much funnier than our *Spiegeleier* [*fried eggs, lit. "mirror eggs"*] or our *Eier im Schlafrock* [*poached eggs, lit. "eggs in a housecoat"*].

The waiters didn't seem to mind at all when I came back for seconds. In fact they always smiled at me, almost as if they were amused. I was actually surprised that all this unaccustomed food did not make me sick; instead I felt wonderfully alive, happier than ever before. Someone said that they should take my picture, blow it up and mount it on the wall for inspiration! But here I am thoughtlessly describing all this food to you when you have hardly anything!

But it is getting late and I work tomorrow, so I must quit, though there is much more to tell. I'll write soon again, I promise. Meanwhile—stay healthy, and don't forget   your old friend Liesl

In recalling the trip, I can't help marveling at how I was able to stand, without even one shaky moment, the stormy weather that accompanied us much of the time. Back then, I ascribed it to

my being a good sailor, but the few sea voyages I have taken since, all on larger and better calibrated ships and usually in far calmer weather, have quickly disabused me of that notion.

Flying became my deliverance. Even a small, otter-watching boat trip along the California coast many years later turned into an ordeal. But perhaps it is no mystery at all—simply a case of mind over matter, just as trying to survive the war in Vienna as a Jew made many later hardships seem insignificant.

2.

[*from the December 1948 issue of* Weltenwende, *translated*]

"**Lisa Mondo:**

A D.P. Sees America
(Continuation)

The first steps in the new country are timid and awkward. But when I discover that most streets are numbered, and that one can orient oneself at every corner, that in the subways huge signs point the way, that I can communicate perfectly, and that the Americans, contrary to all depictions, are outgoing and helpful, and when I reach the first group of friends by phone—my enthusiasm returns.

A meeting is called at the hotel, and we are informed that we cannot expect any support in New York since the committee has definite orders to distribute us across the country. I don't question why nonetheless so many people have been in the hotel for weeks, and still seem to be receiving support. Instead I secure a week's grace period so that I can convey the commissions and messages given to me in Vienna, and to seek out friends whom I have not seen in years. Those advise me not to leave New York since it is easy to utilize foreign languages here, whereas the rest of the country would hardly be interested. Then—and this seems to me to be decisive—that the chances for working as a journalist are better in New York, and so is access to higher education.

When I walk into the office of the *Aufbau*, the local German-Jewish newspaper, I am told that they have a free employment service, and a few hours later I have an offer from a jewelry store, at a weekly salary of $37.50. I request time to think about it, for another acquaintance I had phoned thought he might know of an office job. He does and there I ask for $40 since I speak and write English well, and can also take shorthand. I am told to expect a decision in two days.

Now I try to find a place to live. Again I am lucky. Clutching the ad page of the *New York Times*, I set out early in the morning, stop on the wrong floor (our ground floor is here the first floor!), and see a notice on a door advertising a room. At the hotel they confirm in writing that I may come to the committee whenever I am ready to leave New York, then I move out. Two days later I start working, and after a week I deposit my first ten dollars in the bank.

I soon feel at home. My accent which at first made me insecure is hardly taken notice of, and everywhere people are friendly. Soon I know New York better than people who have lived here for years. Likewise, my fear of the total absence of any cultural life was unwarranted. If one chooses carefully, one can see outstanding films—mainly French and Italian—as well as good plays. The theaters are usually colorless, drab buildings; however, the acoustics are good, there is air conditioning on hot days, and you can see even from the cheapest seat. British ensembles perform frequently, and not too long ago there was a splendid series of performances by the Habimah. Though they spoke Hebrew, that barely lessened the public enthusiasm. Reviewers were, in rare unanimity, very positive, and so it was almost impossible to secure tickets.

The so-called American tempo is mainly practiced by the refugees. The real American has no nerves. To be sure, he is capable of racing down the steps to the subway like a maniac in order to squeeze through the closing doors of a departing train, but that is sport, not haste. Once on the train, he spreads out his *Times* with total equanimity—and it is a huge paper. Even if the car is so mobbed that he can barely find room for his feet, he will, across the heads of his neighbors, lose himself in the baseball scores.

Ah yes, baseball …

Almost every street in the residential areas has its youthful and even older ball players who dash back and forth with the same enthusiasm, and interrupt their game only reluctantly whenever the green traffic light opens the street up to the assault of waiting vehicles. School children know the names of their baseball heroes before that of their President; when, not long ago, Babe Ruth, "the father of baseball," died, the entire nation seemed in mourning. This fanatical passion is difficult for an outsider to understand because the game is really very boring, with single moments of tension and long stretches of inactivity. Yet it dominates young and old.

Not long ago, the *New York Times* carried in its political section a discussion about the average person's degree of interest in politics. A poll yielded the following remarkable sequence for the most common topics of conversation:

1. baseball,
2. the weather,
3. high prices.

Then there was a big gap, and finally a few people declared an interest in the presidential election and the Berlin crisis. Ah yes, baseball ...

The average American's second topic, the weather, requires less expertise. Since New York's weather god is full of mood swings and constantly surprises its subjects, there are quite a few variations even to this, so general a topic. In fact, I have a slight suspicion that New Yorkers relish their unpredictable weather and its tendency toward extremes: they want to be first in the country even in that respect. They keep mentioning with great enthusiasm that the snow level of the preceding winter almost surpassed that of 1887; they point out that this year's heat wave was the worst since 1936, and I am constantly told that the weather is most unusual. No doubt about it—the New Yorker loves the unusual, and it represents for him the "usual," unique atmosphere of his city.

The relationship between Jews and non-Jews is, especially for someone arriving today from Central Europe, remarkably good and frictionless. They seem to respect each other's religion, offer best wishes for the holidays; churches frequently make themselves available for Jewish services, meetings or charity events, and vice versa. Of course it remains to be seen to what extent that is done from tolerance and to what extent from economic and political motives. But the fact of equal rights cannot be denied; though one can find anti-Semitic remarks and actions even here, one feels free.

The Jewish population can be divided into two groups. First, there are those Jews who fled to this country thirty or forty years ago, mostly from Eastern Europe, and who have succeeded after a long, grinding struggle. They tend to live in their own small homes and to form strong, tightly knit groups, primarily on the "Lower Eastside" of Manhattan, and in parts of the Bronx and Brooklyn. These groups often speak Yiddish rather than English, and are still clinging to the customs, habits and songs of the old country. However, it is remarkable how little they have acclimated themselves. They know less about the New Yorker, his life, interests, culture, and weaknesses than would an interested foreigner who had never stepped on American soil; despite this, they are the most ardent American patriots imaginable, determined to give their children a truly American education, and to instill in them an unconditional love for the country which gives them their daily bread.

The second group, which is far more visible, is generally considered New York's Jewry. Its activities are one of the most pleasing features of local public life. The group is composed of most of those born here, as well as of those immigrants who knew how to assimilate without abandoning their Jewishness and the responsibilities it entails.

Almost all belong to one of innumerable religious communities—there is no Central Agency. They not only support their synagogue financially but organize social get-togethers, raise funds and, with strong membership participation, do charity work. Huge sums are often collected, and I know several people who donate all of their spare time to work for service organizations.

Young people are almost without exception enrolled in Zionist groups. Each member attempts enthusiastically to do as much as possible for Palestine, and not only by means of propaganda and donations. Constantly there are some who leave their own environment in order to offer their lives to the struggle for the safety of the new state. The murder of Bernadotte elicited everywhere anxiety, dismay and impotent anger. The concept "Israel" is no longer mere theory, but everyone's personal problem and goal. This common idea has made of the many separate Jewish Americans a unified, conscious American Jewry. Full of hope, they are turning toward the new light that emanates from a small strip of land on the Asian coast of the Mediterranean; its promise succeeds in warming even this enormous country called America. (To be continued)"

* * *

17/8/1947—New York

I must write in English, otherwise my English will never become better. It's long time since I wrote here the previous pages, not so long in endurance as in experience and events. Today it has been one month that I landed on the American shore. I wont go into detail about the events since then, but I should like to discuss the mentality of the people here, which I found (to my great astonishment) being really different and—attractive. People take life easier and I enjoy that. Maybe I will be rebuked later on, when I'll see great problems solved too quickly and unheedingly, but now this easygoingness appeals to me.

There is great familiarity and frankness between boys and girls. But even that is nice, because you may have a lot of fun, without anybody thinking anything different than that it is fun, as it would be in Europe. Maybe there are disadvantages to it as well, but I did not yet get enough company and experience to judge. I still am a little uncomfortable behaving so freely, but I try to imitate Hanna and her friends.

I felt lonely today, because I was alone without any date. I am not yet "Americanized" enough to use every party for arranging future dates. But I do not really mind that.

Actually, it seems dangerous to me, that I think in very American terms already, that is, whether I'll have nice company, lots of fun, make the most of every invitation etc. and no serious thoughts at all. Am I as superficial as that? And also—I do not feel like studying at all in my free time, no languages, no writing—simply lazy. But that might be because of the awful heat which was only broken today. Let us see, if it becomes better with the cooler weather. And sometimes I feel an awful longing for somebody just to take me into his arms and kiss me. And it need not even be Walter. Just somebody I like. Crazy, maybe, thoughts developed because of this day all by myself. Thanks heaven, tomorrow another week will start, with work and people around me.

Otherwise I really am having a marvellous time, enjoying N.Y. and everything I see. Jackie I have forgotten by now. But probably I'll have to meet somebody nice soon, I see it from the way how quickly I am responding, though I should want to keep distance longer. Or maybe, when in autumn I'll start studying in school, I'll have other thoughts and interests than now, when all I see are people hugging each other, and all I hear conversations about boy- and girl-friends.

* * *

Dearest Truderl! New York, September 9, 1947

I apologize for not writing sooner, but so much has happened since I arrived that I was waiting for things to calm down a little so that I could catch my breath. Perhaps that is what they call the "American tempo." Do you remember Goethe's poem *Amerika, du hast es besser?* ["*America, you are better off.*"] I keep thinking of it, and it becomes more meaningful every day.

[Actually, the poem is called "To the United States." This is what it says, in a fairly close translation: "America, you are better off / Than this old continent of ours, / You have no dilapidated castles / And no mountains of basalt. / You are not shackled and held back /

From the surging stream of life / By unrewarding memories / And unproductive strife. / Make good use of every day you have! / And when your children try to versify, / May a good fate keep away from them / Tales of robbers, ghosts and knights."]

The streets, at least in "midtown," which is the heart of the city, are deep, narrow chasms between walls of skyscrapers, or, as they are called here, "high-rises"—much as Kafka describes it in *Amerika*, even though he was never here. Everything is constantly in motion. People are rushing, cars honking, brakes screeching, police and ambulance sirens howling. Total bedlam. But also very exhilarating, and none of the buildings are in ruins.

There are two kinds of streets. An "avenue" is wider than a street, but even there you have to crane your neck to see the sky. Surprisingly, it does not feel claustrophobic but exciting. Especially at night when all windows are lit, the city is a magical place. I have to keep reminding myself that it is no dream and I am now really in America, in a country without war and destruction, where nobody starving or is persecuted. And I too am part of it and safe, need no longer look behind me or avoid crowds, am allowed to go into any store, can get anything I need, do anything I want. Where else could I have arrived with no money and, within a week, have my own room, full-time work and enough money for my expenses? I can even save a little.

My room is in an old six-story building. I like that. The apartment is on the fourth floor. It has a narrow hall full of doors, all leading into rented-out rooms. Mine is rather dark because its window faces a courtyard, but it is quite comfortable and very inexpensive. The furniture is plain—a bed, a night table with a lamp, a chair, a chest of drawers and what they call a "closet" which here doesn't mean *Klosett* [*toilet*] but a built-in wardrobe. A small green bedside rug, no curtains but a white pull-down shade.

My first purchase was a little radio, and I now wake up to music. During the week it is always the same singer, Eddie Arnold. Not a great voice, and he draws some words out strangely and trills others funnily, almost like yodeling, but the tunes are pleasing and resonate in the ear. His themes are mainly cowboys and horses, the prairie and unhappy lovers. They too are obviously part of America, though its heart is definitely New York, pulsating with life, a magnet attracting people from many countries, all knowing that here you can try anything and no one will criticize you, everything is available and anything is possible. I can't tell you how exciting that is.

My landlady is Irish, short and quite stout, with stiff gray hair and a loud voice. She is inquisitive but friendly. On the first day she showed me the telephone and wanted to know if I had ever seen one before! I was tempted to tell her that we didn't live on trees in Austria. But since she didn't seem to know the difference between Austria and Australia, I gave up. Her English is more like British English, and I have no difficulty understanding her. However, one lodger is a tiny old Scottish lady who is almost impossible to understand, much worse than the Americans. Then there are two men; both are quite old, but they still work, and I hardly ever see them.

The bathroom is accessible from the hall. It serves all of us, but so far I haven't had a problem. But imagine—it contains not only a bathtub and wash basin but also the toilet, all in one room! Not very hygienic, and impractical if more than one person needs it. But who am I to complain? My rent is only $10 a week and I earn $40, so I feel like a millionaire.

Do you remember my mentioning Hanna? We went to grade school in Ostrau together, also the first three years of high school; the fourth year both of us switched to the Czech school because the atmosphere in the German school had become so unpleasant. And sure enough, that spring Hitler marched into Czechoslovakia. Hanna was sent to England with a *Kindertransport*. After the war, she moved to the States and managed to get hold of my Viennese address.

It turns out that the hotel, where the refugee committee put me when I arrived, was just one block from Hanna's apartment building! (In American English there is a great word for such a coincidence—"serendipity." It means a mixture of chance and providence, and has such a nice ring.) She immediately came over to welcome me and has invited me several times to her apartment, once even to a big party on the roof, with music and alcoholic drinks. One of the young men I met there invited me to a movie after that, and so I had my first *rendezvous* (here they call it "date"—the same word as for *Datum*). I had a hard time convincing him that I wanted to pay for my own ticket, but otherwise he was very nice. However, when I said good-night, he stood by the door until I closed it, as if waiting for something. Was *I* supposed to thank *him* for the nice evening instead of the other way round? He hasn't phoned since so I had better ask Hanna whether I did or said something wrong. They seem to have different social rules here.

On the whole I cannot complain. On the contrary. After only two months I am comfortably settled and doing extremely well. And I am really glad that I remained in New York, even though the JOINT did not want me to stay. "We have too many refugees here already," they said. I was to choose between Milwaukee, St. Louis and Salt Lake City. There they would take care of me and help me find work. And what happens if I don't want to leave New York?

"Then you must move out of the hotel and are on your own."

I knew nothing about St. Louis or those other towns, whereas in New York I knew Hanna and had several phone numbers from Vienna. Hanna, too, thought I should stay in New York because chances for finding a language-related job would definitely be better here.

When I began to look for work, I was lucky right away. An acquaintance of my father knew of someone who needed office help. And, imagine, the man asked *me* what salary I wanted. I said 40 dollars—and he agreed! The office is tiny and I am the only employee, but the work is easy. I sit by the switchboard, take telephone orders, open the mail, and record incoming checks. Sometimes my boss dictates short letters to me, mostly thank-you notes. That's because we send CARE packages to Europe, which I find especially meaningful because it is a link to home. And now I can give instead of having to take.

My boss comes in only once or twice a day, mainly to collect the orders and checks. He is also a refugee, but prewar, and very nice. He gave me a week's pay in advance so that I could rent a room. That way I could move out of the hotel at the end of the first week and am now standing on my own two feet!

By the way, I receive many compliments on my English but, to be honest, I think people are just trying to be nice. Although so many people here speak imperfect English that it may even be true. Often I am told that I have "such a charming accent." Even if it is only a compliment—who would say something like that to a foreigner at home? Hanna tells me I must then say "thank you" and not try to explain that I haven't been here very long, and that in Vienna we were taught British English. People also keep saying "what a nice dress, nice coat, nice whatever" and it is again the same: you are not supposed to explain that it is really old and nothing special, or that you bought it in a second-hand shop, or made it yourself. Instead, you are supposed to smile, say "thank you" and nothing else. It makes me feel like an impostor.

At any rate, I have no difficulty understanding and being understood, at least much of the time, although the accent of the natives is often odd; sometimes very nasal, some mumble or have long, distorted vowels and a muffled "r" which sounds like an English "w." *Entre nous*, I like British English much better, but I can't say that aloud.

Likewise, I need to watch my language. Did you know that "sympathetic" is not *sympathisch* but *mitfühlend*? They don't seem to have a word for *sympathisch*, though it is such an important concept. And when I said to Hanna that I needed to douche, she laughed and explained that I must say "shower" because to douche means washing your lower parts. It was fortunate that I said it to her! Other words are less dangerous, like "elevator" for a lift and "truck" for a lorry.

Enough for today. I still need to buy some fruit. Luckily, the grocers here are open till very late, not like at home. Nor do they close for a lunch break, even in hot weather. Apparently New York never sleeps. The stores don't even have shutters to pull down when they close, and so the streets never look inhospitable and deserted, even late at night. And you should see the fruit displays—not just apples and pears, but oranges, grapefruit, peaches, plums, bananas, even pineapples. They look like a large cactus, but when you peel them, they are lemony yellow and extremely sweet. The fruit is all arranged in rows on shelves outside the shop, and you are allowed to touch and select whatever you want! Then you take it inside so that your purchase can be weighed and paid. I am surprised that people don't walk away without paying—they must be more honest than at home. Or not as hungry.

The first evening at the hotel I spent almost my entire ten dollars at the fruit stand at our corner, which is 104th Street and Broadway.

My very best wishes to your mother and hugs to you,
From your faithful friend Liesl

Hanna was half a year younger than I and my best friend until she left Ostrau for England in May 1939. Seeing her in New York after eight long years was not merely wonderful but an enormous surprise. She was quite different from the way I remembered her. The timid, awkward and rather plain-looking girl whom I had tutored in high school, and who seemed to depend on my guidance, had turned into an attractive and self-assured young lady, with a seductive smile, dancing eyes, and an ease of manner which awed me. She was quite obviously very popular among the young men of her circle. Though I realized that now I would have to learn from her, her transformation inspired me: if she could change so completely, perhaps I, too, could become a success, despite my glasses, uneven teeth and being so short.

The above-mentioned linguistic oddities bring back memories of Frau Kautezky's language school in Vienna. During the war, it was not only my haven, but it kept me sane. Almost immediately after the Germans had marched into Czechoslovakia on March 15, 1939, the harassment of Ostrau's Jews began. Many people emigrated; others tried to send at least their children abroad. My grandparents had neither the means nor the energy to attempt emigration, nor was grandma able to get me into a Kindertransport. While she was considering shipping me off to our relatives in Poland, the war broke out and—fortunately—closed that route. Eventually, my father, who had moved from Berlin to Vienna in the mid-thirties, succeeded in obtaining the required border-crossing permit for me, and on December 31, 1939, I was on my way to Vienna.

I knew my father only from his brief summer visits to Ostrau where, after my mother's death in 1929, my grandparents had provided a loving home for me. Now, not used to having a teenage daughter around, he treated me more like a housekeeper and provider of meals and clean linens. Nor did I see much of him during the day, and he would not divulge where he was going or had been, even when I asked. That was none of my business, he would say. And since I had not attended school in Vienna, I had no friends there, and felt lonely and abandoned. Even so, I was well aware of my father's efforts at obtaining emigration papers for us, and so I threw myself into the study of English.

My initiation into the language took place at the Berlitz School, with its brutally effective rote approach of "this-is-a-pencil-repeat-please-this-is-a-pencil-now—what-is-this?" After that I switched to a course offered by the Kultusgemeinde or "KG," as we used to call it, Vienna's Jewish Community; however, all of its retraining programs were shut down in 1941 when the "resettlement" transports began. Eventually I discovered Sprachschule Kautezky. The school offered two excellent intensive language programs, one for English, one for French. They were conducted entirely in the foreign language, at four hours a day. Besides grammar, conversation and dictation, we had lectures on Great Britain's culture, literature and history. Mrs. Kautezky taught the English program, her daughter Tulli, the French. Upon completing a course, students could sign up for the proficiency test at the university, which would qualify them to translate from or teach the language, I am not sure at what level. My mother had received similar language proficiency certificates in Ostrau for both English and French, and Grandma had been very proud of her "educated" daughter, the only one of the three girls.

We students diligently took down as much as we could of Mrs. Kautezky's lectures, then memorized our notes in preparation for the weekly test. And since Mrs. K. was a great Anglophile, I too soon adored English literature, the Royal House and its ceremonials, High Tea and the stiff upper lip. Until the daily bombardments in 1944 ended our instruction, those four hours each weekday gave meaning to my existence.

I now wonder whether Mrs. Kautezky might have had a least a tiny admixture of Jewish blood; why else would she have let me register without an Ariernachweis, proof of purely Aryan ancestry? Or was it because, my father having been born in Czernowitz (originally

Austro-Hungary, but by then Romania), we were classified as foreigners, at least till 1943? At any rate, I considered myself extremely lucky to be able to participate in the program since Jewish youngsters were not allowed to attend any schools at all.

Classes and homework kept me not only busy but motivated and fulfilled. They took my mind off my loneliness and the pressures around me, which kept increasing. To be sure, as a foreigner I was exempt from the labor service, which was especially punitive if you were considered a Jew, i.e., baptized after 1935, or had at least two Jewish grandparents. However, there was little I could do with the time on my hands since almost everything was "verboten," even to me who, as a foreigner, didn't have to wear the yellow star. Although I could not resist the temptation of walking along the Donaukanal or entering a bookstore to browse for a few minutes, my father got furious if I mentioned it to him. There could be a Razzia, a roundup, and our Romanian citizenship was rather tenuous. "If you get arrested," he threatened, "I won't move a finger to get you out!" I brushed off his threat, but it did scare me a bit and reduced the number of my forbidden escapades. I also stopped telling him about them.

Before I discovered Mrs. Kautezky, my days had consisted largely of standing in line between 11 and 1 to do the minimal shopping our J-stamped ration cards permitted and, at home, of cleaning, doing the laundry (boiled in large pots on the gas stove), mending my father's socks, cooking, and waiting for him (often frustratingly long) to come home for dinner and criticize my attempts at turning the little we had into something palatable. I chafed under that routine, felt trapped, and was convinced that my entire youth was slipping away unused. When I was able to spend half of each day in school, I revived. Even the chores took less time because I could hardly wait to get back to my books.

I was very proud of the study habits I had developed. In addition to the required homework, I avidly tackled any English-language book I could lay my hands on. I still remember one of them, Bulwer-Lytton's The Last Days of Pompeii, which I could barely put down because I had to find out who would survive the calamity. I would read with a small, lined notebook beside me. After folding each page in half, I would enter on the left side every unfamiliar word, one per line, until two pages were filled. Then I would stop reading and add on the right side the one or more German equivalents my dictionary provided for each word. After that, I would reverse the process and add the English equivalents for every German synonym I had recorded. In bed at night, I memorized that day's pages, then reviewed the two pages immediately preceding; if still sufficiently awake, also some of the earlier pages. Once a week, I reviewed all pages. That method made my vocabulary expand by leaps and bounds.

To be sure, my conversations and compositions tended to be laced with far-fetched or bookish terms, often puzzlingly or hilariously inappropriate. In fact, I admit to suffering from moments of such verbal overabundance to this day. Sadly, I have never again mustered the self-

•NEW YORK (1947–1949)•

discipline required for such rapid and thorough language acquisition. When, at age 60, I took an elementary Spanish course, I did get an "A" for the course, but forgot most of my Spanish in no time.

My father suggested that I learn English by memorizing the entries in the dictionary, a page per day, and save him the money my classes cost! Luckily, I won that battle.

* * *

[*translated*]   Sept. 13, 1947

One is constantly reminded of how young this country is. During the first week, when I was still at the hotel, a lady who called herself a "daughter of the revolution" (although she must have been lying for she was not old enough!) took the four of us who happened to be there to show us Manhattan. I have no idea why she did this. It seems to be part of the "being nice to strangers" motto. Could it be that they have a bad conscience about letting so many of us die?

At any rate, she drove us to Trinity Church—"the oldest church in Manhattan." (Manhattan is one of five boroughs which compose New York City, but everybody says that it is the most interesting. I believe the others are mainly residential, but I haven't been in any of them as yet.) At the tip of Manhattan, which is a peninsula, stands the Statue of Liberty, on a small island. She is the first thing you see when you arrive in the United States, even before the skyscrapers, though they tower over her once you get closer. But guess, diary, how old their famous Trinity Church is! One hundred years, that's all. Apparently, there was a church there before, but it left no ruins. This one is rather small and simple, not much of a style, if you ask me.

On the other hand, the Cloisters at the northern end of Manhattan are a very impressive medieval monastery, and now a museum with a carefully laid-out garden, high on a hill above the Hudson River. Except that it was built in this century and just made to look old. America seems to be very much aware of how young it is, and tries to make up for it in any way it can. But inside the Cloisters are many real medieval paintings and statues. They were brought over from Europe by the Rockefellers. I can only hope they were not "organized"!

New York differs from normal cities not only because of its skyscrapers. Washington, the capital, is, I was told, a planned city. I don't know whether it looks at all like New York, but New York is definitely artificial and planned, at least Manhattan. And it must have been designed by someone who lacked imagination but was addicted to chess. Not only do all streets go east-west and are parallel and straight like a chessboard, but they have no names, only numbers: 34th Street, 35th Street, all the way to 150 or more. They are intersected at right angles by "avenues," similarly straight and parallel, but going north-south. They, too, have numbers instead of names, but since Manhattan is a long and narrow peninsula, there are only about ten of them.

Could it be that the planner expected Americans (and tourists?) not to be very bright so that he feared they would get lost if he did not provide a neat and logical grid for their orientation? To my relief he did not succeed entirely. The shops on each street are different, as is the proportion of high to low buildings. Even so, most streets look so similar that, when you come out of the subway, you often have to walk as far as the street sign on the corner, or even to the sign on the second corner, before you know which way is uptown and which downtown. But I am learning, and I already feel quite at home here. And very, very happy, perhaps for the first time in my life. I just mustn't jinx it!

* * *

Dearest Trudilein, Sept. 15, 1947

Many thanks for your letter. Even if it is just a short letter, I am happy to hear from you; so please, don't apologize!

No, Broadway is not just the theater district. It is a very long and busy street (actually an "avenue") which goes from way downtown to way uptown but diagonally, so that it intersects many of the other avenues. Near 94th Street where I live, Broadway has a grassy strip in the center, with shrubs and wooden benches, which gives it a nice small-town feeling, almost a little like Ostrau, despite the noise and traffic. Some houses are tall, ten or more stories; those usually stand on the corners and are hotels or apartment buildings. The other houses are only four to six stories high, with small shops at street level. In them is everything you might need—groceries, flowers, drugs, clothing, shoes, even such luxury items as scented soap. Some stores put racks with clothes or shoes on the sidewalk so that you can inspect and try on everything right there! You couldn't do that in Europe. Prices are much lower here than in the more elegant stores midtown and downtown (i.e., roughly 70th to 30th Streets), and especially on Fifth Avenue, which is the equivalent of our *Kärtnerstraße*. It runs along the eastern edge of Central Park.

Yes, there is an enormous park in the middle of Manhattan. It is about four city blocks wide and fifty-one long, and I am not exaggerating. It extends from 59th Street to 110th. I have only explored small sections so far. There is a duck pond, a small zoo, hills, lawns, flower beds, even a rose garden. Moreover, you are allowed to walk and lie on the grass everywhere! It also has big shade trees and many benches. The entrances are usually where the busses cross the park. One is only a few blocks from where I live, and I can easily walk to it.

Busses run along each avenue and stop at every other block, which is great, though it makes for a slow ride. Every ten blocks or so are stops for the so-called "cross-town" busses which are actually "cross-avenue" busses. Though they are supposed to go straight across town they don't always: once I started out on 79th Street on the east side of Central Park, and came out on 80th Street on the west side; another time, a bus suddenly switched on me from going west-east to going south. In a way, it is reassuring that even in this so very logical city not everything is predictable.

Whenever I have to wait for a bus, I am amazed at how patient people are, even in a large crowd. When the bus stops, they don't push and shove, though the bus may be quite full and it's obvious that not everybody will get on. Even well-dressed people, with leather handbags or briefcases, tend to use the busses.

On a Saturday it is fun to walk along Broadway or, even better, to sit on a bench and watch the people. Then you realize how much of a "melting-pot" America is: many Jewish immigrants, of course, some from long before the war and quite elderly, with ungrammatical English and an accent that is much worse than mine. You also hear Russian, Polish, even Yiddish. Then there are many Negroes, much younger, and some have fascinating faces. Especially the women are often beautiful and less artificial looking than even the prettiest white women. In Vienna I had seen very few blacks, all of them American soldiers and men. Before that, in Ostrau, I had seen only one Negro, and he was not typical: a tall, very impressive man in a splendid red and gold uniform, who stood in front of the big Meinl store all day long, motionless like a statue. He was probably a symbol for the exotic countries where their coffee came from. He ignored us, and when we tried to touch him, a saleslady would chase us away. I wonder if he understood German. Here the coffee tastes terrible, just a brown watery mixture which has never seen a coffee bean.

However, in Vienna the American soldiers were always friendly, whether they were black or white. Here the Negroes seem very reserved and don't talk to us, I mean to white people. When I started a conversation with one sitting at the next table in the cafeteria, he only said "yes" and "no." As if he were afraid to talk to me. The same happens in the subway, where often the only free seat is next to a Negro. I know, of course, that in the South they still don't treat them well, and I will never go there. But here? Perhaps there are things I am not aware of since all my friends are Jewish. I do know, though, that black people cannot hide their color the way we could hide the star; now, thank God, we no longer have to wear one, whereas they continue to be marked. That must make it much harder for them. Even if they don't get persecuted or gassed.

The one exception are the waitresses. The black ones are usually much nicer than the white ones. They call me "honey" or "hon" and "sweetie," even the first time they see me. First I thought that they recognized me from before, but they all seem to do this. Perhaps they can tell that I am Jewish and therefore o.k.? Their English is not always easy to understand, but I love their faces. Some are very dark, as if they had come straight from darkest Africa, but with beautiful white teeth. Others can be so light that it is difficult to tell if they are whites with a suntan, have come from a southern country, or are blacks. Some women look so exotic and mysterious that I cannot stop looking at them.

I cannot tell the difference between a Negro and an American Indian, but perhaps there aren't any American Indians in New York. We do have a few Chinese or Japanese (they all look alike). Their faces are exotic but less striking, just very unfamiliar, with totally different features from Whites, Browns and Blacks. I would love to be able to talk to them and find out how they think. One thing seems to characterize them: all are quite thin, whereas many Browns and Blacks are fat; and some whites, especially young women, look as if they were starving.

Enough for today. I miss you very much, in spite of all the excitement here. Remain healthy and greet your mother from
Your faithful friend Liesl

PS. They use commas differently in English, not nearly as many and not as systematically as in German, which makes it difficult to learn the rules. I am not even sure there are any.

* * *

9-24-47, New York

Today was Jom Kippur and as I had much time for meditation, I drew you out of your drawer and in an interval between praying read some of the pages I had written before, and began to think back. And the great change in my life struck me and I feel the necessity to tell you about it. When asked why I had left Vienna I would probably have answered—because it offers no future! And meanwhile the main reason was an entirely different one and I should keep it in mind to be never ungrateful and pretentious! The reason was that I had to prove to myself that I could earn my own living, build up my own life, get along well with other people—within short, begin living again. And only when I remembered all those petty worries, quarrels with my father and disasters, and how I allowed them to overshadow my life and to make me suffer, I realize to the full extent, how good my decision was.

I never spent a Jom Kippur more devoted to prayer and nicer than today's. I did not fast, I stopped during the war, and somehow I was feeling now, that it would be insincere to begin again. Prayer is much more meaningful. I had been afraid to feel lonely, but it was a happy day. First I was permitted to enter the synagogue—I was lucky because here you normally have to pay and get a ticket!—then I met the Roseggs, very nice people who knew part of my family in Vienna. And I did not mind eating all alone in a restaurant, for I had to think of the great discovery about my present happiness I had made, and I wanted to be alone. Did I feel guilty about not fasting? Not at all: During the war, we fasted every day, and how much good did that do? I was praying, though.

Well, how does New York agree with me? Marvellously! I only must not commit the mistake to become ungrateful because everything goes too smoothly. I got a 40$ job at 37.5 hours only, can profit there a lot with my English as well as with shorthand. And start being dissatisfied already, because it is no creative work! How many people have a job they love, after all? I remember, in Munich I was afraid that I would have to do dishwashing or things like that, I did not yet dream about 40$ a week. And I got lots of friends too, go out very much, have even a boyfriend, though, thank heaven, it is nothing serious—I would not like to commit myself too early—well, I do not know, what else I would wish. And I *do* enjoy being independent and able to do whatever I like. I am happy, really happy.

I do not suppose that that is the right mood after the Day of Atonement, but the review of this last year must needs lead to this statement, if I was not too pretentious. I only beg God not to let me forget all those people starving in Europe and never to take this great stroke of luck (that I was able to come here) for granted.

There are however some things I would like to hand down and read from time to time, some warnings: FIRSTLY and as mentioned before, never to take my job too lightly and secondarily!

SECONDLY not to allow myself to be drifted along that beaten track that makes the girls crazy for men and marriage here. That makes them view everybody from that angle and keep this question in mind all the time. I am still young enough to wait till the really right one comes with whom I won't be only good at sleeping, but at living with too. And I should not forget that marriage involves all those petty matters again which made me so unhappy while I was staying with my father!

3.) Never to forget the chief aim—to build up a carreer—about the petty diversions and pleasures. Never to stop striving for knowledge and improvement, never to contend and relax in the life of the present! But yet, and before all, lead a reasonable and not too strenuous life, not wearing oneself out or forgetting to enjoy life.

4.) To improve my character, be friendly to everyboy, helpful and sunny! Amen.

I admit to being surprised at these references to prayer. I thought I broke off my ties to religion in Vienna when, only a few days before the Russians liberated us, two of my best friends as well as my father's lady-friend (whom I loved dearly) were killed, Ilse by a bomb, but her twin brother and Grete deliberately by the SS. They went from house to house looking for "protected" Jews (all the others had been deported long before), dragged them out into the street and killed them. We escaped only because the entrance to our building was under fire, and the rear entrance was walled off from the inside. Since we were in the cellar at the time, we would not have known anything, had not Mrs. Pospíšil, who lived in the apartment above us, been upstairs. She heard the loud knocking on the rear door, and saw the uniforms. Eventually, they moved on.

3.

[*translated*] Oct. 28, 1947

I must again return to you, my dearest and most faithful friend. I ought to seek refuge with you more often. No fear—I don't want to shed tears in your arms. Since I have been here and alone, I have regained my equilibrium, though I have not yet learned to cope with major assaults, as I realized on Sunday..

Sunday marked the end of my first New York period—the intoxication and giddiness of novelty. Since I was rather fortunate in finding friends and was drifting in a social whirl totally unknown from Vienna, I enjoyed it to the brim without thinking of anything else. Then, on Sunday, I woke up. In the afternoon I was in the museum with Mrs. Ausländer and had, for the first time in weeks, a (mentally) stimulating afternoon; and in the evening I heard a lecture on the symphony, illustrated with records. I must start going to museums. I know nothing about paintings and painters, just a few names. After the war, I did go to the theater and the opera whenever I could, but never to a museum—perhaps they weren't even open.

Afterward (in the Habonim club), I found myself totally alone and lonely in midst of a loud and exuberant crowd and, for the first time, I longed for intellectual contact. Just being there, or at Hanna's parties, and chatter about meaningless things is such a waste of time, with my life slipping by. I felt so bad that at home I sat down and wrote to Walter. That made me feel better. And today arrived a letter from Frau Doktor Schieber, with a thousand new ideas as always, and angry with me for wasting and squandering my talents by working as a stenographer. Though I don't quite agree with her (probably mainly because I am not nearly as good at business as she is, and hide my missing talent behind indignation about money-makers), I feel unfulfilled because I waste my time without any spiritual gain. Come, Liesl, you need to achieve something! Perhaps I must really decide to live either for the future or for the moment; and if the former is linked to spiritual gain, then everything in me opts for the future.

The Habonim Club was a Zionist youth organization. I no longer recall how long I participated in it, nor what our activities consisted of. The name means "builders."

Rose Ausländer (1901-88) is now considered one of the greatest 20th century German poets. When I met her, at a dinner given by the Roseggs who lived in the high-rise at the corner of my block, she had only published a few poems, in journals, and one collection of poetry, which the Nazis immediately suppressed. I didn't know any of that, only that she, too, was a refugee, was working in an office, was tall and attractive if rather thin, and very intellectual. Moreover, like my family, she had come from Czernowitz in the Bukovina, when it was still part of the Austro-Hungarian Empire and a university town with a sizeable population of Jewish intellectuals. When I told her that my grandfather had been chief editor of the Czernowitzer Morgenzeitung before World War One, during which the entire family fled from the Russians to Vienna, she seemed interested in me. I was therefore doubly disappointed when I did not hear from her again after our joint museum visit. I was sure it was because my company had disappointed her.

Frau Dr. Schieber: I remember her as quite elderly, very short and round, with a broad face but a long, pointed nose, which gave her a mousey look. Her eyebrows were so pale as to be almost invisible; her whitish-blond hair was remarkably long, reaching all the way to her waist when loose. The Schiebers were part of my life in 1940-42, when we shared an apartment in Vienna's "Innenstadt," the first district. More accurately, after our apartment had been confiscated, we were assigned one room and they another in the three-bedroom apartment of an elderly Romanian couple, Herr and Frau Hofrat Winternitz. Amazing, how that name suddenly crops up, after sixty years! Frau Dr. Schieber actually had no doctorate, just as Frau Hofrat Winternitz was no Hofrätin, but it was (and still is) common courtesy—or flattery—in Austria to extend the husband's title to the wife.

Since Jews were not allowed to attend any schools, my father asked Frau Dr. Schieber to tutor me in English, math, chemistry, cooking, baking, cake decorating—you name it. He claimed that I needed to learn something practical instead of the fashion-design course I was taking at the Jewish Community Center, and which I loved. As so happened, when in 1941 the deportations began, the Jewish Community had to cancel all retraining courses anyway. That assuaged my disappointment at least somewhat. Not that I recall much of what Frau Doktor had taught me, but I still have somewhere the perforated paper doilies you put on top of a cake's icing to decorate it. When you poured powdered cinnamon on the surface of the paper, it would retrace the paper's intricate design through the holes onto the icing. I recall a birthday and a wedding pattern; perhaps I had others as well.

In 1942 the couple was deported, but Frau Doktor survived. At the end of the war, at age sixty or more, she dragged herself from Auschwitz to the Bohemian spa of Karlsbad, which in the liberated Czechoslovakia was again called Karlovy Vary. She hoped that its mineral waters would restore her health. She weighed 80 lbs at the time. Indeed, she soon regained her strength. She made a living, at first by selling items she collected from trash heaps, later by running a small resale shop. In the summer of 1946, to express her gratitude for the packages I had sent to her in camp, she invited me to visit her. By then, she looked much the way I remembered her, seemed to be doing reasonably well, and was full of ideas and projects.

She urged me to stay with her and help her open a language school in town. True, I had spent a happy childhood in Czechoslovakia and had, like all of us, revered President Masaryk. But it was no longer the same country. My entire Ostrau family had been deported, and that made even a visit painful. Moreover, on my way to the spa I spent two days in Prague visiting friends of Viennese friends. Both were medical students but at that point spent most of their evenings distributing communist literature. Czechoslovakia was probably still better than Austria which had, after all, embraced Hitler with open arms, but I was unable to see either country as a "homeland." The only place where I could envision starting over and sinking *roots was America, and I was going to try as hard as I could to get there.*

The above-mentioned letter from Frau Dr. Schieber came from Florida, where she was now importing feather quilts from Austria. She wanted me to be her New York representative, but I declined. I did not hear from her again and, unfortunately, don't seem to have kept her address. By now it is obviously much too late to search.

* * *

[*translated*]   Nov. 4, 1947

Today was an unpleasant day. To my disappointment, I discovered that I am not nearly as well balanced as I had thought. I must be more careful. Though my nerves are calm at the moment, they tend to slide back into a tense state at any provocation. Today was election day. Officially, our office closed two hours earlier, but since I don't vote, Abe, our office manager, kept me till 5:30. I don't like Abe. I am even a little afraid of him. He smokes like a chimney (Fred smokes as well, but cigars like grandpa used to. That I don't mind). Abe has a long, narrow face, and there is something harsh in his eyes which makes me uncomfortable. He is Jewish, but an American Jew. Perhaps that's why there is no warmth in him. With Fred I am comfortable.

I was close to tears, even though I tried to talk myself out of my anger since the work I was doing would have to get done sooner or later anyway. Even so, I calmed down only when I found a birthday letter from Ditha at home. Though too early, it could not have arrived at a better moment. But why do I get so easily upset when nothing is really wrong? Now I am again sensible; it seems that, if you have no worries, you invent some!

Ditha was one of our Viennese "cemetery group." On Sundays we would meet inside Gate Four, the Jewish Section of the Central Cemetery, which was the only outdoors spot where we were allowed to congregate. Since by 1943 star wearers needed special permits from the Jewish Community to use the streetcar, my friends had been assigned an "official" task, namely to weed and water the Agency's garden plot, the Grabeland [*lit. "digging land"*], *as we referred to it. In those days of shortages, it supplied the Jewish orphanage, hospital and* Ausspeisung—*the free-lunch program—with vegetables. Once the chores were done, we could sit on our blankets on the lawn and talk, play cards or word games, or take walks under the trees along the rows of graves. At first that did not seem right to me, but then I told myself that we might be bringing a bit of life to those below, in case they were still attuned to a human presence, and I relaxed.*

Though only half-Jewish, Ditha and her brother had to wear the yellow star, and were periodically threatened with deportation. (So was I, even though, as a foreigner, I did not wear the star. Being seen with star-wearers was dangerous, as my father warned me, but I ignored him: I felt that the least I could do was show my loyalty to my friends. Luckily, I was never confronted.) Ditha's entire family survived the war in Vienna and eventually emigrated to the United States. We have kept in touch.

* * *

Dearest Trude,   Dec. 3, 1947

    First of all, many thanks for your long letter and the birthday wishes. It was a quiet day, but I did not mind. Incidentally, your letter arrived only three days ago. Inside was a note from the censor: "Because of lack of sender detained for four weeks." (The censor must have had fun with that letter!) Be careful that you don't forget again.

    You are quite right to scold me for interspersing my German with English. I will try not to do it in the future, except that some words have no German equivalents; those I have to give in English.

    Now to the rest of your letter. I must admit that your "confession" surprised me completely. I would have expected anything but that. I waited for a few days before answering, but by now I have thought about it very carefully and can, I believe, express an objective opinion. First of all, I beg you not to think for a moment that "it's easy for her to talk" or something similar, or that I am too prudish to understand. I think you know how much I love you; I could not love my own sister more, and what you told me has not lessened my love for you, only my concern.

    I must confess that I was indignant about O's behavior toward you all those years. I don't know if you realize how despicable it was of him. He must have known what he was doing if he not only managed to dominate you, but—even more important—was the first one, thereby leaving a doubly great impact.

    You write how decently he acted when you met Hubert. That's no surprise. He knew that his conscience was not clear, so he tried to justify himself by enabling you to find somewhere else what he could not offer you or didn't want to. It upsets me all the more that O continued the affair when Hubert left for Russia, even though he knew that you had become interested in him. In my view, this is inexcusable. I have one question: did Hubert know about your relationship with O? I assume he did not or he would probably have tried to get closer to you himself and replace O. But perhaps he was too decent for that. Though it is in a way fortunate that you did not go all the way with him. It would have made it even harder for you, when he was killed.

For an impartial outsider there exists only one, all too obvious motive for O's behavior: the endeavor to recapture his own youth, at least indirectly, and to hold on to it, not considering that he might be harming you.

I suppose that my judgment on O will seem harsh to you, dearest Trude. I do not doubt that you like him, and probably more than you admit even to yourself, and you found consolation with him after losing Hubert. But if you are able to see him the way he really is, you cannot continue this relationship. Go there as little as possible, and try not to be alone with him. And avoid all explanations because then he will entangle you again.

Well, Trudechild, here you have my carefully considered opinion. I hope you will take my advice, or you will get hurt again.

Here there is nothing to report which you don't already know. I notice, Truderl, that you are jealous because my father gets letters more often than you do. I cannot spend so much money on postage. You too should not write by air mail as long as the financial situation in Vienna is so appalling. As soon as I can, I will help you myself or through others, but I can't promise anything since at the moment I am primarily occupied with my cousins in Berlin. They are very badly off. Their father was killed in a camp, but they and their (Aryan) mother survived. However, it was too much for her, and her heart gave out at the end of the war. Now the grandmother and an aunt care for them. The boys want to come here, but I don't earn enough to send them an affidavit.

I enclose a few photos, some for you, the rest for my father. Last time, I did it the other way round, and he still has not forwarded yours to you. All his friends want to see them, he writes. But don't spend any postage on forwarding: next week I will send a package to my father with some cocoa for you. When you fetch that, you can hand him the pictures. This time they are not as good.

That's all for today.

Good night, and write soon to your very concerned

old friend Liesl

* * *

[*translated*] Dec. 14, 1947

Here I am again, for a change. Yesterday I moved, to an apartment owned by a very nice old couple. It was a good decision. The atmosphere is much more pleasant. I am still cheerful and balanced, and cannot complain about a lack of entertainment. I guess I am catching up after all those empty years.

Though I have no boyfriend and sometimes wish I did, I am also glad. I don't feel comfortable with the way the girls run after the men, when it should be the other way round. They make them talk about themselves and pretend to be terribly interested, even if they must be bored. How can a friendship develop that way, not to mention a real relationship? But perhaps Hanna and her friends are not typical, and I have to wait till I can compare.

Or am I too egocentric, and that is the reason why in Vienna Harry and I drifted apart, after he returned from Theresienstadt? Perhaps I did not show sufficient interest in his life and thoughts, and so we limited ourselves to physical closeness, which could not, of course, suffice for either of us in the long run. But he did not try either. At any rate, right now I enjoy my freedom far too much to want to tie myself down. Also, I am if anything short of time and not bored, so there is really no serious problem.

Far more important is my dissatisfaction with myself because I am making no progress with studying and writing, and am simply wasting my time on unimportant things like visits, parties, movies—all fine and good except that the occupation I consider most important for me is suffering. Sure, it felt great to be finally able to have some fun, after all those years during which the only good period were those three months with Harry in 1943. But now I am already twenty-three; I cannot waste more time but must begin to create a life for myself, to become something and someone. Honestly, I must pull myself together and do more; especially my writing must not be neglected. From now on my motto must be: "Is this the best way to spend the next hour?"

4.

Dearest Truderl, [*undated*]

I have moved, as you see (on the 13th), and this room is much nicer. The apartment is in one of a row of old-fashioned buildings, all joined. They are called "brownstones," though they are really of reddish brick. With their gabled roofs they even look a little European. However, they are more sober, and all very similar, lining the street like sentries. Most of them are four stories high. Each has ten or more outside steps going up to the entryway. Some also have two or three steps leading down to a basement entrance. The square space in front of that lower entrance tends to be of concrete, often softened by a potted shrub or a few flower pots. Ours has a raised flower bed. The main outside staircases have high iron railings on both sides, some with nice curves or patterns which add a little variety and style.

My building is the last one of the group. Adjacent to it is a large high-rise of twelve floors, which takes up the entire corner facing Central Park. That's where the Roseggs live. Have I written to you about the park? It is huge, in the middle of this sea of stone a green oasis, even if without palm trees. If you stand on one of its little hills, you can see the high-rises on Fifth Avenue on the other side of the park, and also those at the southern edge of the park, on 59th Street. This panorama is called a "skyline." It is truly impressive, especially at night, when the windows all around the park sparkle like hundreds of stars. But Mrs. Milstein says I should not walk in the park at night.

To help you imagine my new home: the apartment is on the first floor, which here is the second floor since there is no *Parterre,* and which is actually the third floor if you count all the outside steps. We have two bedrooms, and I am the only renter, so I am allowed to use the living-dining room, the kitchen, and of course the bath-toilet room. Now and then the Milsteins' daughter, son-in-law and two grandchildren visit, but then it gets so crowded that I try to be out. Also, I find it embarrassing to watch how hard Mrs. Milstein tries to please them, and how loud and demanding—really ill-behaved—the children are, and their parents say nothing. Nor is the daughter very helpful. She sits and waits to be served, working at her make-up instead of helping. Her lipstick is very red and her earrings and rings are huge, all of which makes her look rather vulgar.

Although the Milsteins must have been in this country for many years, they speak ungrammatical English, with a lot of Polish and Yiddish words mixed in. Mr. Milstein was a tailor until he retired. Both are white-haired, stout and even shorter than I am. They seem fond of each other, or at least she of him. He does not show much emotion. Square and stocky, he hides behind the newspaper most of the time and says very little. Despite her warm smile—which reveals a missing front tooth—she has permanently worried eyes. These worried eyes now include me.

Mrs. M. is very motherly and often invites me to eat dinner with them. Though she is a good cook, I usually pretend that I am meeting a friend, and eat at a nearby café. I am sure they don't have much money. Also, I don't want to become too much like family. She means well but tends to treat me as if I were her child. When I come home late, she wants to know where I have been, just as Father used to. I am, after all, twenty-three years old! Also, she keeps hinting that it's time for me to find a nice Jewish boy to marry, not wait too long or waste time on men that are not right for me.

By that she means Dr. Rosenthal, whom I met at a party. He is a journalist and quite a bit older, but very handsome and distinguished-looking, like a movie star or a professor. I feel flattered that he is interested in me, but I certainly wouldn't think of marrying him. When he heard that I was still a virgin, he immediately said that in that case he would not dream of touching me—in great contrast to your friend O! When he comes to pick me up and waits in the living room, Mrs. Milstein is very polite, but I can tell that she disapproves. Of course, she says nothing, only looks at me with those worried eyes.

He and I often walk along the park in the evening, and he describes his work. He is extremely well-informed, and very witty. Sometimes we sit down on a bench, and lately he has begun to kiss me. I am of course flattered, but I don't really like his kisses. I would much rather just sit and talk, only I don't want him to lose interest in me. Except that the other day he led my hand down along the front of his trousers and asked me to massage him. I naturally refused and, to my relief, he did not insist. Even so, I wonder if I should not say I am busy when he calls again, because now I worry that he is perverted. But he helped me forget Jackie, who was perhaps just as bad—who knows.

I also have a new job. I work in the office of Imperial Linens Incorporated, a linen import firm on Fifth Avenue, corner 31st Street. The building is a high-rise but with an interesting façade, almost like a baroque building. However, the façade is misleading. Inside it is quite modern, with long, straight hallways and many identical doors, distinguishable only by their signs. The halls tend to be totally empty except at noon and at five, when mobs of people spill out and race to the elevators, as if the place were on fire.

My firm is in what is called "downtown." There both avenues and streets have much nicer stores than those where I live. At noon, they get terribly crowded. Everyone tries to squeeze as much shopping as possible into the lunch hour. I usually bring a sandwich and eat it in the office, or sometimes in the stock room with Hertha, our "in-house" designer; or I go to a nearby coffee shop, with the funny name "Chock-Full-o'Nuts." They are famous for their coffee. "Chock-full" is a slang term for completely full, and the shop is certainly always full of people so that I often have to drink standing up. They don't sell nuts there at all, but crazy people are sometimes referred to as nuts—so perhaps that is what the name means.

The streets are just as crowded at five. Cars get stuck and honk like mad, and people push and shove the moment the light turns green. It is like a stampede, enough to make you dizzy. All that in order to catch a subway train a minute earlier! The moment its doors open, there is a huge wave of bodies pushing in as if a wild beast were after them. But they push you in with them, not aside as they would at home, where they would elbow you out of their way. That excuses a lot, don't you think? Democracy at work.

By contrast, 94th Street where I live is much quieter, actually quite idyllic, with few cars even during rush hour, at most a taxi or two. And once you have escaped from the subway, you can walk and breathe at your own speed. It feels like having emerged from a hurricane or steam bath. Or both. The few pedestrians you meet are mainly people escorted by their dogs toward the trees or shrubs that need to be inspected and watered. Yes, our street has trees, each inside a small grassy square, which takes up part of the sidewalk. An iron railing encloses it, but it is so low that even a mini-dog can ignore it. Some of the trees have flowers around them. I don't know who plants and takes care of the flowers, but they look nice, despite the unhealthy watering. And where I live, the avenues even have real names, meaningful names. My block is between Central Park West (Avenue) and Columbus Avenue; then comes Amsterdam Avenue, because New York was originally settled by the Dutch and called New Amsterdam. Then there is Broadway, West End Avenue, and a narrow, long park along the Hudson River. I would never have imagined that a metropolis could be surrounded by so much nature!

I will describe my new work environment to you in my next letter.

Remain healthy and don't forget—

Your faithful friend Liesl

* * *

Dearest Trude, New York, Dec. 19, 1947

You will be surprised to hear from me so soon after my last letter, but your letter has just arrived, and I want to reply right away. I can't tell you how glad I am that you have met Kurt and like him so much. He sounds like a great person. Remember what you said, when you returned to me the little booklet in which I had poured out my heart, right after Harry was deported? You were anxiously waiting for letters from Hubert, and you said:

"Your story has an ending, mine hangs in the air, and who knows how it will end." And when Hubert was killed at the front and we were crying together, you said:

"Now my romance has an ending like yours." I will never forget that. You were so brave! It is high time that you find some joy. I hope Kurt will treasure you as much as you deserve and will spoil you a little as well. (I assume that the affair with O is over? Make sure it is!)

Now let me tell you about my new job. I am no longer a switchboard operator, but a real secretary, and I earn $5 more per week! I take shorthand and type business letters. They have a special format, but that was easy to learn. Now I sometimes am even asked to compose one on my own. There are two other secretaries, Florence and Alice. I think both are Jewish, though Florence has blond hair. Alice's hair is dark and quite long, although she is not at all young, but probably younger than Florence. Florence works for the big boss, Mr. Roland, Alice for one of our two office managers, Abe. I work for the other one, Fred. Yes, you heard right: we are expected to address not only the other secretaries but also the office managers by their first names, and they do the same! I am Elizabeth for everybody. Can you imagine calling your boss Fritz or Abraham (I assume those are their real names), not even *Herr* Fritz? Here that seems to be the custom, and they keep reminding me of it. I find it disrespectful and embarrassing. Perhaps it is due to the fact that English does not differentiate between *du* and *Sie*, consequently you never know what the relationship between two people is. (Originally, English too had two forms, "thou" and "you," but I guess you know that. I wonder why the "thou" was dropped—long before any democratic ideas came into circulation.)

The big boss is addressed as Mr. Roland, probably because everybody seems in awe of him, even Abe and Fred. I am not sure he is Jewish. At any rate, he is a bit distant, though quite handsome. He has thin dark hair carefully distributed over what is probably a bald spot, a sharp profile and a tan. He is always well-dressed, with bow tie and suit jacket. (Abe hardly ever wears a tie, and a jacket only to come and leave, and not even that at all times. He looks quite sloppy with his rolled-up shirt sleeves. Fred also takes his jacket off in the office, but at least he keeps his tie on, and he never rolls up his sleeves. He wears bow-ties, though; perhaps that is considered less formal.) Mr. Roland's office is very elegant, only quite dark. It has leather armchairs, a huge desk and wood paneling all around. The main office where all of us sit is large and bright, but the desks have no personality at all.

When Mr. Roland walks through our office, all talk stops immediately, and Alice and Florence begin to type like mad. Otherwise they waste a lot of time gossiping, mainly about men or clothes or hairdos. Especially Alice seems obsessed with the fear of becoming an old maid. If you ask me, she is trying far too hard to catch a man. The women, in general, dress much less tastefully than at home, often in garish, loud colors, even old ladies.

Yesterday, three were standing at the bus stop. When the bus came, one called out:

"Come on, girls!"

Girls? They must have been at least fifty. Two had blond hair, definitely dyed, and all wore tight skirts, although they were anything but slim. I have noticed that especially older women try to appear young rather than mature. Odd.

So far Mr. Roland has not been paying any attention to me. That is fine with me since my typing is still very slow, as is my shorthand. I would hate to be called into his office for dictation. Even Alice gets nervous when she has to substitute. (Though Florence is very self-assured and a *Besserwisser* [*know-it-all*], she often has to retype her letters. I can always tell when that happens because she comes out of Mr. Roland's office with a red face, and types for a while without talking.)

Luckily, Fred is very patient with me. I was given his phone number by friends in Vienna to convey greetings, and a few weeks later he called me to ask whether I wanted to be his secretary. When I told him that my typing and shorthand were still very slow, he assured me that he would dictate slowly until I was worked in; so I changed jobs, and am glad I did. Besides more money, this is much more interesting work than sitting in front of a switchboard. It is also nice not to be alone all day.

Something else is interesting here: people don't use "big words," and every word which has more than two syllables seems to be considered big. When I said at the office that we were having propitious weather, everyone stared at me. Either they did not know the word or it was too big for them.

Altogether, people, or at least our two secretaries, speak a very simplified language. For instance, they use hardly any verb other than "get," often with strange meanings. To be sure, Mrs. Kautezky taught us that "get" can have many meanings, depending on the preposition. But that's not what I am talking about: in addition to such logical meanings as "get in, out, up, down," there are totally unguessable combinations such as "get going" for start, "get through" for finish or, if followed by "to", for reaching someone or even getting connected on the phone; "get with it" is pull yourself together or concentrate, "get along" to enjoy someone's company, "get over" to overcome, "get behind" to ferret out, "get at" to reach, also to find out or explore. Fred gave me a long list, and there may be more. Remember how angry Mrs. Kautezky became when we used too many "gets" in our essays? "It impoverishes the language!" she would say. Here she would have a heart attack!

Another funny thing: I, of all people, am asked, even by Abe (and he is an American!) how to spell. They never seem to know whether a verb is spelled with "ei" or "ie," an "s" or a "z." Fred spells really well, but then he too is a European, even if he came here before the war. Schooling can't amount to much in this country.

In a few things, however, Mrs. K. was wrong, at least regarding American English: you are allowed to split an infinitive, and you can also end a sentence with a preposition. And you mustn't place a comma before "that", but you can before "and." Believe me, American punctuation drives me crazy.

What I also have trouble with is if someone tries to spell a word or name for me. I always have to say "more slowly, please!" and write each letter down, or at least try to visualize it. Of course, I know the English alphabet and can recite it quickly, but it is so frustratingly illogical—why would anyone want to say "ej" for *a* or "ii" for *e* and "ejtch" for *ha?*

High time to get to bed. My very best wishes to you and your mother for a merry Christmas, and a very happy New Year—

Your Liesl

* * *

[*translated*] Dec. 22, 1947

I had an unpleasant little adventure, which made me wonder whether I would need to look for another job. Fred invited me to his apartment for dinner. He cooked a delicious meal, with wine. After dinner he asked me to sit next to him on the couch, and after a while he placed his hand on my knee. I moved it away and changed back to the chair. He said "sorry" and began to talk about something else. After that he did not try anything. He must be in his forties, is chubby, wears black-rimmed glasses and has a round, unfinished baby face. He is almost bald except for a little mustache. Quiet and pleasant but certainly not sexy. I wonder if he has ever been married. I felt sorry for him but was very uncomfortable at work for a while. Much to my relief, he has behaved totally properly since then, and is as polite and helpful as before. I just hope he won't invite me again because it might offend him if I refused. Life is so complicated!

Something else which is far more positive: at work I met a very interesting lady, Hertha Fürth, also from Vienna. She doesn't work in our office but in the stockroom, all by herself. She is different from everyone else I know, probably because she is an artist. She designs the patterns for our table cloths, pillow cases, guest towels and handkerchiefs, which are then sent to Madeira to be embroidered. She has great charm, a subdued, low-key kind of charm, quite different from Frau Farkas, but just as nice.

Hertha always wears a white smock, like a physician. Perhaps that makes her look so dignified. I feel flattered that she likes me. Not very young and undoubtedly a spinster, she has a great deal of poise. She never talks about herself or her past, and I of course don't ask questions. She must have had a difficult and frustrating life. Her smile is sweet but seems timid, as if she were apologizing for her existence. I don't think she associates with anyone else in the firm and must be very lonely, having to spend her days by herself in a back room drawing designs for table linens. Whenever she invites me to eat my sandwich with her, I feel privileged. She urges me to keep up my writing.

Now that I know a lot more about Hertha than I did then, I am embarrassed at my hasty assessment. And yet—don't all human beings remain to some extent a mystery to all others, even to themselves? All we can register are individual gestures, thoughts or feelings, and we don't know if they are marginal, accidental, or possibly deliberate disguises and masks. Perhaps one should not even attempt to characterize or classify another person, much less analyze or judge, only observe, marvel, and learn the lesson where there is a lesson to be learned. Even so, I greatly regret not having tried harder to get to know Hertha then and, in fact, later.

After I left Imperial Linens to go to college, we corresponded for many years. She suggested books I should read, encouraged my writing efforts, and occasionally sent me a book that had especially impressed her. Eventually she wrote that she was getting married and moving to Chicago. It was quite a romance: a prominent surgeon whom she had met shortly before the outbreak of World War One, when he was studying in Vienna, saw her name in a New York telephone directory and contacted her. I don't know if it was love at first sight or a romance resumed, but at any rate she sounded very happy, and I was delighted that, however late, she had still found a soul mate.

When I visited her in Chicago a few years later, I should have taken my clue from the fact that their huge house seemed cavernous and impersonal, almost spooky. The darkness of the hallways was only brightened by the large number of paintings on the walls, with strikingly vigorous and vibrant lines and colors. They were Hertha's works. Now that she no longer needed to design doilies, she had become a member of the Chicago Art League. She was exhibiting frequently and had, in fact, won several prizes. One painting in particular enthralled me: a market scene in Oaxaca, Mexico, with pale yellow awnings under swaying blue-green palm fronds. In its mood it reminded me of Cézanne's forest-scapes, except that it was more exuberant. A few young women in pink, blue and white skirts were scurrying up the sunny road toward the shade of the trees, with fruit-laden baskets balancing on their heads. I was getting married that year, and Hertha insisted that I take the painting with me as a wedding present. I still have it and find it as enchanting as I did then.

I did not meet her husband the surgeon but, alas, by then the romance had already begun to fade. Hertha's later letters sounded at first wistful and sad, then more and more discouraged and bitter. He only seemed to have eyes for his two adult offspring, who were sponging on their doting father, and expected to be supported throughout their lives. To his wife he became increasingly stingy and inattentive, and Hertha felt that she was little more than an unpaid housekeeper. When he died, he left everything to his no-good son and daughter, even though Hertha had nursed him faithfully during his long illness. It took a court battle for her to get at least the house.

Many years later when, after nineteen years in California, I was again living in Massachusetts where my first job had been, I met an elegant elderly lady at the opening of a Klimt-Schiele exhibit I had arranged at my college. She introduced herself as Viennese and invited me to her apartment for tea. When she returned the visit, she noticed the Oaxaca market scene, signed Fürth, and gasped: Hertha was a first cousin of hers!

My visitor began to tell me about Hertha's youth in Imperial Vienna, and I was spellbound. Not only had she been a much admired beauty who moved in Austria's best circles, but she was quite notorious. What today would barely elicit a smile, then shocked her environment. During a trip to Spain she had learned to dance the tango, and she demonstrated the dance whenever she had a chance. She also smoked openly and went horseback riding in the Prater, probably the only woman aside from the Empress to do so. At one time she wrote a little skit for her cousin's wedding, and acted in it as well.

Hertha's mother died when she was three, and she was raised by a series of governesses. She married very young—"to spite Aunt Cecile!"—divorced soon, married again, and divorced again. When, why and how she reached the United States, her cousin did not know for she was living in Hungary by then. Even after she had emigrated to the States, she was not in touch with her Hertha, and so the years until I met her at Imperial Linens remained a blank for both of us. All my friend had learned, indirectly, was that Hertha's third marriage was not happy either, and that she had died quite recently, in her late eighties.

By then, however, I was able to add a few more details to her story. So often such encounters leave the bystander with an indefinite, incomplete picture—train tracks disappearing in the distance; therefore it feels especially good to be a witness to the final brush strokes, and doubly good if they enrich the painting.

During a visit back east while I was still living in California, I traced Hertha's address to a nursing home in a New York suburb. A friend offered to drive me out to see her. We had to wait while Hertha was having a pedicure. When she appeared, I barely recognized the hunched-over, tiny old woman leaning heavily on a cane, her face almost lost in a spider web of wrinkles. Except that even under those big horn-rimmed glasses her eyes were still large, black and sparkling.

She neither remembered nor recognized me. When I said that I was her old friend from California, she merely stated that she too had a friend in California. But as she was taking us down the long hallway which led to her room, she proudly pointed at the many paintings on the walls: all of them were her work.

Her room was small but sunny and bright. Alas, they would not let her paint there, she complained, nor give her another room to use as a studio. From behind a chest she pulled out, not without effort but refusing all help, two large maps containing sketches and paintings. Every one of them revealed a highly skilled and original artist. As we were admiring them, Hertha straightened up as much as she was able to, looked into my eyes and said with a big smile: "I have had such fun in my life, haven't I?"

* * *

[*translated*] Dec. 23, 1947

I am in a festive mood: this afternoon I received my first citizenship papers. What a wonderful feeling! My evening class on American history includes a lot of current politics so that I have really gained a good insight into the problems of this country. To be sure, there is plenty to criticize; even so, America is a great place, and I can understand that its inhabitants are proud of it. I am so glad to have been able to come here. When I returned to Czechoslovakia last summer, I realized to my dismay that I was a stranger there. But now, I have found a country that accepts me warmly, without prejudice and without distrust. The prospect of eventually belonging to it makes me feel proud.

And the people could not be nicer and more helpful. Yesterday I found a charming letter from Miss Evert in Lincoln, whom I had never met but who had sent me several CARE packages to Vienna. She announced that she was sending something for me and also for my cousins in Berlin, and that she had also asked her nephew in Philadelphia to send them a package. And that is not all: I spent an evening at the Roseggs and they, too, gave me a parcel for the boys. What a wonderful feeling that so many people here do good deeds!

Outside a white velvet cover has spread over the city. A few snow stars are floating through the air. They drift onto coat collars and hats, and settle on them lightly like butterflies. Only now and then do they encounter a pedestrian. In this neighborhood it is easy to forget the existence of a Times Square bathed in neon lights, and noisy subway trains that are rolling incessantly below the surface of the streets. White and still, the cars hover motionless along the sidewalk, each with a pristine snow cap pulled deep over its ears. Only occasionally a shovel clanks through the night, scooping up the snow before it can turn into dirty, water-riddled city slush—*ó svatá dobo vánoční ...* ["oh holy Christmas time ..."—the beginning of a Czech carol]

An episode of the following evening haunted me for a long time, and even now I recall it with discomfort. I had met Inge, likewise a refugee, at Hanna's. Whereas Hanna, with her big smile, flirting eyes, and self-assured demeanor still awed me a little, I felt totally at ease with Inge. She was as short as I but dainty and gentle, with the dark, soulful eyes of a basset hound. Hanna seemed impressively grown up; Inge was more like me.

When I mentioned to her that in Ostrau Anna, our maid, would take me to the carol concert at her church on Christmas Eve, Inge suggested that we try it here. Where does one go? To St. Patrick's, of course, the imposing cathedral on Fifth Avenue.

It was a damp, cold evening and, when we arrived, the long line outside was barely moving. We had just about decided to give up, when people began to surge forward. Before we realized what was happening, we were not only inside the church but propelled on by a solid wall of ushers until, much to our horror, we found ourselves in the first row. Inge and I looked at each other with dismay: how could we get away now? Worse, in the first row we could hardly remain mere observers. Glancing stealthily right and left to see what the others were doing, we followed suit. Neither of us crossed herself, but we did kneel when our neighbors knelt, and rose with them. Nor was there much singing. It was what I now know as a High Mass. When everyone began to move forward, the two of us exchanged puzzled glances but then, much to our relief, noticed that a few people remained seated, and some were leaving. We followed them out, incredibly relieved.

I don't know what became of Inge. After I left New York, I lost touch with her, and when I recently asked Hanna, even sent her an old picture of the three of us together, it elicited no memories in her.

The episode brings back a few more recollections. On Christmas Eve, our traditional meal was jellied carp, each serving surrounded by circles of cooked carrots. Grandma and Grandpa would eat at our big table in the bedroom, but I was allowed to have supper with Anna in the kitchen. A white table cloth covered the kitchen table; on it stood a large bowl, filled to overflowing with fruits and nuts. They were for Anna, as was the sealed envelope wedged in between the pieces of fruit. After dinner we would sing carols together until it was time to go to church. My singing was nothing to rave about, but with her in the lead I managed to stay on key. Anna taught me a great many Czech carols and some of them I remember to this day.

It was a thrill to enter the festively lit church, to which the faint scent of incense added an aura of mystery. Anna's clear, strong soprano soared above all other voices, and I felt privileged to be with her. And, since Grandma had sanctioned the visit, I had no qualms about being there, no feelings of disloyalty or envy, only pleasure. Nor did I find it difficult later on to accept the sight of a cross or the crucified Christ as anything but the manifestation of another religion—perhaps because I was used to seeing Anna's small crucifix on the wall of her little room. If that was all right with Grandma, it was fine with me too.

Over the years, my relationship to religion became more complex, which should hardly surprise. In Ostrau, I had gone to the Jewish elementary school, as had my friends. In fact, that school provided an excellent education, probably better than any other local school. It was the only school to be truly bi-lingual, offering every subject in German as well as in Czech, in alternate years. The religion class, on the other hand, consisted mainly of learning the Hebrew alphabet but little of the language itself, of reading aloud incomprehensible texts, of painful attempts at translating them and, finally, of our committing to memory the names of assorted Old Testament prophets and judges.

The class was obligatory for only one year. After that I dropped it with considerable relief as did many of my classmates. Since all of us were Jewish (though some probably from far more religious homes than mine), religion and ethnicity were never discussed at school, and therefore did not have to be either affirmed or defended. Only when I, at age eleven, entered the German secondary school (a logical choice, since Jewish families tended to speak German at home), did I begin to hear anti-Semitic remarks. But at home Hitler's rise to power was never mentioned—at least not in front of me—and Germany was far away. I could therefore easily dismiss such remarks as aberrations. I was sure that no intelligent person, and definitely no Czech, would utter anything of the kind.

My grandparents never discussed religion with me or what being Jewish meant. To be sure, they observed the major religious holidays, but I suspect that they may have been motivated by tradition more than faith. On Friday night, Grandma would rush home from the shop to light the candles before sundown, and Grandpa conducted the family Seder on the first night of Passover. The long stretches of boredom Cousin Walter and I endured while Grandpa was reading, in Hebrew, the story of the Israelites' flight from Egypt were, fortunately, punctured by moments of fun: we were allowed a sip of red wine each of the four times the grown-ups emptied their glasses, and we dipped our little finger into the wine glass to spurt one drop on our plate for each of the ten plagues, while Grandpa was reciting them.

The highlight of the evening, though invariably a bone of contention, was the question of who should recite the manishtano, the "four questions" about why this night was different from all other nights. Every year, Cousin Walter and I argued whether I, the youngest, or he, the boy, should have that privilege. Grandpa's solomonic judgment was that both of us should read, Walter first, I next. I considered this Walter's victory, and so did he. However, Yom Kippur made up for it: when the Prayer for the Dead was recited, Walter had to leave, but I was allowed to remain in the temple with the grown-ups because my mother was dead.

My father was, for all I know, not religious at all. I wonder if he even believed in God. Once, when I returned home from a ouija-board session at a friend's apartment, convinced that "there was something there," he explained that the universe consisted of energy, and energy could take on concrete and often surprising forms, both within and around us. Thus any thoughts that have ever been thought are now floating around in the universe as energy, and can, under the right circumstances, be reconstituted into thoughts and words. It made a lot of sense to me.

No Shabbat candles were lit in our Viennese apartment, and fasting on Yom Kippur was never mentioned, not even before March 1941, when Grandmother Vera, my father's mother, was deported. And since my environment in Vienna was totally different from that in Ostrau, I accepted this omission as unquestioningly as I accepted the many other restrictions. My religious contacts consisted of an occasional participation in the Friday night candle-lighting ceremony at the home of my good friends Ilse and Kurt, and my spending a few hours at one or two Yom Kippur services because they urged me to join them. As for my belief in God, any god, that was severely shaken during those war years, and it never quite recovered.

The Milsteins did light candles on Friday night, and on my first Yom Kippur in America I went to the synagogue with them. Whether I did this from embarrassment or genuine belief I no longer recall, nor any later observances on my part. On the other hand, my loyalty to secular Judaism has stayed with me; it has, in fact, intensified over the years.

Yet, as I was kneeling in St. Patrick's that Christmas Eve, I felt like a hypocrite and traitor for paying obeisance to a religion that was not mine. Why did I suddenly feel guilty? From superstition? Reverence? The realization that my childhood was gone forever? Who knows. By now I can evoke the experience without great discomfort; but it is not forgotten.

5.

[*translated*] January 1, 1948, 1:30 a.m.

    I am sitting by my window. It is a mild, foggy night, with yellow, hazy lights and large, dirty puddles of slushy snow. Along the street the dreaming cars are partly hidden by a grayish-white snow crust. They have not yet recovered from the Friday-Saturday blizzard. Individual and clustered human outlines are weaving picturesque lines and curves, in slow motion, toward their homes. Only one element disrupts the harmony—large, cold lights which keep changing color with unconcerned regularity: red-green-orange-red-green-orange. That's how the New Year has arrived, welcomed by long drawn-out sirens, and undoubtedly received with jubilation by a thousand-headed crowd on Times Square. I wonder what it will bring.

    I am a little dizzy and tired—but not from excitement. Probably it was the champagne I had at Inge's house. I'll recapitulate briefly.

    The evening before I was feeling very lonely. When I decided to go to the theater, I faced another disappointment: at $4.80, the available tickets were beyond my reach. I finally went to the movies and saw *Mourning becomes Electra,* based on the play by Eugene O'Neill, which is not exactly cheerful either. But at least it made me resolve to take up again my long-neglected writing, and to give it high priority. And that is my main New Year's resolution.

    New Year's Eve, which I had feared, turned out nicer than expected. I spent it with Inge and her father. First they introduced me to the sketches by Käthe Kollwitz, a German painter, whom I found both impressive and depressing. Then Inge and I prepared supper amidst much hilarity since neither of us knows much about cooking.

    Shortly before midnight I read Rilke's *Cornet* to her, and I hope she enjoyed it as much as I always do. And since I knew that she was afraid of spending the evening alone with her father (her mother had died just a year ago), the knowledge that I was helping them to a few cheerful hours made me feel festive as well. I recalled Goethe's admonition that every day one ought to at least see one good painting, read one good book and, if at all possible, utter a few sensible words.

    Dear God, make it into a good year, and a thousand thanks for the past one! If, upon taking inventory now, I am not satisfied, it is my own fault; but I promise I will take the future more seriously. By the way, I received a $3 raise! Good night!

* * *

Dearest Trudi, January 10, 1948

Prosit New Year! I hope that it will be a very good year for you, your family and all of us. This is going to be a short letter, because I will be picked up soon.

I forgot to answer your question about Jackie—I thought I had written about him long ago. It is an embarrassing story. He was in our D.P. transport to the States, was French or part French, and very handsome and sexy. I had a difficult time staying away from him. It was humiliating and scary. What was worse, I did not even like him, his suggestive remarks and jokes, his references to a bride in Vienna and "someone" in New York, and yet I could not restrain myself and kept trying to be near him as much as possible.

In the Munich barracks his bunk was in the room next to mine. One evening, when I just couldn't stand it any longer, I walked in. Two of his three roommates were in, both of them older women whom I knew, though not well. He was not there. I said I would wait, and sat down on his bed—he had a lower bunk—then I lay down and pretended to fall asleep.

"What's she doing here?" he asked when he came in.

"She wanted to talk to you and would not tell us what about. And she wouldn't leave."

"I am not interested in her. Get her out of here." With these words he left again. They said some nasty things about my running after him and not leaving him alone. A little later I pretended to wake up, tried as nonchalantly as I could to apologize for falling asleep, asked them to tell Jackie that I had wanted to get some information from him, and left with burning cheeks. You can imagine how embarrassed I was. After that, though I still had this terrible urge to be near him, I pulled myself together. And after a row with him it was over.

It still shocks me that I could so completely lose all self-control, but I think that I am cured. Never again will I give in to my feelings or instincts like that. Now I am all right—I go out but remain uninvolved.

I wish you, your dear mother and your friend Kurt all the best in the coming year, and please don't forget

Your old friend Liesl

* * *

NEW YORK (1947–1949)

[*translated*] Jan. 18, 1948

People are strange in America—I must learn not to trust them too much. They all seem so friendly and keep smiling at you, and then they don't mean it. There was first that American lady who called herself a "Daughter of the American Revolution." She came to the hotel shortly after we arrived, was elegantly dressed and very refined, and took four of us along in her car "to show us New York." We drove to big plazas and saw tall skyscrapers, then Wall Street and Stock Exchange. At one point we caught a glimpse of the Statue of Liberty, and it again gave me goose pimples to have her before me: she had bid me welcome, and she had kept her promise. Finally, the lady invited us to a nice restaurant for lunch. (Americans have odd table manners: they use knife and fork to cut the meat into bites, then they put the knife down, switch the fork to the right hand, and eat with it like children who are not allowed to hold a knife. Were the first settlers all convicts who could not be trusted with a knife? And another thing: the lady did not take her hat off inside, even while we were eating. Nor did the other women!)

At any rate, when we said goodbye, she gave me her phone number, and invited me to call her up and come and visit. When I phoned a few weeks later, she said, "Oh yes, I remember," though I don't think she did. Nor did she seem really interested in finding out how I was doing. People always ask "How are you?" but when you begin to tell them, most of them hardly listen. It seems that all they want to hear is, "Fine, thank you." She said, "How nice of you to call," wished me good luck and—hung up!

Something else is strange here: people don't shake hands when they meet. They just stand there and mumble, "Pleased to meet you" or, if you had met them before, give you the usual "How are you?"—"Fine, thank you" routine. Or, even stranger, a slight acquaintance may suddenly hug you and kiss you on both cheeks!

Another thing you have to watch out for is someone's asking how you like America. You mustn't ever say anything except "fine." When I once tried to explain what I liked and what I didn't, I was told: "Perhaps you should go back to where you came from!" Back? I was upset for hours.

I also had a puzzling experience with the Roseggs. They live in a very attractive apartment c lose by and have invited me to dinner several times. They even gave me clothing to send to my cousins in Berlin, and once they took me along to a cottage they own outside New York. All this make me think that they really liked me. Then, quite suddenly, they stopped inviting me. I wrote several notes asking whether they were all right, or if I had perhaps said something that offended them and, if so, that I apologized—but they never responded.

Is all that friendliness only a façade? The interest seemed so genuine! I now have the feeling that people don't want to know what you are doing and who you are, that they only pretend to be interested and nice. Or is it I who disappoints them, who does not act correctly? During the war nobody cared about manners, so perhaps my manners are not good? However, with the Roseggs I could not find anything I might have said or done to offend them. I wish people would be frank and honest. How can you believe anything anybody says?

* * *

Dearest Trudchen,   February 20, 1948

I am very happy, and not only because it is a holiday. I received a very encouraging, sweet letter from Walter. What is even more important, I now see my path clearly before me: I may have enough talent to become a real writer!

Why do I believe this? In my short story class in night school we had to write a composition, and Mr. Goldberg, the teacher, liked mine very much. After class he invited me for a cup of coffee, and of course I felt flattered.

We talked for a long time. He said I unquestionably had talent and could become a writer if I didn't give up. What was wrong with me, he said, was that I had no self-confidence, and was too tense and guarded. He could feel it. "Let your hair down!" he said, even though my hair is short. I guess it means to relax, though it is not clear to me why hair that's hanging down would relax you.

Now we often have coffee together after class. There always seems so much to talk about that time just flies. He has this odd habit of looking intensely at your mouth or into your eyes when you speak. At first, that was disconcerting, but now I am used to it. He is quite elderly, at least forty, perhaps even older. Nor is he good-looking—short and heavy-set, with thick lips and a wide nose; but he has such kind eyes, despite those thick lenses. You can tell that he is really listening, and that he cares—like a real father.

I keep reminding myself how lucky I am. My work is not too demanding, I have time to read, to go to school, to afford a theater ticket now and then, I can even send packages to my cousins. I pray to God that He should not make me pay for this happiness with great suffering. Normally, I am not superstitious, but I can't forget the moment during the war when I thought I had earned the little bit of happiness I was having, and the next day Harry was arrested, and everything was over.

I am taking two evening courses to prepare me for the "Regents," a state examination which I must take in English and American History. If I pass it, I can take evening classes at a college, and they will count toward a degree. The history class is quite boring because we mainly memorize dates and names of labor laws. That seems to be the teacher's primary interest. But Mr. Goldberg's English class is really interesting. We read stories, discuss them and write essays about them. I have also met a very nice girl in that class, Lore, a refugee from Germany. We have become friends, though she is very reserved, and therefore I too am careful. Mr. Goldberg sometimes invites both of us to join him for coffee after class, but I am not jealous.

I go to school four evenings a week, usually right from work, after stopping for a snack at Horn & Hardart. That is a great place, a kind of cafeteria, but far more pleasant. There it's not awkward to eat alone. They have several freestanding automats with revolving tiers, with the food displayed in individual cubicles—a glass of juice, a sandwich, a slice of cake, a piece of fruit etc. Each item is on a plate and in its own glassed-in compartment. You can take your time deciding what you want, and nobody rushes you. When you put your coins in the proper slot, the little window opens. The food is very inexpensive, and the place is clean and never crowded.

By the way, America has a strange dessert, called "pie," which is served just about everywhere. It is round, like a *Torte*, but with a crust both on top and bottom so that you cannot see the filling and have to rely on the description. You are served a wedge and, unless you object, they put ice cream on top. That is called "à la mode"—don't ask me why. There certainly is nothing French about it, not to mention any kind of *Mode* [*fashion*]. Inside are stewed apples or other cut-up fruit in a gelatinous sticky sauce. A little like a *Strudel* but not as good and much too sweet, and the pastry is soggy instead of being thin and crisp. They don't seem to have *Torten* at all, only something resembling a *Gugelhupf*, which they call "Bundt cake." (I have no idea how that Bundt was.)

Enough for today. Stay well, don't work too hard and give my best wishes to your mother. And don't forget   Your old friend Liesl

In Austria, a Torte *is considered an elegant dessert and can be found in pastry shops in a great number of variations. It tends to be very rich, with a base of six or more eggs, butter, sugar, ground nuts or almonds, and bread crumbs rather than flour; there is usually one or more layers of a flavored butter or chocolate filling, as well as an elaborate icing. More low-*

brow, i.e., served for breakfast or with your afternoon coffee, is Kuchen, *a fairly plain cake with a yeast, baking soda or baking powder base. If baked in a tall, fluted form, it is called Gugelhupf, if in a square pan, it tends to have stewed fruit in a layer of gelatin on top and is cut into squares.*

* * *

[*translated*] March 10, 1948

New York's subways are impressive, an enormous network which goes almost everywhere. They are very fast and clearly marked, but also noisy and bumpy so that your bones get a good shaking; and often disgustingly dirty. People simply throw things on the floor—tissues, banana peels, anything. The stations are even messier, but since most of them are poorly lit, you don't notice the dirt. Also because, at least during rush hour, they are so crowded you don't see the floor. Sometimes they smell of urine; that is the worst.

During rush hour, when everyone tries to get home, it is impossible to find a seat. Luckily, one can hold on to poles near the doors. If you manage to sit down and look across, you face a weird sight: almost every mouth is going round and round, like a row of moving train-wheels. Otherwise the faces, whether black, white, brown or yellow, are quite expressionless, as if asleep. Perhaps they chew gum to stay awake. Sometimes I wish I could follow them home invisibly, and find out where and how they live. And then perhaps write about it.

* * *

Dear Trude, [*undated*]

Many thanks for your prompt letter. I am glad that my father finally gave you the photo. You write that he was very pleasant, and seemed to worry about me. That has always been his way: to make people think he is the best father in the world. Once, when someone asked him if he wasn't thinking of remarrying, he said: "I don't want to give Liesl a stepmother." And I would have been so happy if he had married Grete! She had a really good influence on him, taking my side whenever he was unreasonable. She would even bring me food when he wasn't around. It is difficult to believe—but, whenever he bought butter on the black market, he would lock it up and eat it all himself, saying that I had not earned any money toward buying it! Early in the war, when we still got one egg per person per week, he would eat both, because "a grown man needs eggs more than a child does." Is it surprising that I hated him, and went to America to get away? If Grete had survived, I might have remained in Vienna.

Now I save all the money I can to visit Aunt Jenny in England this summer. When I was little, she often came to Ostrau in the summer. I liked her best of my father's family. I met all of them during the summer of 1936, which I spent in Vienna. However, when I arrived there again on New Year's Eve 1939, Jenny was already in England, Uncle Otto in Paris, Uncle Paul in Morocco, and Aunt Olga in Italy. And Grandma Vera was deported fairly soon after I came, so that only Father and I were left. Uncle Paul and Aunt Jenny are the only ones to have survived, aside from us. Once the war was over, Jenny began to send me food packages, even though England was not much better off than Vienna.

I am in a hurry, so this is a short letter. With my very best wishes, I remain
> Your devoted old friend
>> Liesl

P.S. Best wishes also to your mother.

6.

I found no diary entries nor letters dating to the early spring of 1948. All I recall is that the after-class coffee sessions with Mr. Goldberg continued, and that I would look forward to them all day. The initial euphoria about my freedom and opportunities in this most exciting of cities had by then subsided, the parties with Hanna and her circle paled, and my mood swings took off from trifles. Fortunately, Mr. Goldberg continued to buoy me up, and seemed more than willing to listen to my emotional ups and downs.

Hindsight makes me think that he derived considerable pleasure from an almost voyeuristic participation in my life at the time. Not that I was the only one. Frequently, our jam sessions would be joined by one or another of his students or friends, all of them female, young, and attractive. They were either quite introverted, in which case he would try his best to draw them out and make them relax, or lonely extroverts who needed to unburden, and were as thankful for a willing ear as I was.

The latter part of spring was taken up by a new friendship—of sorts. Mrs. Milstein had introduced me to Michael, a sweet, timid boy whom she seemed to see as a good prospect for me. To humor her, I went out with him a few times. Just when I had decided that we didn't have much in common, he mentioned that, since he was working for an airline, he had a lot of free flying-miles. The rest is history, albeit a short one.

Dearest Trude,   New York, July 7, 1948

Has my birthday card arrived on time? I bet you were surprised to get it from Washington! Here is the explanation: I have met a young man, Michael, shy, not very good-looking, a bit of an *Armitschkerl* [*sadsack*]. He is Viennese, not much taller than I, thin, with a long, narrow face, straight black hair and dark, sad eyes. One can't help feeling sorry for him. He works for an airline and told me that he has a lot of free flying miles but does not use them, because he doesn't know where to go, nor has he anyone to go with him. I offered to come along if that was allowed. He was delighted—he could say I was his sister.

I suggested Niagara Falls, and six weeks ago we flew there for a weekend. Barely a year in America, and here I was on an airplane! At home we hadn't even had a car. I was not afraid at all. On the contrary, it was a real thrill, a feeling of both danger and freedom. And what luxury! We were served a complete hot meal. The views before we rose above the clouds were spectacular.

Michael behaved well on the entire trip. We had separate rooms, and I paid for my own meals. That is quite acceptable here, and is called "going Dutch." (I wonder why—are the Dutch so stingy? Or is that the Americans' revenge for having had to pay them for Manhattan?) I have a very funny photo of both of us walking under the falls in hoods and rain capes. We look like clowns. I will have a copy made for you.

The falls are enormous, incredibly powerful and elemental. They say that a man once climbed into a barrel, went over the falls, and arrived alive on the bottom. I certainly would not want to try that. People don't seem to know how lucky they are not to have to live in constant danger; so, instead of being grateful, they go looking for it.

The town itself is nothing special, just a lot of gas stations, restaurants and what they call "motels." Those are inexpensive hotels, just one or two stories high, architecturally not very imaginative, with huge, vulgar signs outside, and flashing neon lights at night. The motel we were in was a long white box. In spite of that, the rooms were quite attractive, large and clean. Each had its own bathroom—though once again with the toilet and tub together. I have begun to get used to that. There was also a big ceiling fan, which was much needed because of the heat. Despite my open window, the heavy curtains kept not only the daylight out but also any fresh air. It seems, though, that all rooms in a motel look the same (at least our two did). They have a desk and a chair, two nightstands, flowered curtains, a matching bedspread and a picture, likewise of flowers, above a double bed. A little like army barracks, but of course luxurious if compared to Munich. Car doors were slamming all evening and morning, and it was too hot to close the window. There was no foyer or dining room, just a small office, where you registered. (You have to pay upon arrival but, much to my surprise, you don't need to show your passport or any other identification.)

On the return trip we had trouble because of heavy fog, and it took almost all night. At 23:10 we were above Coney Island, which is right next to New York. Then they announced that "the ceiling has lowered below limits," and we would fly to Philadelphia. There, we had to take a train, and I hardly reached home in time to change for work. Mrs. Milstein was, of course, very worried. I wonder if she really believed me, when I told her that we had had separate rooms.

That is not all. Two weeks later I went with Hanna and a friend of hers to a mountain resort in the Catskill hills, not far from New York. It was beautiful there and much cooler but, instead of enjoying the landscape and the lake, some of the girls were only interested in meeting men, and they were embarrassingly aggressive about it. Hanna's friend said quite openly that, for her next vacation, she would go to Lake Placid because chances of finding a rich husband were better there.

I was shocked, also about something else: they shave under their armpits! I thought only prostitutes did that, but Hanna claims that it is far more hygienic and I should try it too. Henry, her fiancé, was not with us but, though Hanna now no longer flirts, her nice roguish smile still makes men notice her. I wonder if Henry is proud of her or jealous.

Finally there was the Washington weekend with Michael, but that did not go so well. It was raining, and Michael wanted to fly back right away. I insisted that we see at least a few things. We did, and I even had a glimpse of the famous White House. The town is quite different from New York, less exciting and dynamic, but much cleaner, with wide streets and squares. Very attractive, but quite artificial-looking. The monuments and public buildings are modern and surrounded by parks. Many are of white marble, which makes them look very serene. A little like our *Heldenplatz* or *Volksgarten*—actually more like Greek temples. But Michael got impatient with me for spending so much time in the National Gallery so this may well be the end of my flying trips.

I am glad that you are well again—pneumonia is no joke. Have a wonderful vacation in Aussee! It is supposed to be very lovely. Since I arrived in Austria during the war, I saw very little of it other than Vienna; just one outing to Gastein during that first post-war winter. Gastein was in the American zone, and Gerd knew of a place where we could stay and get meals without ration cards. And they had heat as well. (Did you know Gerd? I met him in the six-week cram course I took after the war to get my high school diploma. He was awfully nice, but I haven't heard from him in a long time.)

  Best wishes and many hugs and kisses,

                Your Liesl

Gerd: How well I remember him and how that memory saddens me. He was tall, broad-shouldered and handsome, with a wild mane of blond hair always covering part of his forehead, and with a big, warm smile. He was probably half-Jewish or he couldn't have been taking the course, but I never asked. Walking together, we must have looked like Pat and Patachon or, in this country, Laurel and Hardy. There was no question that he liked me and was trying to please and protect me. We never kissed but I knew he felt as close to me as I to him during the short time I knew him. Though he now and then complained about a painful back, and dropped hints that something was seriously wrong, I had no idea of how ill he was until I received, a few years later, the ominous black-rimmed envelope from his mother. He had died "after a long illness" in Beirut, Lebanon—of all places. I wrote to her to find out what had taken him there and how he had died, but she did not answer. When I was in Vienna eight years later, her name was not in the telephone directory.

7.

Dearest Trude,   Sept. 5, 1948

  Here is finally a letter from me. I am so sorry that I didn't send at least a postcard from Guildford, but my two weeks there passed so quickly that I held on to every minute. But before I start my report, let me immediately say that I fell in love with England!!! First with London, which is not just European, i.e., full of fascinating streets and romantic alleys, but which also has marvelous mansions, palaces and parks. The bank of the Thames with the contours of the Houses of Parliament and Big Ben is even more impressive than on pictures.

  Surrey, of which Guildford is the capital, has an exquisite countryside, gently rolling hills, and incredibly bright green meadows, dotted with solitary trees that seem to have been strategically placed there by a designer. Cows and sheep are grazing as if on a postcard, there are willow-framed creeks and rivers with swans and boats. One river, the Wey, flows right through Guildford. And everywhere you can find elegant manor houses, old churches and ruins. In Guildford there is a picturesque Norman castle ruin, surrounded by magnificent flower beds. Close to it, at the bottom of High Street (Guildford's main street) is a lovely old stone church, overgrown with ivy, St. Mary's.

Roses were in bloom almost everywhere, even on the tiny patches of grass in front of the smallest cottages. That's because England never gets hot, and has a lot of rain. From the train, the landscape between Guildford and London looked like one enormous park, strewn with clusters of red and brown roofs. Even the larger towns looked attractive, far less haphazard than in the States.

I immediately took to Aunt Jenny, and she was, as she put it, "thrilled" to see me. She kept hugging and kissing me—almost too much so. She had managed to leave Vienna in 1939, just before the war started, having a job offer as a "nanny" in Guildford, Surrey. The mother had run off on her husband. The father eventually proposed to Jenny, but though she liked him and adored his little girl, she declined. Perhaps his proposal came too soon after her fiancé, a Czech officer in the British army, had been killed. It seemed to me that later she may have been a little sorry she had refused.

Jenny never married. Having always been "good at figures," as she put it, she became a bookkeeper, and still is. Though she barely earns enough to make ends meet and has continual health problems, she never complained, and was a pleasure to be with. She is still very attractive, has a lovely voice, plays the guitar, and has an inexhaustible supply of jokes.

She spoiled me, bought the best food she could find and, the moment I admired something of hers—a scarf, a vase—wanted me to have it. "Blood is thicker than water," she kept saying. Of course I refused her presents, but I did appreciate all that attention and was equally impressed by her generosity. Right now she is sending packages to the boys in Berlin whenever she can.

Her flat takes up the first floor of a narrow two-story "row house." Someone else lives on the second floor, which is accessible by a staircase from Jenny's hallway. In front, a little white fence encloses a diminutive garden. All buildings on her street are of red brick, with brown and white woodwork. Each seems to contain four apartments, on two floors; a vertical drainpipe in the middle of the façade is the only divider visible from the outside. Between the buildings narrow walkways lead to the respective backyards, and they are so narrow that to a casual visitor the entire street seems to consists of only two enormously long two-story blocks, one on each side of the street. Surprisingly, this doesn't look monotonous but neat, even attractive. Oh, I forgot to mention that all buildings have rather odd chimneys, each with four thin smokestacks reaching upward from a large, square base. It looks like crenellations of a fortress.

Jenny's flat consists of two rooms, side by side, off a long, narrow hallway which ends at the kitchen. The kitchen is quite small, has a dirt floor and a small electric water heater above the sink. It feels bright because its door opens into the backyard, and the upper part is glass. The backyard or "garden," as Jenny calls it, is a fairly large grassy rectangle, with a few shrubs leaning against the high, grey stone walls. When I bought an assortment of blooming perennials at the Friday open-air market and planted them along the walls, Jenny was "thrilled to bits." Off and on, her friend Margaret brings her lawnmower and trims the grass for her.

Next to the kitchen is a tiny room with a toilet but no sink or tub. (Here they call the toilet the "loo," and if you want to use it, you say you "need to spend a penny"!) The upstairs apartment does have a regular bathroom. By arrangement, Jenny can take a bath upstairs once a week. (However, we washed ourselves in a large bucket on the kitchen floor, and did our laundry in the kitchen sink!

The only heat available came from the kitchen's gas stove and two "storage heaters," one in each room. They were boxes the size of large radiators, but solid. Jenny would turn hers on at night because that was less costly, and it stayed warm for much of the next day. I slept on a cot (loaned by Margaret) in the dining room, which faces the street. Though we turned its storage heater on as well while I was there, I appreciated Margaret's small electric heater, which kept away the dampness. In winter, the place must be awful. Poor Aunt Jenny: not to have adequate heat even now that the war is over. How lucky I am to have a heated room, and not even having to take care of the stove!

In Vienna, we had a **Kachelofen,** *a tile stove some six feet high. It stood in a corner of the living room. Whenever coal or briquettes were available, it kept the room cozy for close to twenty-four hours, and the warmth would spill over into the bedroom. But the stove had to be cleaned and restarted every day.*

Margaret is English. She has a nerve disorder which makes her hands tremble. She also eats very slowly, as if swallowing were an effort. Though much younger than Jenny, she looks much older. Jenny is sure that she has never had a boyfriend and feels sorry for her, even though Margaret is wealthy and has a much easier life. "She is very high-strung," Jenny said, "but she has a heart of gold." Margaret is not Jewish but knows that Jenny is. In fact, when the refugees began to arrive in Guildford in 1938, Margaret helped them adjust. She often brings Jenny things she needs or can use. Even Jenny's small refrigerator was a gift from Margaret.

On my first Saturday, we were invited by Margaret's parents for "High Tea," and Margaret drove us there in her cute little car. And I mean little. Rascal was practically in my lap every time she took a curve. Luckily, he is a small dog, but the ride was bumpy and jerky. Jenny kept telling Margaret to slow down. She obviously didn't trust her driving. Margaret's parents live in a real mansion, larger than a Viennese villa but not as modern, more like a small estate. Margaret's father used to be a physician in India, though he looked more like a retired officer, polite but stiff and proper.

It was a very formal affair, with the maid bringing in a silver teapot and sandwiches on a silver platter. They were strange sandwiches, not at all like American sandwiches or our *belegte Brötchen* [*i.e., slices of bread, each topped with an assortment of appetizers attractively arranged*]. We were offered double slices of soft and very thin white bread, cut into quarters, all crusts cut off. Inside was a cucumber slice, in every one of them, and nothing else! And, much to my surprise, Mrs. Billinghurst poured the tea herself, and she poured hot milk into my cup before I could say no. However, the tea was so dark that it almost looked like coffee, which may have made milk a necessity.

Both seemed very nice and asked many questions about my life in America. However, later Jenny commented that this was the very first time in all those years that she had been invited there. She was certain that the reason was my visit. Apparently the English never let you forget that you were not born there, and are therefore only British, but not English. And here I had begun to think how nice it would be to live in England because it is so much more European than America, has many traditions, a long history, a lovely countryside, and interesting people. Even simple people conversing on the bus were a pleasure to listen to. They used "big words" with ease, and sounded far more educated than their equals in the States.

How important is tradition? Am I lucky or unlucky not to have a country? Will I never be at home anywhere, or will I be able to feel at home everywhere? Perhaps having no roots means having no regrets, never being betrayed? Mr. Goldberg says that roots are for trees, people have legs and should be moving. Even so, I still love England, at least to visit.

Though Guildford is the "market town" of the county, it is small and charming. Many of its timbered buildings are tall and imposing, with coats of arms or other ornaments above the entrances. There is also a romantic old inn with brown timbers and ivy-covered white walls. It is called "Angel Inn," and stands on High Street which slopes down to the river and the train station. Mounted to the façade of Town Hall in the middle of High Street is a large, elaborate clock. You can see it from a considerable distance, in either direction, and it is featured on many of Guildford's postcards.

To get to Jenny, you have to take the bridge across the railroad tracks (the train station is on your right if you come from town), continue straight for half a block, then turn left onto Testard Road just before the street starts to climb a hill. Though Testard is called a road, it is just one block long, and dead-ends. The houses on the left side look down on the tracks (actually, their backyards do), those on the right—Jenny's among them—have the rising hill as a backdrop. The area is considered "on the wrong side of the tracks," i.e., a poor neighborhood. Perhaps it is, but it certainly did not look poor to me. The houses were clean and attractive, most of them had flowers or neatly trimmed shrubs in front, and the location was great: if you continued on the main road to the top of the hill, you found yourself on a wide trail running along the ridge in both directions. No houses, only trees, shrubs and wildflowers.

The hill is called "Hog's Back" and is part of a group called "Surrey Downs." From the trail you have great views of the town and its surroundings. You can even see the cathedral, which Guildford is very proud of, though it is modern. It rises up on the other end of the town, its tower a rigid finger pointing at the sky. Behind it you can, in clear weather, make out the roofs of the University of Surrey.

One day Jenny and I took the train to London. We walked for hours. Remember Mrs. Kautezky's description of Hyde Park Corner? We went there, but nobody was giving a speech, and no soap or other kind of box was in evidence.

I also took a bus to Stonehenge, by myself. I remembered the vivid descrip-

NEW YORK (1947–1949)

tion from *Tess of the d'Urbervilles*, and wanted to see the site. That's where the police catch up with Tess, if you remember, under those huge stones. It was just as dramatic in reality. A lonely and silent place. As I walked between the enormous columns, the air made me shiver—as if I might be caught just as Tess was, even though I had not killed anyone. No one knows by whom and when Stonehenge was built, where they had found those massive boulders, and how they managed to hoist the horizontal ones up to the top. It is supposed to have been a religious site of prehistoric sun worshippers called Druids.

There was only one other visitor there, an elderly English gentleman. He told me interesting details about Stonehenge and other aspects of English history; then he offered to drive me to Salisbury Cathedral which, he said, was nearby and likewise a very special place. It was indeed. A Gothic cathedral, majestic like the *Steffl* [*St. Steven's Cathedral in Vienna*], but otherwise very different. There are no houses around it and, and its steeple soars up into the sky, yet the building is solid and firmly anchored in the ground. I found it truly inspiring.

Then we drove to Kenilworth, Sir Walter Scott's castle. Very little is left of it, but it was exciting to follow up on some of the names Mrs. Kautezky had so often talked about. How I wish I had had more time to explore England, especially since its public busses are cheap and go everywhere, and so do the trains. I promised Jenny that I would come back soon. She offered to contribute to my plane ticket, but I would, of course, not hear of it. I assured her that I could manage to save enough for another visit soon.

The Englishman was a real gentleman, very polite and attentive. He drove an unusual car which looked very old-fashioned, like a jeep, though very shiny. He was impressed with my knowing something about English literature, and he also wanted to hear my impressions of America. (Funny, in England they took me for a "real" American!) From Kenilworth he drove me back to Guildford. Just as I was beginning to wonder if I could invite him in without embarrassing Aunt Jenny, he explained that he was expected at home, and left.

I also have some real news—maybe. On the airplane magazine I read an article about an international education conference in England. A small American college had received much attention because of its unusual philosophy: no examinations, no grades, and each student has an adviser called "don," like in England. The college, Sarah Lawrence, is a girls' college outside New York City. It was named after the founder's wife—strange that someone would choose the name Sarah voluntarily! Perhaps the "h" at the end helps. [*In the Third Reich, Jews* were forced to use Israel or Sara as middle names.]

The college sounded so interesting that I took down the address, and later wrote for the catalog. When it mentioned that scholarship aid was available, I applied. They encouraged me, even after I made it quite clear that I had no money. (It is very expensive.) Next spring I have to take an examination called the "American Council Test.". If I pass it, I might get a scholarship. Keep your fingers crossed.

       With my very best wishes,

                     Your Liesl

The references to Mrs. Kautezky and her admiration for English "high society" remind me of an amusing episode in Vienna.

One day a tall, middle-aged lady in a gray tailored suit entered our classroom in the middle of Mrs. K.'s lecture. Thereupon she, usually so composed and self-assured, got surprisingly flustered. As she walked to the door to greet the visitor, she kept tugging at her glasses, and when she shook hands and invited the lady to take a seat, she almost bowed. Moreover, she who never lost her thread stayed agitated throughout the session. When the bell rang, we rushed out to ask the secretary who the woman had been. "The Duchess Liechtenstein," she said with an awed expression and added, as if to give more weight to her statement: "The 'ruling' duchess. She is a friend of Mrs. Kautezky's." A friend? All I was aware of was the gulf between them, or at least imagined by Mrs. K. However, at that point I too was quite willing to be awed by the distinguished visitor. I had never met royalty before, or someone as close to royalty as that. And if she considered it worth her while to visit our class, didn't that bestow a special aura on us students as well?

Perhaps my excitement was also due to the fact that the name rang a personal bell. Before we were turned out of our apartment at the corner of Liechtensteinstraße and Strudlhofgasse during the first year of the war, I had never paid attention to the huge walled-in park diagonally across from us; nor did I wonder who might be living in the big Liechtenstein-Palais hidden behind the park's enormous trees. Now suddenly the name had a face to go with the place. But I was puzzled as well: on the one hand, the association bred familiarity, so much so that I felt an impulse to follow the lady out, and tell her that I had lived right across from her Viennese palace. However, Mrs. K.'s attitude implied that not only would such behavior be unseemly, but that there must be something basically different about people who are nobility—especially if they "rule"—if it could make someone as self-assured as Mrs. K. so servile, almost obsequious. Or did this simply reveal a weakness in her character, a chink in her armor?

I quickly dismissed that thought. Even so, whenever in later years the name Liechtenstein was mentioned, I felt a special closeness to it.

8.

Dearest Truderl,   New York, Sept. 18, 1948

    You are wrong about my English. It may be quite good by now but I still cannot always make it express exactly what I want. Mark Twain said somewhere that the difference between the right word and the almost right word is like— and I must say this in English — "between lightning and a lightning bug" (*Blitz* and *Glühwürmchen*). I am still catching *Glühwürmchen* most of the time ... Perhaps it is really impossible to absorb a second language so completely that it becomes like your first. I also noticed something else: I have always loved poetry and thought I could tell a good poem from a bad one, no matter how traditional or experimental; in English I can't, especially recent verse. It is a little like abstract paintings. Sometimes you are not sure whether they were made by the painter or his monkey. Worse, I think I am losing my first language as well, now that I don't use it much. But Joseph Conrad wrote in English and wrote extremely well, so I must not give up.

    Incidentally, something very nice has happened. I have stopped dating and have a real boyfriend. His name is Hans, but here he calls himself John. He is also from Vienna. We were in the same accelerated high school graduation class in 1945, though I barely remembered him. In early August, we ran into each other on 34th Street. He seemed as pleased as I was, and asked for my phone number. Except that then he didn't phone. Naturally, I was disappointed. We met accidentally again as I was coming out of the subway on 96th Street, and this time he accompanied me home, and asked if I would go out on a date with him. That's how our relationship began.

    John lives in a very small room in a rooming house not far from me. We spend many evenings together, eat together, listen to music, and take walks in Riverside Park. Often we play a game where one of us hums an aria or a song, and the other must guess what it is from. (Having heard so many operas in Vienna after the war helps a lot: the librettos usually included the first bars of the main arias and the corresponding text, so I could learn them.) I am not very good at carrying a tune; therefore, it pleases me all the more when John can recognize what I am humming.

We also go to talks together, and sometimes to a movie. He won't let me pay and, since he has very little money, I try to find free events like lectures and museums. The marvelous thing about New York is that there is a lot you can do even without money. For instance, there is a lovely five-cent ferry ride to Staten Island, one of New York's five boroughs (Manhattan is another). The boat passes right by the Statue of Liberty, and on the way back Manhattan's entire skyline lies before you. It is simply spectacular. We have done this several times, took sandwiches along, sat on the grass on the other side, and picnicked. Once we took a bus all around Staten Island, but that was disappointing. A largely industrial area without interesting buildings, at least from the bus. Except that it looked older than Manhattan and not as crowded.

Life is definitely much easier if you don't have to look for a date, especially in this country where there is so much pressure on dating. Also, it is nice to have someone to discuss things with, and go to events and places.

John had an awful time during the war, much worse than I. When he was a child, they were very poor, because none of his father's business ventures worked out, and so they constantly had to move. The father committed suicide (with gas) at forty-three, while John was in the hospital with scarlet fever. Then they lived on an unpleasant uncle's charity. John was imprisoned by the Gestapo in 1938, at eighteen. His mother and sister were deported, and never came back. He escaped to Bratislava and spent much of the war hiding there. In February 1945, the Gestapo caught him once more. Luckily, the war ended before they could deport him. From 1945 to 1948 he eked out a living on the black market, and went to business school at night. Those three years were the worst years of his life, he says. (I got all this information out of him bit by bit because he does not want to talk about that time, which I can fully understand.)

Unfortunately, John is very disappointed with America and would probably prefer to be in Vienna, despite his awful memories. In contrast to me, he does not find the people here helpful, and is disgusted that everything seems to be about money. But I think that is only because he still hasn't found a real job. He was working as a cashier in a restaurant for six days a week, including weekends; then he got fed up and quit. He tried to sell nylons on the street—many people do that and apparently make a lot of money—but he ran into trouble with the police for not having a license, and now he is searching again. And when he is depressed, he becomes difficult. I, too, would be dissatisfied if I did not have interesting work, friends, and my night school. I try to cheer him up, but when I don't succeed, I get depressed as well.

You are quite right that since coming here I seem not to be quite myself, am restless and jump from one thing and one person to another. But all that has become much better now that I know John, only things are still not quite right. But watch me complain when I should be happy, and usually am.

Let me end on this cheerful note, and please write soon to

Your faithful Liesl

PS. I am very curious how you will like law school. Is Kurt also studying law? I would never manage such a dry subject!

* * *

N.Y. Oct. 26, 1948

It feels strange—coming back to you after such long time! And I am a little guilty, for this neglect of you has been a negligence toward myself, an attempt to escape maybe honest self-condemnation maybe or at least self-criticism, by only alleviating my troubles to those ears whose sympathy was asserted and who were even more willing to excuse my faults than I myself. And then one commits the crime that is worst of all, that of confiding too much, of opening oneself up too completely. And one suddenly feels so naked in the midst of people who are all dressed and even took care to dress well!

That is why I today and at this hour—a quarter to one o'clock in the morning—humbly come back to you to hide in you my nakedness and to have your soothing attention and confidence cover me and comfort me.

Only a few days ago, when asked by Mr. Goldberg to write down any problems I might be confronted by, I quickly retorted: Everything is clear and straight and beautiful. And now that I have come home from what was supposed to be an especially solemn occasion—saying good-bye to John who leaves for two weeks—now all of a sudden nothing is clear and bright and beautiful, and though nothing unpleasant really happened, everything seems strange, unfamiliar, somewhat unnatural and sordid. And strangely—we felt it, both and the entire time, this estrangement that was creeping between us, and we both tried to fight it, and could not. It was a mere saving face, our souls were not awake.

I was not at all in love with him at that moment, and I do not think I even now am. Is it all just about having sex? What an awful phrase that is—"having sex," like having breakfast, having a bath ... Or worse, as if one simply turns on a drive randomly, instead of a joyful coming- together, an intertwining of bodies *and* feelings. Why doesn't one say "be intimate" which is what it should be? Perhaps because it usually isn't—people simply throw themselves into a physical frenzy without being in love, without loving. And have I succumbed to this frenzy too? Am I merely having sex with John to forget myself, instead of truly liking him, loving him?

Have I ever loved him? I cannot tell. He is really quite good-looking, of just the right height for me, with a rectangular face and dark, curly hair. His eyes are very small but when he smiles, they twinkle and are surrounded by lots of wrinkles so that then his whole face smiles. When he is serious, though, his eyes are like dark slits sitting in deep pockets very penetratingly, almost cruelly.

I am wondering if there is really such a thing as love, or if we only talk ourselves into it because we either want this sexual gratification and oblivion, or somebody who is kind to us? Perhaps it only happened through loneliness that I felt drawn to John, and I simply fear to take risks waiting for the right man? But then—he represented to a dot the man I would wish to be in love with me (and he certainly was and I hope still is!), and did I not always preach that intellectual harmony is more important than physical attraction? I did say so and his physical behavior was not averse to me either—so everything should be perfect. It was up to tonight, when he suddenly was a stranger once again. I still did not dislike him, was not sorry for anything that preceded this evening, but we were miles apart, both trying to call the other towards himself, and yet by the echo of one's own words misleading the other further in the wrong direction.

Now everybody probably has love-troubles and to anybody outside my personal world this seemingly unreasonable and unjustified construing of things out of nothingness must seem utterly foolish. But we both are sensitive and that is why I know it is a problem. Somehow, I was much better off before I met him, when I just had a good time and not worried about what I said and what not. And yet, not having a boyfriend also was not good. Why is life so complicated when it could be so simple and enjoyable?

John told me that he will do whatever I want, but in certain things it is I who has to obey. I accepted this doctrine like a child does that has not the slightest idea or experience on the subject. Maybe that was wrong. It is easy to go on one another's nerves if you are together too often, and if the man does not have to fight with the reluctance of the woman and everything for him is smooth and easy, naturally he then has time to think up other matters. So I better don't take this request too verbally. But I definitely must not let him notice that I'm doing it on purpose!!!

Another thing worries me more. According to my theory I ought to have found my ideal partner. Why do I not get as excited when I see him as I was with Harry or even with Walter who really was not sexy at all, just great fun to be with, or even at the meetings with Dr. R. who gave me much less personalization than John does? Is physical attraction an a priori demand? Or am I just too touchy and critical? Well, anyway, I have a couple of days to think it over and to arrange my thoughts gradually. And there is no need undressing in public, with you taking me back, diary—and I will come to you more often in the future! Good night! (It is 1:10 a.m.)

P.S. Though I really ought to be happy—my first submitted short story was accepted!

* * *

Dec. 28

Here I am again—and as confused and uncertain as can be. I will try to put the problem down clearly and maybe that will also clarify it in my mind.

Things with John do not go well. I always believed that physical attraction is something passing, and that one should rather choose for a partner somebody with whom one in general corresponds well. Now, I have never corresponded better with anyone than with John: He is at least as much interested in music as I am—even knows more about it and has a better musical ear—he is very critical and intelligent, can talk about most subjects, interested in plays and books, observing and, at least in the beginning, very appreciative and attentive, kindhearted and true—well, what else would you want your partner to be? I never met a man with all those qualities assembled and yet, I had been in love before, and I am not now. Still, I do not resent him. I like his ways, his physical nearness—sometimes. And that's where the equation goes wrong. One-hundred single percents should add up to a full 100% and they do not.

Sometimes I do not care for his company at all, sometimes I even resent it. And then little, ridiculous things begin to get more and more important and tiny differences almost irreconcilable. He does not care about the way he dresses though he will notice every dress I wear and will want me to look nice. He is negligent about most little things, does not take them seriously, the way he eats, talks—he does not even try to improve his language, etc. Then, and this problem is much more portentous: He is a pessimist, he will find fault with almost everything, whereas I always try hard to see the bright side.

Now, this is bad, for it not only makes me very nervous and sometimes lose my temper, but it also throws me off my balance, and what is going to happen then, where am I to find support, when he instead of supporting, leans against me? And another thing: He cannot forget even though he will not acknowledge it. Whereas I, if I like someone, try to overlook his faults, he likes a person in the measure of her faultlessness. With other words, if after a quarrel I would only the stronger feel the relief of reconciliation, he would think of the quarrel and like the person the less for it.

I started writing this in order to find back to him, but the further I progress, the clearer and more inexorably the thought seems to gain shape: It is no use. It seems incredible, yet I seem to reach the conclusion: It is the little things that matter, whether both like people or prefer solitude, whether they have a sense for adventure, whether their attitude towards life is positive, whether they are in love, and now I really mean simple physical infatuation. I always believed in a choice of congenial spirit, and I must admit, it does not work with me and John, and only because I am not infatuated. If he would see this notebook, he would say, how can you solve such problems by reasoning, what a cruel, selfish, heartless method. It is true and probably due to the lack of feeling on my part. Or do I take everything too seriously, too scientifically? Am I going to destroy everything beautiful by lacerating it, sow unhappiness with all that desire to find beauty and give warmth? That would be horrible, but what shall I do? I do not see a way out of this and I cannot pretend anything that is not true. And leave the decision up to the moment—no, one has too often acted rashly on the first impulse and hurt more by unconsidered words than by the will to do harm. I wish Trude were here, she would know what to do. I don't, I really don't.

I just reread this. The only way out of this without a rash decision would be to see less of him, but to try to stay friendly. Yet this is very hard, for he gets offended the moment something is refused to him—but that's just it, I cannot overcome this. If we were married, it would probably lead to his only appreciating me after I am dead because during our life-times he would be busy thinking of the times we had differences and misunderstandings.

____I will be nice and *will* refuse. If he then comes back to me, maybe ... if not that is the solution.

* * *

Dearest Trudilein! January 1, 1949

A very happy New Year to you and your family! And many thanks for your beautiful birthday card, and my best wishes to you for a healthy and happy year! It is great that you and Kurt study so well together; that must make it much easier and more enjoyable. But do you really have to work so hard? Why not let your studies take a little longer? Don't forget that you are not supposed to overtax your heart. Even if it is behaving right now, you shouldn't take risks. It is hard to believe that one can get a weak heart from infected tonsils! (Mine were removed in Ostrau when I was quite little, and all I remember is eating lots of ice cream. Luckily, my heart stayed healthy.)

Yes, you are of course right to urge me to be patient with John. I am sure I am doing everything wrong. I should be glad to have found him, and he would really make a good husband. He is well educated (much of it on his own), and knows more than I about a great many things. And what was especially nice was that, even after I had said yes when he asked for a kiss, he did not push for more. Only after quite a long time of seeing each other did he ask me to consider that the longer a girl waits to become intimate, the more difficult and painful it is. That had not occurred to me, but if he was right, it was high time at my age; so I agreed. He was very gentle and sweet, and though at first it hurt (and he warned me that it would), it soon stopped, and I am not sorry. But, as with my first kiss, I wonder what all the fuss is about.

For a while I felt really grown up. Now I again don't. Will I ever? And do you feel that way too?

For my birthday John gave me a small phonograph and several 45 rpm records, even though he has so little money. He brought me a wonderful song cycle called *Dichterliebe,* which I adore, and *Winterreise,* which I like less. You probably know both. He also introduced me to Richard Wagner, and I am very grateful to him. We listened to the *Walküre* on the radio with the libretto, then he pointed out some of the leitmotifs. It is a wonderful opera. By the way, every Saturday afternoon there is an opera on the radio. Usually, we sit in his room and listen to it. We also heard the rest of the *Ring,* but I thought the other parts much too long and talky. Last Saturday *Salome* was on. Afterward we argued because I found it quite perverse.

Am I attracted to him? I guess so. I always believed that physical attraction is something passing, and that one should preferably choose as a partner someone with whom one has a lot in common. That is definitely the case with us, and yet I am not happy. However, I am also afraid of losing him, of being alone again. Yesterday we saw "The Thief of Bagdad" and had a really good time, but in the evening he was difficult and moody, and nothing I said helped.

However, I don't want to complain. It was really a very good year for me. In November, the first short story I submitted was published in *Opinion*, a Jewish magazine. The story is called "The Day of Atonement." I also passed the entrance examination for Hunter College and take evening courses there—"General Psychology" and "Public Speaking & Oral Interpretation" in the fall, and "English Literature" and "Historical Foundations of America" next term. So far I have not been impressed, but it is good not to have so much time with John. I also still see Mr. Goldberg for coffee now and then. He has such empathy that it is a pleasure to be with him. (Don't worry—he is married and has a child.) However, I cannot talk to him about John. When I tried, I could tell from his expression that he was getting impatient.

Enough for today. I wish you a very, very good year!

Embracing you,

Your Liesl

9.

]*from the January 1949 issue of* Weltenwende, *translated*]

"**Lisa Mondo:**

A D.P. sees America

(Continuation)

Due to a delay in the receipt of the next installment, we close this series with a number of sketches on different aspects of American life, excerpted from earlier letters.

January 1948:

I am comfortably seated in a warm room—though we could have been freezing (I will explain later)—and hear the rain drum against the window panes. After finally finishing last Sunday's *Times* (200 pages!), I have started to tackle my correspondence. At Christmas we had a small party at the office and every employee was given a box of candy.

On Friday we worked till noon, then we were sent home, fortunately: it was snowing so heavily and persistently that by late afternoon much of the traffic had ground to a halt. Saturday evening, when it finally stopped snowing (after about 75 cm!), the city was practically cut off. For the first time you could take long walks in the middle of the street or, rather, cut a path through knee-high snow, and the cars, which looked like huge snowdrifts along the curb, had to watch passively. In Central Park and on the Hudson shore there was sledding and skiing, in the middle of the city.

Not everybody was cheerful. A food and fuel shortage was threatening. Today the trains, subways and major busses are again running, though not all streets are plowed. To our relief, the fuel truck parked in front of our building at noon, just before we would have run out of oil. I ought not to report all this in such detail, since you are probably freezing, but Trude wrote about a wood and coal drive, and so I hope that this winter won't be as bad. I was assured that the blizzard was most unusual, but then I have been told that the weather is unusual ever since I arrived.

May 21, 1948:

I spent a marvelous weekend—guess where? At Niagara Falls. It all sounds too improbable to be true, doesn't it? A Viennese friend who works for an airline and gets 5000 miles of free flight time annually, secured the tickets, and after one and a half hours of a calm, gorgeous flight in brilliant sunshine we were there. By train it takes about eight hours. A natural spectacle which cannot be put into words. Millions of kilowatt hours are produced by this titanic force and transformed into light, heat or energy in both the U.S.A. and, on the other side, Canada. My few photos can only convey a faint image and, without the accompanying roar, they lack the proper background music. I spent two glorious days quite inexpensively (I paid, of course, for my room and meals). The return flight was very interesting, and it inspired me to write a humorous short story.

June 17, 1948:

Have I told you that I was in Washington? It was great though it poured when we left, and there we got soaked as well. Michael wanted to fly back the same evening, but I protested. When people get free flight tickets, they don't properly appreciate them. I found an inexpensive bed in a service area of the YWCA, after an acquaintance who was staying there for the weekend convinced them to help me out. Michael complained that I was spending too much time at the National Gallery, and so I suspect that this may be our last flight together. Washington is a beautiful city. The second day was sunny and warm, and I took some good pictures.

November 3, 1948. Wednesday, 12:30:

The election results have just been announced and it is now certain that Truman has won. It was the strangest election campaign imaginable and, I was told, the most interesting in years. It began with disagreements within both parties as to which candidates to choose. People were joking that the Republicans had more candidates than members, and the Democrats were searching frantically for candidates. Eisenhower was urged to run, though Truman had not yet officially relinquished his right. (If the president decides to run again, his party cannot refuse.)

Truman's cause seemed hopeless, especially because his "Civil Rights Program" has alienated the South. People were just shrugging when they heard that he wanted to try once more. And when Henry Wallace founded his party, the only salvation for Truman seemed to be to draw Wallace into his camp at the last moment. Nothing of the sort happened. The Republicans were so sure of their victory that last night people were betting 60:1. Most of the population seemed totally uninterested. Many complained that it was a hard choice since none of the candidates were satisfactory. Some declared they would vote for Wallace, since he at least was fighting for a good cause, even if he did not have a chance to win. Others insisted that a vote for Wallace meant four for Dewey, and they voted for Truman, if reluctantly.

In the meantime, the candidates had for three months been all over the forty-eight states, each making the most grandiose promises, and accusing the others of all imaginable evil, irresponsible, and selfish motives. That, I was told, is customary here during election campaigns. Therefore, when the first results began to emerge yesterday, people were barely paying attention because the outcome seemed so certain. Well, Truman was leading in several states, but they were traditional democratic strongholds, and the results were, after all, very preliminary. Usually the count is only advanced enough by 23 hours to yield the final results. This time, there were constantly new figures and reports, and the later it got, the more upset the Republicans became, and the more amazed the pessimists among the Democrats.

By midnight, it was clear that the race was by no means decided. It appeared that there was an unexpectedly high participation by the population, and that every vote might count. In the morning there was still no final outcome, but the Democrats were leading. They also had a clear majority in both houses of Congress. This even the most optimistic Truman supporters had considered the best result achievable.

A few hours ago word came through that Dewey has conceded. We haven't yet seen the exact figures, but people are, naturally, very excited. In the streets, small groups congregate, they dispute in restaurants, and all phones are busy as everyone tries to come to terms with the unexpected outcome. Dewey had all the money and most of the influential people behind him, his campaign cost several times as much as Truman's who did not even have enough money to buy radio time. And yet he has won the race, and with him the man in the street. Whether he will justify this enormous confidence, no one knows, but since his main argument during the last few years was that he was unable to achieve anything with a hostile Congress, we will now see what he can do for the country with a Democratic Congress.

Thursday, 12:30.

I am very impressed, not so much by Truman's victory as such, but by the fact that there is real democracy here, and that it is the people, the average man, who has elected the president. And that is great.

* * *

[*a handwritten draft, translated*]

Dear Dad, Jan. 23, 1949

I just received the January issue of *Weltenwende* and am furious [*crossed-out and "upset" substituted*]. Publishing selections from my very personal and informal letters and without my agreement conveys to the reader a wrong [*crossed out and "odd" substituted*] impression of my activities and interests, and an even odder one of my social life. There is a great difference between a private letter and something in print, as you who also writes should certainly know.

It seems to me that you still do the same thing you used to do in Vienna, namely assume that it is up to you to make all decisions, and that I have no voice, not even in things concerning me. You always said that I should work and earn my own living if I wanted to have the right to speak up. Now I am doing that, am far away and independent, and you are still trying to make my decisions for me!

If you want me to continue writing to you in detail, I must be sure you won't publish anything of mine unless I agree to it, or send it to you specifically for publication. Also, there is no need to continue giving me advice on what I should and should not do. You don't know this country nor my immediate environment. Please realize finally [*"finally" crossed out*] that I am grown up and need to live my own life. That is, after all, the reason why I went to America. Or one of the reasons.

I apologize if I sound angry, but I had to say this and hope that you will understand.

Upon reading—as if for the first time!—my description of that presidential election, I am truly sorry that in my anger and embarrassment I stopped sending "official" reports to my father. Anyway, his magazine did not outlast the year. However, the episode also brought back all of the resentment that had accumulated during the war years and almost driven me to suicide. While his friends admired his intellect, his self-assured composure and his balanced judgments, I saw only his self-centeredness, rigidity and condescension toward me. "Children are to be seen, not heard" he would say. When I left for the States, he gave me a manuscript of his on the origin of the world to send to Albert Einstein! I did so with embarrassment, but to my surprise I received a typed note signed by Einstein, asking me to convey to my father that his theory did not seem to contain anything new. I dutifully forwarded the note to my father, and now it is lost.

10.

[*translated*] January 25, 1949

America, I now realize, is a flight from myself. That only became clear to me today, through an event which made me pause for a while and deliberate. On Sunday I visited a friend, and she gave me a book, *Demian*, which is the story of Hermann Hesse's youth. I am half finished. Actually, I cannot claim that it is the fate and development of that young man that have made such a strong impression on me. No, it is really his brooding, his burrowing into himself and listening to his inner self, which showed me how far I have departed from being a good writer, even a whole person. New York's stimulating atmosphere has entrapped me, even though I did not admit it. I covet every moment, I strive to utilize every second, but what do I do with it? I waste it, yes, waste it on school, books, magazines, friends—doing exactly what so many other so-called intellectuals here are doing: in order not to let life pass by aimlessly or suffocate in daily trivia, we cram as much as we can into every hour. Then we think we have lived fully that day, and we throw ourselves dead-tired but satisfied into bed at eleven to get the necessary eight hours of sleep. And body and soul are so well trained that they relax on command, and we fall asleep.

Meanwhile one has spent the entire day greedily swallowing without having chewed properly or digested, one has raced through twenty-four hours of satisfying trivia without doing the one most important thing—think! Reading *Demian* made me realize how false such zeal can be. "Smart talk has no value whatsoever. One only gets away from oneself," he said. How true, and how easily and without warning that can happen! You think you are in the midst of things, have a thousand interests, perhaps also opinions, you want to tackle all problems—but later, when you have more time and find it easier to concentrate. And after a while you forget that you have left something unfinished, a thought, a conviction, a decision. Instead, you live entirely in this hypocritical, superficial "world of the spirit" which is really a flight from yourself. But now and then you meet people who embarrass you for they say little but mean much, or you find a book which holds up a mirror to you and rouses you from your torpor.

Now I am totally awake and fully determined not to allow myself to be put to sleep again, not by passion nor by an easy spirituality. I want to stay awake and fortified!

* * *

[translated] Feb. 1

How infinitely alone the human being really is! Here one lives in the midst of a world of people who were after all created equal and should be similar, and yet, if one is truly oneself, one is totally alone and can't be anything else.

You can share a world with someone to a certain degree; if that degree is high, you speak of spiritual commonality, perhaps of love. You feel that the other would understand everything if you could convey it entirely truthfully and directly. However, beware. Only if you accept that feeling of confidence in the other's understanding without baring your soul entirely, and without displaying every trifle before him, will your union be happy.

That's because only you know yourself sufficiently well so that even your least expected actions and thoughts won't shock you. The other person is tapping in the dark, has to search from the outside, and is therefore bewildered. He takes little manifestations of yours far too seriously, precisely because he is not familiar with other, similar gestures of yours. It is easy to forgive oneself, not to blame oneself; the other will, however, remember as significant, characteristic, and irrefutable the one little fact which may have long ago lost its meaning and significance for you.

What then? Can one ever be sure? Is there such a thing as being totally at home with another person? I wonder if one can find someone like that, or if there is always that one little word, one little gesture, which dispels the illusion. Is that why so many people unburden themselves to strangers? Is it from the knowledge that the other person is distant enough not to hold on to their confession, that they are able to overcome their timidity? For many that other is the priest. He represents a distant, impersonal ear to which one can escape from one's solitude. But does one really escape? No, you take it along, the consciousness of your loneliness, and you burden the other person with it because that makes it more bearable. If one could accept one's loneliness, one could bear it. Perhaps keeping a diary is the only possible solution.

* * *

My dearest Trude,   New York, Feb. 3, 1949

Thank you for your letter and its wonderful news. My warmest congratulations! From what you write, Kurt is a great person, and the two of you seem perfectly suited for each other. I am sure it will be a good marriage. When will the special event take place? I would love to be with you on your great day, but I doubt that it will be possible on account of my finances. Nor is my general state too good right now. But please let me know the date of your wedding the moment you can because I want to send you something nice. And let me have a picture of you and Kurt, please!

Sorry that this is such a brief note. More next time, I promise.

        I kiss and embrace you, Your Liesl

* * *

[translated]   Feb. 11

What an emotional hell I have gone through during the last 48 hours. As if years had passed since our discussion two days ago. Actually, the conflict started long before that, was perhaps always present. I kept trying to show him that it was far easier to take a positive stand, not to underestimate the good because of the bad, but all I achieved was his answer: "You are 100% right, and your attitude will be very helpful to you, but I simply don't share it; we are very different." And then, on Thursday evening, he exploded: here he saw only meanness and egotism in Jew and non-Jew alike, the simple worker was even worse off than in Europe, only power meant money, and money, in turn, satisfaction. And one could not be satisfied with a mere struggle for an existential minimum, without goal or purpose.

When I suggested that he accept the eight hours of daily work as a necessary evil, he snapped at me that that was his entire day. He could not turn himself on and off on command, and live only in his spare time. And study in the evening the way I do he can't either, simply because he is not as disciplined as I am. He needs the freedom not to have to eat, sleep and study by a timetable. And movies, concerts etc. are not life, not entertainment, only a superficial narcotic.

I felt very hurt, for then I too was only a narcotic, just when I had thought to be someone who was making life beautiful for him and worth living. But I did not realize that right away. At first I just saw that he was unhappy, and I did not know how to help him. He added that if he had to sacrifice his life, he might as well do it in Israel, where he would at least be fighting for a good cause. That seemed a way out, so I suggested: "O.k., let's save for a summer in Israel and, if we like it, we can stay!" He immediately countered: "No, that would not be anything for you, for you America is the right country, and you will succeed here." As if "succeeding" were the most important thing, as if I could not be happy anywhere. He called me a Pollyanna. But what's wrong with being a Pollyanna? I had read her book in Vienna, and was very impressed by her managing to make the best of everything.

I have now spent the entire day thinking that perhaps he really would be happiest back in Vienna. There he would not be a nonentity like here (his term!), and I could teach, read and write there as well as here. It is, after all, a lovely country, and I still have a few friends there. Or should I convince him to go back by himself and try it out first? What if he is just staying here for my sake? How can I justify that? Perhaps he needs to go back right now, while he still has some links to that life he is crying about? Father wants to come here, and John could take over his apartment in Vienna. The rent is low and could in the worst of cases be paid by my sending him packages. And if, after he has established himself, he wants me, I can follow. Yes, but what happens if Vienna disappoints him too and he fails there? Then, I fear, he will be totally lost, to himself and to me.

    I spent a terrible day, and finally phoned Hanna. She did not know what to advise, but Henry thought I should not undertake anything, that it is not up to me. If John is ready for a decision, he will make it, and if he wants to leave, he will, even without me. Henry is probably right. And his advice lifted a heavy burden from my shoulders. I now see things clearly: I must continue on my own path no matter what happens. When a truly fundamental decision will confront me and I will say "yes," it will be a spontaneous and unshakable yes.

I gather from the above reference that Hanna and Henry were married by then, though I have no recollection whatsoever of their wedding. Strange how selective one's memory is: I remember every detail of my first American-bought dress, down to its pearl buttons, yet I cannot recall either the bridal shower (I found a photo of it and it includes me) or the wedding of my best friend. All the more puzzling since it was the first Jewish wedding I ever attended, and it must have left an impression.

    To this day, a Jewish wedding ceremony evokes in me, of all things, the memory of a Hindu wedding held at a hotel in Aurangabad, India, while I was staying there. As I was observing it from the sidelines, I was invited to join in. The ceremony took place in a spacious garden decorated for the occasion with colorful garlands, graceful arches of flowers, and a profusion of paper lanterns; the women wore gorgeous saris, and as part of the elaborate ritual, taking place under a large fringed canopy, bride and groom circled the platform several times.

    Hanna's wedding, according to what she remembers, "wasn't too exciting." It took place in the basement restaurant of a brownstone building on the upper Westside. After the brief ceremony, a dozen or so of us apparently had lunch together at one long table. (Hanna sent me enlargements of a few wedding pictures. I only recognize her, Henry, and, to be sure, myself.) Hanna claims that I was at the time interested in her cousin Walter, whom she indicates as sitting next to me, and who does not look at all familiar. Hanna is wearing a dark green suit with a large corsage, she writes, a beautiful beige blouse "with sparkles," and a feather hat which she still owns. She looks every bit as attractive on the pictures as I remember her.

* * *

Feb. 21

    John gave me a book called *Gentlemen's Agreement* which I have just concluded. The book deals with a reporter who pretends to be Jewish and goes to a town in Connecticut called Darien, to try to live there. But at the moment when they hear his (assumed) Jewish name, the room is no more or not yet available, and everywhere he encounters anti-Semitism. So is John right and I am living in a dream world? Perhaps it is true then what someone told me and I didn't believe—that even in New York some apartment buildings don't rent to Jews? Have I just been lucky or was I closing eyes and ears? Was I wrong to think that this was a place in which one could live peacefully and freely? But where else can one go? Israel? To my shame I must admit that that is not a real temptation to me, though I wish it the best and am glad that it finally exists.

I feel myself lost. Will I feel better when I am in college? Perhaps life there is less money-focussed and the intellectuals less prejudiced? I don't know what else I can do.

* * *

[*translated from loose 3x5 cards*]

2-27-49

How is it that one can forgive a murderer more easily than one who slurps his soup?

* * *

3-15-49

How many people are searching for *the* path to the secret of life. And yet, *the* path does not exist, only innumerable paths; one can find one's own path only by finding one's own self and accepting it, and by fully living and experiencing that self.

* * *

[*carbon copy, written in English*]

Dear Walter,   N.Y. May 8, 1949

I owe you a letter for a very long time, but lots of things have happened, namely, I have been busy preparing for a big change in my life. But first let me thank you: It is wonderful of you to keep writing, and your letters help me greatly staying sane, or saner. I truly had to laugh about your story on dancing with the Queen. No, you had not told me about it before. How nervy of you to ask her for a dance, you, a private! As you say, since it was an armed forces ball she could not refuse. At any rate, you are as I remember a very good dancer, so that she probably enjoyed herself. Did you converse with her, and what did you say to her? And she? What did your wife think of her crazy husband? Was she along? Typical you—I can see before me your innocent/insolent grin! How much longer will you both remain in England, and are you then planning to return to Vienna and settle there, or will you perhaps move here?

This year I enrolled in five evening courses at Hunter College—three this spring—therefore I am very busy, although I do not have much homework. The classes are quite disappointing. Composition, Literature, and American History are not bad but also not very stimulating, and the information in Introduction to Psychology last term was so obvious that I wonder why one would take such a course. No discussion at all, only in-class lectures, doing reading assignments and writing papers. In Public Speaking the instructor was a real clown who always wore a red tie and jumped around, almost attacking one. Or he made us stand with closed eyes and breathe deeply, let our arms hang down, and pretend we are under a waterfall with water dripping down from us and relax, and similar nonsense. When we had to come forward and recite a poem, I chose "How do I love thee? Let me count the ways" and he liked it very much. For a few moments I thought of becoming an actress and not a writer...

I took an entrance test for Sarah Lawrence, a regular daytime college, and I have passed it. I first thought I failed because it was a very peculiar test, each question not to answer directly but by one of four choices, identified as A, B, C or D with a pencil. I worked very carefully to get every answer right, but did not know that time was limited and so I did not finish. I was certain that I had fallen through and wrote a letter to explain that I had never taken such a test, and asked if I could take it again. To my surprise the answer was that I had done quite well, and would soon hear from their financial aid office which was trying to make housing arrangements for me. That means that I was accepted!

You know, this is a big joke—though not as big as your dancing with the Queen. In Ostrau I had five years of elementary school and four of *Gymnasium* before I had to quit. In Vienna I was not allowed to go to school until after the war, and then all I had was the *Stadtschulrat's* [*Municipal Education Department*] three-months accelerated course, after which they gave me a graduation certificate. And here the government has awarded me two years of college credit for that certificate! Having missed six years of schooling, I will probably be the least educated college graduate in America. I only hope that I won't be much weaker than the other students who, about five years younger, will already have absolved two years of college courses.

Another joke: When I gave notice at my working place, Mr. Roland, the big boss, called me in and asked why I wanted to leave. If I stayed he would raise my salary and appoint me to his private secretary! First I was flattered, then I began to wonder if he could be serious and if I needed to explain to him why I wanted to get an education. Finally, I only thanked him and said no, sorry, I really want to go to college. Now I am convinced that he is not a Jew.

And something else is quite funny. I heard so much about the famous Easter Parade that John and I went to Fifth Avenue to look at it. What a disappointment! No bands or marchers, really no parade at all, just a lot of people, many coming out from the churches, and especially the women were enormously dressed up, with huge, ridiculous hats. Some strutted up and down the avenue several times, like us teenagers on the *Korso* in Ostrau, except that we did not dress fancily and went there not to show big hats but to see our friends and meet new ones.

Yes, I am still going out with John, and we still have problems. I probably should end our relationship but till now I somehow could not do it. However, since I have so much to do most evenings, I don't see him very often, and that makes our being together less stressed. And of course I look forward to my new life in college.

I have saved enough to again visit Aunt Jenny this summer. I shall take my vacation in early June, and then work the rest of the summer until late August. Will you still be in London then? Please, let me know.

My father wants to come to America and although I am uneasy about it, I am trying to find someone to send him an affidavit. He will have a much more difficult time than he believes and I only hope I won't have to stop school and work to support him. That would be ironic, wouldn't it? But how can I say no?

With very best greetings—

11.

[translated] May 23, 1949

Here I sit, ready to draw the balance sheet. An episode, or rather, a drama with tragic undertones, has come to an end, and I don't want to make the mistake of waiting for a sixth act. It is time to take stock.

The episode with John is over. It lasted for almost seven months, and even that was too long. The final three weeks were forced, from a painful, unreasonable hope that all might still go well and separation not be necessary. Well, seven months are a long time. You get accustomed to the other, you learn to count on him and to include him, you hope so very strongly for fulfillment that you are ready to find that fulfillment in almost anything. And even when inside you pain and sadness rise, you hesitate to call them doubt or, worse, disappointment, you continue to hope, you blame yourself for everything, and get more and more entangled in the thing wished for till it is far from reality. So far that you cannot find a bridge, can no longer see clearly, but are merely confused and unhappy, and terribly afraid of the end.

However, let us draw the balance honestly and truthfully. I would not want to undo anything. I have learned about sorrow, and insight. I learned what pleasure is and how much importance it should be accorded. I have learned that it is not the spirit that links two human beings, however much I always clung to that. The most intelligent, most highly respected man can annoy you, and evoke constant contradiction unless there is also a personal link that binds. That link is twofold: first and foremost, it is sexual; only if you are in love with someone, are you willing to close your eyes to much, and to forgive more. If, however, you are not, the other person can be hated more than the most hateful stranger.

Secondarily, an emotional affinity is needed that would tie a more permanent and balanced bond across the physical, and turn being in love into love. Only then the spiritual factor can follow and bestow respect and appreciation. It is very important, but should never be placed before points one and two.   I also learned that a man can be an ideal partner for one woman, a middling one for another, and disastrous for a third. John would have developed me mentally, but at the same time he would have suppressed my entire self, my joy in life, my optimism, my creativity. In some ways he resembles my father.

That I can see all that so clearly now, I owe to him. I only wish I had been stronger and had given the episode a more harmonious ending, instead of the dissonance with which it broke off. But I was too weak. Forgivable, with a first experience. On the whole, I can be satisfied with myself, and that painful feeling inside will surely subside, once I have some diversion and a goal—my good, old, reassuring goal!

* * *

[*translated*]   June 4, 1949

Today I had a very bad day. I felt so lonely and useless that I was tempted to phone John, though my common sense was most definitely against it. But if you are in such a mood, you think stupid thoughts, begin to rearrange the facts according to your desires, you beautify things and blame yourself. The deeper you dig and withdraw inside yourself, the deeper you get entangled in your own sadness, and the more miserable you feel. I have asked myself repeatedly how it could be that mentally sophisticated people like artists and other creative people commit suicide, even though life bestows so much on them.

Now I think I understand how difficult it is to struggle through to an affirmation of life from a great, deadly disappointment, and that some people simply can't do it; especially the artist who is far more open to every pain than the more even-tempered average person. I understand it now, when I see how a small, unimportant disappointment is so difficult to overcome if its accompaniment is loneliness. But I must put all that behind me, I simply must.

Just recently I came across a wonderful quote, in English, no source given: "If I had not read somewhere that no one should quit life voluntarily while he could still do something worthwhile, I would have been dead long ago and certainly by my own hand. Oh, life is so beautiful, but for me it is poisoned forever. (Ludwig von Beethoven)" I taped it to my desk.

Later.

Right now I am lying in the park under a shady tree, and in the soothing calmness and harmony of nature my own equanimity is gradually returning.

* * *

Dear Truderl,   N.Y. July 6, 1949

I haven't heard from you in ages, but you are probably busy with the wedding preparations. And I guess I haven't written in quite a while either.

Here it has been unbearably hot and humid. I wonder if it is as hot in Vienna. But at least you have a garden to lie in and a public swimming pool to go to. Where will the wedding be, how many guests, and will you wear white? I so wish I could be with you, but it is not possible. All I could manage was my short visit to Aunt Jenny in June, and that was planned long before I knew when your great day would be; by then I had already arranged my vacation dates with the office. I hope you can forgive me.

Here this is a big holiday, and we had two free days. On the Fourth John and I went to the movies and saw a double feature, two silly films, but at least the cinema was air-conditioned. And yesterday we took the ferry from the Battery to Asbury Park, New Jersey. According to John, Francis Asbury, after whom the town was named, was the founder of Methodism in America, in the 18th century. We were hoping that it would be cooler there, and had heard that it was a nice place. However, when we arrived in the early afternoon, there was no shade anywhere, and the beach was mobbed.

We noticed a castle-like building on top of a hill, and walked up to it. Despite a "no trespassing" sign, we entered the grounds. The building was not in use, but its walls cast the only shadow far and wide. Since we had to wait for the late afternoon ferry back, we sat down near the wall and had a good time together.

I thought I had totally ended my relationship with John, but when he phoned and sounded so sweet, I could not refuse to see him. I guess I am weak and a coward, but being together was such a relief, almost as nice as in the beginning. For once, I felt totally relaxed with him. Since I will be moving out to Bronxville soon, our relationship will change anyway.

I am a little sad to leave New York. It is such an exciting city, and it makes you feel truly alive. I think, though, that it is good for me to get away, for a number of reasons. But right now I am fine, only much too hot. Luckily, we have strong fans at the office and that helps. On the twenty-eighth I will be thinking of you intensively!

I hug and kiss you, and am sending my congratulations and best wishes to Kurt and your mother.

   Your Liesl

* * *

[*an undated entry, penciled in English on onionskin paper inserted at the end of the diary*]

A writer is made by his style. But I don't have a style yet, I am searching for a style. No, not even that, I am still searching for other people's styles. Therefore I am not a writer. But I feel the need to write, the joy to write. Doesn't that make one a writer too? Perhaps it does, more so than the style, for style makes one write for critics, but urge makes one write for either oneself or everyone. Or both.

But before I can find a style, I need to find myself. Recognize my self or create a self. I am not there yet, but I am on the way, am since I have arrived in the USA on a hot June evening, after days in a cattle car standing on railway sidings for hours, sitting on straw, nervous because not knowing if and when we will move on. Nervous also because when we were commanded to leave the cattle cars with our small bags and given a cot in the dormitories of Munich's army barracks, the faces that emerged to greet us were so full of the hopelessness of many months in the camp that we feared we would also be kept stuck there.

And when our group sent me and two others to the American officer in charge to protest against how we were treated by the Ukrainian guard, and when he said that he had till now not had any trouble and was not going to on our count and that he would take away our visas if we did not stop the complaining and then we could go back to where we came from, we felt trapped.

I almost asked to be sent back, even though my memories of Vienna were bad and sad, and Vienna was still a broken city without food or coal, and I would have to go back to my father who did not understand that I needed love and acknowledgement and appreciation, and there was hardly anyone else left there or anywhere else whom I loved or who loved me. But this first glimpse of America seemed to reveal a country that was callously concerned only with its own comfort, not comprehending or caring who we were, what we were and what had been done to us. I did not search for pity or even help, but after five years of persecution I was looking for justice. And justice was not offered, only a new type of subjugation.

Fortunately, on the next day we were informed that our transport was going on to Bremerhaven. I packed my bag and climbed into the freight car with all the others, still depressed and apprehensive, but I went. Why? Who knows? Definitely not from a conscious rationalization that this one American was not likely to represent all of them, and not from defiance. Perhaps from a kind of fatalism—or was it simply tiredness? If the decision had come a week later, I might have given up. But I was swept along.

Will I never shake off these memories? But there are others, nicer ones, as well: my arrival on that hot, colorful, noisy evening, when the refugee committee put all of us displaced persons—young, middle-aged, elderly, even a few old people—into real hotel rooms in New York. They were simple rooms but to me they seemed incredibly luxurious with their carpets, lamps, white sheets and semi-private baths.

And then there is the memory of the sea of color offered by the exhibited fruits on the corner stand next to our hotel which I visited that same evening; of Hanna, appearing the next morning with a bouquet of flowers and an invitation to a party; of finding a room and a job the same week; of being able to earn, save and spend money the way I chose, including a trip to England; of my learning what love might be and what it wasn't, the difference between loneliness and solitude, and finding a wonderful teacher and friend who would listen to me and warm me by his belief in me. And mainly, my being free, totally free.

Anyway, it was very full two years, rich in unusual impressions and strange experiences. I may have drifted more often than rowed, but the water was bracing and I have stayed above water and have, it seems to me, covered a respectful distance. I still don't really know who I am and where I am going, but even so I am glad that I did not turn back on that awful day in Munich.

PART TWO

Sarah Lawrence (1949–1951)

1.

Dearest Truderl,   Bronxville, Oct. 8, 1949

I want to hear from you about your new life and how it feels to be married. Is it difficult to live with your mother-in-law? Let's hope you find an affordable apartment soon! Did the dress arrive in time to take with you on your honeymoon, and do you like it? I thought it was very much "you"—I hope Kurt agrees. I can't wait to see the wedding pictures! Where in Italy were you, and was that your first time there? Of course, by now you are probably back at the Uni and working hard, and may not have much time to write.

There is quite a bit of news here as well. I want you to know that I have joined the American Upper Classes! I am not kidding: Bronxville is so different from New York that it is as if I had again stepped into a new world, only this time as a gatecrasher who may be discovered and thrown out sooner or later. Or perhaps I will, like Cinderella, turn into a princess and fit in eventually …

Let me describe my new environment. Bronxville calls itself a village, but that is either a joke or false modesty. It has no farms, no grazing cows or crowing roosters, no smell of manure. Bronxville is actually a *Villenviertel* [*upper-class suburb*], except that the houses are not called villas, just "one-family homes." Nor do they look like our villas. No walled gardens or hedges to hide the house, no tall wrought-iron fences and locked gates. Sure, they have large, manicured lawns, but those are not fenced in: anyone can walk right up to the house, on the path or even across the grass. This openness makes the streets look very cheerful and inviting, almost like a *Sommerfrische* [*vacation spot*], except that most people go to the other extreme: at night they draws their curtains, and you can look right into the living rooms! Either they don't have private lives or they are snobs—perhaps like our aristocracy of old, who would address servants in the third person and undress in front of them as if they didn't exist. Or is everybody an exhibitionist and wants to show off the chandeliers and expensive furniture? (Don't laugh—I once visited a Viennese refugee family in New York who, when I admired their living room furniture, told me how much each piece had cost! In their case, it was probably the after-effect of the war, but here people haven't gone through a war and haven't had to start from scratch; why then are they doing that?)

Unlike a villa, these homes have simple lines, unusually wide windows (they call them "picture windows"), but no real style. Many are merely one story high, long and narrow, with the windows facing the street, and a one- or two-car garage attached to one side. They call this "ranch style"—even though I can't imagine anything like that on the prairie.

There is another type of house which I like much better, even though it doesn't look like a villa either. Those houses tend to have two stories, sometimes even a third one right under a pitched roof, and they are called "Victorian." They look more old-fashioned than the ranches, and not as neat, though I doubt they go back as far as Queen Victoria. Nor did I see anything like them in England. These are compact, gabled cubes rather than rectangular boxes, with small lawns, a few shrubs or perhaps a flower bed in front. Again, no fences of any kind. Some have black or dark green shutters mounted to either side of the windows, which imparts on them a kind of low-key elegance. But the shutters are useless: they are permanently attached and cannot be closed. Many of the Victorians have raised porches in front and sometimes around the sides, with roofs that are held up by thin, square, very plain pillars. The porches, too, are wide open, and any passerby can see what's going on on them.

The Victorians are built of horizontal wooden slats, usually painted white. The ranches are stucco, but probably also of wood underneath. I bet all these houses are hot in summer and cold in winter, and they would burn down fast. But of course here there is no danger of incendiary bombs. Only some Victorians have garages. If they do, it consists of an unattached small building, a kind of shed. The streets are unusually clean—few cars, fewer pedestrians, no busses or streetcars. It is easy to sleep at night since you hear no ambulance or police sirens, no honking and screeching bus brakes. In fact, the first few nights it was so quiet that I couldn't fall asleep. Needless to say, the air is much better than in New York. Somehow Bronxville looks like an oversized toy town where time stands still. What a difference to the smelly, noisy, dirty but exciting "City." (That's what they call New York.)

I live in one of the Victorians. Our little street, actually a circle, is far less fancy than most streets. We have a front porch, and ivy climbs up the left wall. A small stony hill, called a "rock garden," faces the ivy. The house itself is relatively small, but it feels sturdy and comfortable. It would definitely look less out of place on the prairie than those ranches. Well, our house is not on the prairie, but the first house on the left after you enter Beall Circle. Three more houses surround the grass-covered center.

Would you like to know how I got here? It was actually quite simple: the college arranged free room and board for me with one of their professors. In return, I help Mrs. Bozeman take care of her eight year-old daughter, Anya. The third family member, Kitty, is a small black dog of uncertain age and origin, whom all of us try to understand and please. There is also a tenant, a middle-aged lady who rents one of the upstairs rooms and teaches school somewhere. We hardly ever see her, though Anya and I share a bathroom with her. The two of us sleep upstairs as well, but each has her own bedroom.

The house is considered old (which in this country means thirty years or so); the other houses on the circle must be much newer. They are ranches and resemble big barns, except that their window frames are painted white. The exterior is painted as well, but in surprisingly loud colors. Ours is white, with a steep gray roof, but the house nearest to us is cocoa brown (putting it politely), the one next to it pale yellow, and right across from us is one in baby blue! Each has a garage attached to its right side, while we don't have a garage.

This is the first time for me to live in a "one-family home," and it is a real treat. Almost as if I co-owned it. My room is large and sunny, and it is surrounded by treetops. Also, I am allowed to use every room except the rented bedroom—even Mrs. Bozeman's bathroom downstairs. And I am not treated like a maid or governess, but like part of the family. We eat together, set and clear the table together. Mrs. B. even helps me wash dishes, though she does all the cooking. That's actually a relief because I still don't know much about cooking except for wartime *Eintopfgerichte* [*"one-pot dishes", i.e., casseroles made of whatever is available*]. Mrs. B. is remarkably skillful at turning leftovers into interesting new dishes. I also appreciate that she does not waste food like so many others, perhaps because her background is German. But she is not Jewish, in fact, originally a *"von"* [*i.e., titled*]. Her field is political science.

The inside of the house is not ostentatious at all. You wouldn't know that it is a professor's home. The small square hallway is quite plain, with a staircase on the right leading to the second floor. Its railing is painted white, as are all walls. But though you don't see any nice wood, everything looks clean and cheerful. On the left side, an open arch takes you into a large, square living room with one wide three-part window facing the street and another, narrower one, the rock garden. No curtains. On the right is Adda's study-bedroom, also quite large, with a sliding door which she pulls shut when she works. That room has a bathroom, but no real bed, only a couch. At the end of the living room is the kitchen, with a door out to the back. Much of its space is taken up by a huge refrigerator, with some of Anya's drawings taped to the door. If you don't open and close it slowly, the drawings fall off.

The kitchen is as narrow as a railway car passageway, but that is only because, on the right, half of it is partitioned off by a low wall. Behind that wall there is just enough room for a cubicle with a table and two benches, all built-in. The benches are covered in real leather, dark red. Each bench can seat two people. That's where we eat, very informally, without a table cloth. Surprisingly, there is no dining room, not even a dining table in the living room, only a round table with wicker chairs out on the porch. I suppose one could eat out there, at least in the summer, but it would be in full view of the neighbors.

Most windows are tall, narrow and quite odd: each is subdivided into two halves, and each half has nine little square panes of glass. Perhaps glass was difficult to obtain when the house was built? It couldn't be more impractical. To open a window, you must either slide the lower half up or the upper half down, instead of opening them inward. That way, you never have a completely open window; nor can they be cleaned properly. Perhaps the windows in the living room and in Adda's room were enlarged later.

To the left of the house and in the back is the so-called "rock garden." It is indeed full of rocks of varying sizes, with clumps of grass and plants between them. Once a week the three of us do "garden clean-up," usually on a Saturday morning, which means that we pick up dry leaves and weeds from between the rocks and plants. (I am learning to distinguish weeds from real plants, but it is not always easy.) There isn't much in bloom right now. In spring, the garden must look much better. Such rock gardens are, for some reason, called Japanese.

Actually, Adda looks a little Japanese as well, despite her German background. She is still quite young, very attractive, has strong black eyebrows, slightly slanted black eyes, very white skin, and a high forehead. Her hair is also black, long and straight. She parts it in the middle and ties it into a low bun with a bow or a black velvet ribbon. At home she sometimes lets it hang loose, and then she looks like a young girl. She dresses very simply, but always looks slim and graceful, even in her long house coat or the *Dirndl*-like green dress with lace in front which she wears at home. And on her, I don't mind a dirndl. [*Dirndls were the signature outfit of Nazi women and girls.*] Anya is blond, with bangs and pigtails, a round face and lots of freckles. She does not look at all like her mother, and I have not met the father since Adda is divorced.

Most men seem to work in the City. When I walk to the college, I meet whole processions of them, heading for the train station, with briefcases, dark jackets and ties, even on a hot day. Hardly any women, though. And here the streets have real names, and they don't necessarily intersect at right angles. Also, some are quite hilly. The road from the railroad station up to our house is really steep, and only a little less so is the long, tree-lined boulevard leading up to the college. There are no sky-scrapers, only a few large apartment buildings near the station, and so far I have not seen a single traffic light. Could that be the reason Bronxville is called a village?

All shops seem to be clustered together on one short street near the station. Some call themselves "shoppes" (pron. shopies), though I couldn't find the word in my dictionary. There is also one large grocery store, Gristede's, which sells not just food but almost anything. I was in it only once so far because Adda usually shops herself, or she has the groceries delivered.

I don't have to clean the house, not even my room, only make Anya's bed and help with the dishes after dinner. A "cleaning lady" comes once a week— and "lady" is the correct word: she drives a Cadillac! Only in America ... Adda does not have a car, but the shops are close by; so is Anya's school, and even the college is only fifteen minutes away on foot. If you are in a hurry to catch the train, you call a taxi, or take the shortcut down the hillside behind the house. It's steep, but if Adda can manage it on high heels, I am sure I can.

My fear that I would not know how to deal with children was unwarranted. Anya is gentle, smart, and likeable. I just need to be at home when she gets back from school, offer her a snack, and think up things to do after homework. We play games or walk Kitty, or she practices the piano—and so do I.

Yes, we have an upright piano in the living room, and I am taking lessons at the college. My playing is very elementary, and I will probably never be good at it since I am not very musical. Even so, it is reassuring that, though I can't carry a tune properly, on the piano I immediately detect a false note. In Ostrau, Hanna taught me how to read music in exchange for my helping her with math. But we had no piano, and so I could not practice. Now I do, whenever Anya and Mrs. B. aren't in, and I love it.

Dinner is, in this country, eaten in the evening. Adda's meals are quite different from Grandma's, much quicker and with a lot of herbs and spices, but once you get used to that, quite tasty. Now and then a colleague drops in for a drink before or after dinner and, if you can believe it, if I am downstairs, I am invited to join in! At first I felt very awkward, nor had I been drinking alcohol before except for a few sips of Grandma's homemade bread-crust wine, but now I even enjoy a "martini," which is what they usually drink: a mixture of gin and a few drops of wine, shaken with ice, then strained, and an olive dropped into each glass; don't ask me why. It took me a while to get used to it for the gin puckers your mouth, as does the olive. I am of course delighted to live with grown-ups and not in a dormitory with students much younger than I am.

In the living room there is not only the piano and several comfortable armchairs, but also many paintings on the walls, which make it look like a little museum, only more cozier. And books are everywhere, in bookcases, on end tables, even on the coffee table in front of the sofa. Many are about art and artists. In Adda's room, an entire wall is covered by a bookcase, and the large table under her window is piled high with papers and more books. Once I have my own apartment, I too will have a lot of books, and paintings on all walls!

As you see, I have once again been lucky. My room is quite luxurious, my work easy, I am treated well, and I am free to study, read and write. What more could I want? The college, by the way, is quite different from what I had expected, but that description will have to wait till my next letter. How I wish you could be here, at least for one day, see the house and my room, and meet Mrs. Bozeman! I admire her greatly. Incidentally, she has a law degree in addition to her doctorate.

Write soon and tell me about your trip—I hope the weather stayed good to the end. Your postcard was beautiful, but it didn't say enough.

Best wishes for a successful semester for both you and Kurt. By the way, I still see John, but only for a few hours off and on, and that works out fine.

Embracing you, I remain your

Liesl

P.S. This has become an awfully long letter, even though my typing it should make it easier to read. If you are bored by so much detail, please let me know—I promise I won't be offended.

* * *

Oct. 17.

I don't know what is wrong with me. Everyone is nice to me, I have enough free time to study and read, much stimulation, I am with people who are intelligent and nice—so why do I feel myself more as a stranger here than in New York? The city is only 30 minutes away by train but it seems worlds distant, and I miss it and my friends terribly. Is it because there everybody around me was Jewish so that we were among ourselves, and here all is foreign and untransparent? No, that can't be the reason. Though Mrs. B. isn't Jewish, she couldn't be kinder, and I have heard no antisemitic remarks anywhere. It is just such a totally different culture, and I don't belong in it. I don't think that I am seen as a person, only as another student. Can the girls tell that I am on a scholarship? At any rate, they must hear that I have an accent and despite I am never asked where I come from, how long I have been here, or anything else. I think that Rudi and Kurt, or at least Rudi, might be Jewish—both have German accents—but they have not asked me either. I am saying to myself that it is probably better this way. I need to forget Vienna and the war. But I feel invisible.

In New York nobody asked questions either, but there it was not necessary. We knew that we were all Hitler victims, that we earned our own living and it did not matter how. We were free and independent, and yet somehow one large family. Here I am an outsider, maybe the only one. None of the other students have foreign accents, even those with Jewish-sounding names. I know nothing of them, or is that because I see them only in the class? But before class no one says anything to me either. Am I too easily touched? I must try to concentrate on the things that are good here and not ruminate, but I feel terribly lonely.

Recently, when Rudi was having a drink with us, Adda mentioned a newspaper article which criticizes today's students on account of their apathy. Perhaps that is the key. She complained that even in her class (and she teaches politics!) the students show little interest in what happens in the world. Perhaps that is why I feel like in a *Dornröschenschloß* [*Sleeping Beauty's Castle, i.e., an ivory tower*], and not because I don't fit in. I must submerge myself in my studies and forget all these broodings and self-lacerations.

Adda never criticizes me. Even when she tells me to do something differently, she is polite and tactful. I have the feeling that she does not approve of the way I am dressing, though I now try to coordinate my colors. But there are no inexpensive stores here like Ohrbachs or Kleins, and I don't want to tell her that I have more important things to think about than clothes. I would even if I had money. No, I am not just. She is a real scholar and looks *schick* [*has flair*] at the same time, but I am not tall and slim and attractive like she and wouldn't, even if I spent more money on dresses. If the five hundred dollars scholarship from the Jewish women's organization comes through, I could go to New York on a Saturday and buy me a new dress.

The problem is the girls at the college. They make me uncomfortable because they are so self-assured and worldly. I do not know what to say to them. Also, they all look really sharp in their flared or pleated skirts, and their white shirts or blouses and cardigans. I can tell, those are expensive, even though they look modest and understated, quite different from the students at Hunter who were older, and often came directly from work, with sandwiches, like I. Whether Jewish or not, they were genuinely friendly and not just polite. There must be other girls who also have a scholarship, but still I am left with the feeling that most never have worked, and that they are rich. But perhaps it is simply that I have nothing in common because they are so young and inexperienced— four to six years younger than I, with the exception of the few veterans who are here because the army pays for them. I must remind myself that I am lucky to live with Adda and not in a dormitory, so I ought to stop complaining!

* * *

Dearest Trude,   Bronxville, Oct. 28, 1949

Many thanks for your letter and the great photos. Kurt is very handsome and *sympathisch,* and he is looking at you with admiring eyes. And you look simply lovely and very happy. I am so glad that you have found him! Also that you had such a nice honeymoon, and I don't mind at all that you are reporting to me only now. Great that the dress fits, that you like it, and that Kurt does too.

Today is Founding of the Republic Day in Czechoslovakia, but I am probably the only one to remember … It makes me melancholy, those celebrations seem so long ago. Yes, John and I still see each other but not really; he only comes out for a few hours on weekends. That way I don't have to hurt his feelings. Perhaps I am a coward, but I just couldn't say to him, "I don't want to see you any more." It would have hurt him badly, and he is having a hard time anyway. And I don't have another boyfriend.

Since you like my long letters (you are not just being polite, are you?), I will now introduce you to American "college life." We have what is called "a campus," namely a large park-like area with big buildings, up to four stories high, of red brick, gray stone or a combination of both. They look old-fashioned, very European, and attractive. Lawns and big trees are everywhere, and no roads, only pedestrian walkways. Some buildings have ivy climbing their walls— like English manor houses, or Hampton Court Palace.

Even so, Sarah Lawrence does not feel like a university, not even like New York's Hunter College. More like a boarding school or a *Gymnasium* [*university-oriented high school*]. There are only 340 students, and no lecture halls, just classrooms. In one class, we sit around a long table. Of the three courses I take (the fourth is piano, which doesn't count), one has twenty students, one eight, and my creative writing course fifteen. The small classes make it very intimate; the professor gets to know you, and you have an idea what he or she is like and expects of you. Nor do they lecture, but merely ask questions to start a discussion, or to hear your opinion. Sometimes I think the professor is much too patient. What is worse, the students are allowed to smoke in class, and many do.

We have no examinations. Instead, we are assigned "contracts," namely research essays—either a few short ones, or one long one to be handed in at the end of the term. (There are three terms and we take three courses, each running through the entire school year.) We can write about almost anything, as long as it is at least vaguely related to the class topic, and that is delightful. The contract determines the grade, or would if we had grades. But we don't. Instead, we will get a personal report for each course at the end of the term, and I won't know how well I am doing until then. It is an interesting system and I can understand its justification, but I also find it discomforting to tap in the dark and not find out how to improve my work before the term is over. However, the lack of competition and exam pressure definitely makes up for the high school environment; so does the close rapport with each professor, and the freedom to explore any topic and book you choose—not just plowing through dull textbooks.

The "faculty"—here the term does not mean *Fakultät* [a *university school or division*] but the teachers—are not called *Herr* or *Frau Doktor* or *Professor* but simply "Mr." or "Mrs." followed by the name. It seems disrespectful, but is probably meant to be democratic. At least no first names are used, as was done in my office in New York. Not for the students either. I am "Miss Welt," except at home where both Adda and Anya call me Lizzy. (Hanna still calls me

Liesl as in Vienna, and Mr. Goldberg Liz. And some teachers call me Elizabeth. It is odd, but sometimes I think I respond differently to each of these names, am almost a different person. Perhaps one day I will discover which of the four is the real me, or whether I am someone else altogether.)

Once a week we meet with each teacher to discuss the reading assignments or contracts we are working on. That provides an incentive and establishes a little discipline, though not a lot: if you can't finish your paper on time, you simply ask for an "incomplete" at the end of the term; and if you need even more time, you see the school psychologist and discuss why you are "blocked." (It seems fashionable to see a psychoanalyst—students practically brag that they do! I would be ashamed.)

My classes are interesting, much more so than at Hunter, and so are the professors. They all seem to be very knowledgeable. However, I probably work less hard than at Hunter because there is so little pressure. After class everyone disappears into the dormitories or for sports or art, or whatever. (Thank God, sport is not obligatory!) The dormitories are all inside the campus, and the campus is fenced in. The gates are locked at ten at night, and the students have to be inside. According to rumor, there is a hole in the fence ... Fortunately, I don't need any holes: at the Bozemans I am free to come and go when I want, as long as I don't wake anybody. Apparently even students with families in New York live on campus.

You ask if the students dress elegantly. Not really, at least during the week. Usually skirts, white blouses, and low-healed shoes, either white ones with brown stripes and shoelaces, or "loafers," which are a lot like *Sattelschuhe* that the foot just slips into. And white socks, but luckily short socks, so they don't look like BDM girls. [*White knee socks tended to identify members of the Bund deutscher Mädchen—the official youth organization for girls under the Nazis, which everyone was expected to join. The male equivalent was the Hitler Youth, the Hitlerjugend or HJ, (pronounced Haah-yott). The boys wore Lederhosen (short leather pants), and kerchiefs around their necks.*]

However, on weekends the girls are almost unrecognizable. Some look great, others a bit vulgar. Very expensive dresses, often highly décolleté, with narrow waists and wide skirts, black eye-liner and big eye-lashes, fire-red lipstick, often high hairdos with pearl combs or ornate pins. All this to impress the dates who pick them up and "take them out," usually by car, either their own or their father's. "Out" can mean a restaurant, a dance hall, or a "drive in," which is an outdoor cinema with an enormous screen high above the parking lot. You stay in your car and get the sound from a small, portable loudspeaker that is attached to a post next to each car. I understand that students often go there not to watch the film but to "neck," which means kiss, also called "smooching" or "making out." I certainly don't plan to use that language.

Most of the dates are from Princeton or Yale, and on weekends they invade the campus like hordes of Mongols. Then there are noisy parties in every dorm (they call them "mixers," so they probably drink martinis), and if you don't have a date on a Saturday night, you might as well hide in the library. Am I glad I don't have to live on campus!

The American dating custom could be a project for anthropologists. It is as bad here as it was among Hanna's friends in New York, but somehow more calculating. If a girl has gone out with the same boy several times, they call it "going steady" and only then she stops seeing others—to make the boyfriend jealous. Remember how we would get together in someone's apartment and talk, play games, or dance to records? And it didn't matter if we were all girls, or more girls than boys. I am certain we had as much or more fun, without chasing anyone. And if two people decided to go out with each other seriously, we might kid them but respected their privacy, and we would certainly not have tried to flirt with their boyfriend, or ask indiscreet questions. So much simpler and more natural.

This is all very puzzling and disappointing. I had expected that at such a good and expensive college everyone would be serious, and discussions would focus on school work, books, assignments, or important events and topics. Perhaps that happens in the dorms.

Another, very different experience still puzzles me. Once a week we meet for an hour with our "don," an adviser whom we select, provided he agrees to accept us. I selected a very nice don, low-key and pleasant. When I told Mrs. B. whom I had chosen, she gave me a funny look and said, after a pause:

"Lizzy, perhaps you should know that he"—she hesitated again—"is not interested in women."

"What do you mean?" I was puzzled, but then I realized that she was trying to tell me he was *ein Warmer* [gay].

A bit worried, because I really like him, I asked:

"Do you think he won't be a good adviser?"

"I am sure he will," she said quickly. "I just thought you should know."

I assured her that it didn't make any difference to me, but that wasn't quite true. Now I find myself watching him to see if he is in any way different from the rest of us. He doesn't seem to be, much to my relief. That way I know that I can say anything I want to him, and he won't think that I am trying to flirt. (Some girls do—could that be the reason Mrs. B. mentioned it?)

Our college is considered "progressive." That is a new educational trend, and was probably the reason why it attracted attention at that conference in England I read about. The progressive idea was introduced by our president, Harold Taylor. He is very young, probably not even thirty, and quite good-looking, more like a student than a president or professor, with an open shirt and V-neck pullover. Adda says he is the youngest college president in the country. His field is philosophy, and his model Dewey, whose theory was that students must not be criticized or put under pressure, but should be encouraged to develop in their own way. (We have a Dewey nursery school here, and once a boy cut off a girl's braid and was not stopped or even scolded!)

Adda is quite skeptical about that kind of education, but I like it, at least at the college level. It is the reason why we have no exams, grades or attendance sheets. How much I will learn under this system I don't know since I work harder under pressure, but I love it because I can take any class I want and explore any topic I choose, as long as my don does not object. At other colleges you have a lot of required courses, whether you are interested in the subject or not, and you waste time cramming for exams.

Enough for today. Write soon! You are my only link to Vienna, except for my father, and all he writes about is how I should conduct myself ...

Kisses and hugs from your

Liesl

I am fortunate that Trude liked my long letters, and doubly fortunate that so many are again in my possession. Not only have they restored forgotten images and memories, but they also enable me to review now what I had then accepted as fact, often without adequate information.

One such fact concerns Harold Taylor, our president at SLC. He was not the first to introduce "progressive education" at the college. That was done by William Van Duzer and his wife, Sarah Bates Lawrence, who had founded the school in 1928 on their 12-acre estate. After consulting with their friend Henry Noble MacCracken, then president of Vassar, they based the curriculum on Dewey's philosophy, and on an emphasis on the performing arts rather than the usual homemaking skills for young women. Sara Lawrence has remained one of the leading progressive colleges in the country. In 1962, it added a Center for Continuing Education—one of the first—and in 1968 it became coeducational.

Likewise, my assessment of the students as superficial and frivolous was as hasty as my characterization of Hertha had been two years earlier—I was obviously a slow learner. Only years later, when I began to read the SLC [*Alumnae/i*] Magazine, *did I realize how many of my classmates had embarked on distinguished careers in the arts and sciences, or were in public leadership positions, for which the basis and incentives were unquestionably provided by the college's supportive as well as liberating atmosphere.*

* * *

[*carbon copy*]

Dear Mr. Goldberg,   Bronxville, November 18, 1949

I am so sorry that you were not free when I visited Hanna. So, until we can meet, I will inform you in this manner about my life and activities hitherto.

First, yes, I think that Lore would like it here. This is the right school for people who value independence and freedom, and she could probably obtain a scholarship and financial help just like I did. You can definitely encourage her.

My life is busy but everything is manageable. We have to take three courses which extend over the entire year. I also take piano which doesn't count, but I have always wanted to and this is my first occasion. I practice either at school or at the Bozemans when nobody is at home. We have an upright piano because Anya (age 8) also takes lessons and this way I can aid her a little. In the morning, I get her ready for school, then I go to my classes or the library and return in the early afternoon to be at home before her. In the evening I help to prepare supper and wash dishes, and that is all. As you see, my duties are easy and I feel comfortable and at home—actually the first time since I left Ostrau—although everything is very different. But you don't need to worry—I am not in the danger of becoming a snob!

I take "Psychology of Art" where we learn and theorize about motivation, the "artistic process" and similar. The readings for that course (they even include an Indian philosopher!) are both unusual and interesting, and the subject is intriguing.

My second course is "Thought and Image." The texts are very wide-ranging, some quite philosophical and difficult. Now we are reading Thomas Aquinas. The class is taught by Mr. Robert Fitzgerald who is also a poet. He has translated the *Odyssey* and the translation is beautiful—simple and understandable, but also very poetic. Mrs. Bozeman told me that he is Catholic, and his poor wife who is not very healthy continues to have children. You would never guess it about Mr. Fitzgerald, for he is very quiet and shy. It appears to be agony for him to address us in class. He never looks at us, only at the table, and he squirms and clears his throat all the time and talks in a very low voice. It is almost as bad during our personal weekly conferences. (We see each teacher one time a week in a private conference.) I admire him very much but I never know what to say and he waits for me to speak, so we often sit there silently pretending to be in deep thought. Once I mentioned reading *Seven Types of Ambiguity*: his eyes lit up and he began to talk about the book animatedly.

My last course, you will be pleased to hear, is "Intermediate Writing" with a very sweet old lady, Mrs. King. I don't know if she herself is a writer or just a literature teacher. She is too gentle to criticize our attempts, but she makes me write, and that is good. An essay I wrote she liked a lot (I will send it to you), and now I have the first act of a play, a little à la Noël Coward, which she found amusing. So I hope to receive a good term report from her. Those reports are personal evaluations—we don't get grades.

I probably don't work hard enough, and feel guilty that my courses are so easy. But they are a real pleasure, very stimulating and about totally new subjects. And the teachers are extremely knowledgeable. I only wish I had time to read more—there is so much to catch up on! The students, on the other hand, are very young and quite immature. All they talk about are boyfriends and parties, so I am doubly glad that I live with grownups. I admire Mrs. Bozeman very much. Even though I am not her student, there is a great deal I can learn from her. She is brilliant as well as beautiful. And she not only knows politics which is her area but also has a law degree and is well-informed about art and literature and music.

Mrs. B. is also a sharp critic and can be a little intimidating. She has a way of testing you by asking for your opinion, and then saying with a sweet, almost embarrassed smile: "Lizzy, you don't really mean that, do you?" Then I know that I have said something stupid. I have also noticed that she often sounds a colleague out about his opinion before expressing her own. Whether she does this from caution or respect I don't know, but it is a good way not to make a fool of oneself. Of course, I cannot say to a professor "what do *you* think?" only to friends. But it teaches me to deliberate before I annunciate my views.

Before or after dinner a colleague of Mrs. B. sometimes stops in for a drink, and I am frequently invited to join. I want you to know that I now drink "martinis" like they do, though at first I though they tasted terrible. The most frequent visitors are two professors, both of whom are very learned although totally different. I don't know if they are married, but they usually come directly from school and alone, and for only a short time.

Rudi (of course, I call him Mr. Arnheim) is my teacher in the Psychology of Art course. He is German, a very kind and quiet man, thoughtful and interesting to listen and talk to. He might be Jewish. The other, Kurt Roesch, is also German but an artist. I looked at a little book of drawings he made to poems by Abraham Cowley which Adda has—it is called *The Metaphysical Love*—but the drawings are too abstract for me. One, to a poem called "Of his mistress bathing," shows a few fish outlines, some squiggles and not much else. [*At my graduation, Kurt presented me with an autographed copy which I still own.*]

I don't know how far known Kurt is as an artist, but he has a very strong personality, the exact opposite of Rudi. He is good-looking in an aristocratic way, almost arrogant, with a sharp profile and piercing eyes, a little like a Prussian officer. Also, he is very formal and kisses Adda's hand whenever he comes and leaves. Witty, in a sarcastic way, and sometimes condescending, at least to Anya. Perhaps also to me. With Rudi I can argue, with Kurt I only listen.

I feel very flattered that Adda invites me to stay downstairs when she has visitors. It is immensely interesting to observe college life from this inner side, or rather outside, to hear about the problems at the school and about other professors and administrators. Some of them Adda and Kurt are critical about for being yes-sayers or changing their views. (It seems that everybody here not only teaches but also takes part in policy-making and in the way the college is administered.) Kurt even jokes about the president who always walks across the campus with a huge English sheepdog and a tiny one which is smaller than a cat. The three look very funny together. He is a "Dewey man" and Kurt does not think much of his educational theories.

A little episode may amuse you: Rudi invited Kurt into our class to talk about the creative process (remember, Rudi is a psychologist and Kurt an artist). But no matter what questions he formulated, Kurt answered that he does not think nor observe himself when he paints, but leaves it to others to do the interpreting. Rudi stayed sweet and polite but was visibly frustrated, and Kurt's face expressed very clearly what he thought of this psychology of art nonsense.

That is all the news "that's fit to print"—although usually I don't have time to read Adda's *New York Times,* not even parts of it, and books interest me more anyway. I hope you have good pupils this semester—I miss your literature class and even more our after-class chats. But I will soon write again and keep you informed, and perhaps you can free yourself when I next visit Hanna.

   Many greetings,

Here are two miniscule but treasured memories of Mr. Fitzgerald. Among the few activities at SLC which I remember was an outdoor production of "Oedipus at Colonus," in which he read the part of Oedipus. I marveled at the intensity of this shy man's performance, and at the effort it must have cost him to expose himself to such an extent. His love for the play (of which he had published a translation) must have been stronger than his resistance to a public display. I tried to ascertain from the college's archivist when that reading had taken place, but she had no record of it.

* The other episode is even slighter, but I treasure it. Many years later, Mr. Fitzgerald and I found ourselves on the same plane, returning from a translation conference where we had been on a panel together. He complimented me on my presentation and, when I confessed that I had written it on the flight down, his voice and eyes expressed disbelief and admiration.*

*   *   *

My dearest Truderl,   December 10, 1949

 Many thanks for your beautiful card and birthday wishes. I had a nice but quiet celebration with John, who came by train last Saturday afternoon. He said hello to Mrs. Bozeman, then she withdrew. We played records, and he was good company. I think I have found a good modus vivendi for our relationship.

 You sound even busier than I am, so don't feel obliged to write long letters. I don't know Italy at all, but of course I also don't know Austria either since I only spent the war years there. But I have definitely been catching up on traveling since coming to America. Niagara Falls, Washington, even England—I can't quite believe it. Now that I don't earn any money, I can only plan occasional day or weekend trips to Hanna. They have a small apartment, and I don't want to intrude too often.

 As a Christmas present, Mrs. B. gave me thirty dollars to purchase a smart party dress at Lord and Taylor's, an expensive store in New York. I will try to get it instead at Klein's, a less fancy store, if I can find something really nice there. I can't see spending so much money on a dress which one hardly wears.

 This time I will celebrate a real Christmas, with a big tree. It already sits on the porch, in a bucket of water, which Kitty tries to slurp up. Anya and I will decorate the tree once Adda has decided where to put it. We are making paper garlands together, and I have also taught Anya to fold and cut out paper napkins into snowflakes of different sizes and patterns, so they can be taped to the windows later. All this brings back memories of Christmas Eve in Ostrau. Not that Adda goes to church, nor Anya to Sunday school (a program at the church to teach religion to the children).

Actually, Christmas is more of a public celebration here than a religious holiday. People put strings of lights all around their windows and doors. They start doing this already in early December, though they don't celebrate the Sixth [*St. Nicholas Day*]. Some people also place on their lawns or roofs large cardboard figures of Santa Claus with a sled pulled by reindeer, or snowmen, even Disney's seven dwarfs. It is like a competition and quite silly, but the children love it, of course.

I found a great present for Anya, a board with the outline of a human face, and with small black magnetic pieces which you can arrange into different facial expressions—a smile, a scowl, thought etc. I hope Adda will consider it a good educational toy.

That's all for today. I have two contracts to write; no time, not even for piano practice.

I hug you and wish all of you the very best for the holidays.

Your Liesl

* * *

Dec. 18—midnight

I visited Hanna last week, and finally saw Mr. Goldberg. We met in a café in the proximity of Grand Central Station. I had not seen him since moving to Bronxville and it was a pleasure to be together, almost like the good old times. But all he had for me was one hour and that was hardly adequate, for him too.

"It's been too long," he said and hugged me, as we separated. "We must not let so much time come between us again! I don't want you to drift away, do you hear?"

"No, I won't."

"Promise?"

"I promise."

What was I promising? His words left me strangely exhilarated and a little uneasy. As if something unfinished, unclarified was between us, and I could not tell whether it was good or bad. Perhaps I am just imagining this because I have not been in a very good emotional state these last days. But it is too late to talk about that now.

2.

The record for the rest of that first year at Sarah Lawrence is surprisingly meager, consisting of only two diary entries, a few letters and two documents. The diary entries were written in English and, I regret to note, once again show the girl that was me backsliding into emotional chaos. However, that spring a new problem moved into the foreground. By the time fall arrived, it was taking up more and more of my thoughts and efforts, and, quite unexpectedly, it propelled me into an unforeseen direction.

Dec. 25, 1949

It is true, only in trouble I find my way to you. But then, does not distress lead people to strongholds, be they religion, philosophy or suicide? I certainly have in you a less fanatic and uncompromising friend, a safer and gentler one!

Yet, today I do not even come in distress, only to clarify things and bring that salutary new emotion to the fore. I had a very soothing long conversation with Robert Goldberg when I was in the city to visit Hanna a week ago and I did not even tell him anything because I thought I had mastered the whole problem and felt very good and balanced. But the truth is that just now I again went through a crisis. I hope it is over, really over. To make certain I won't forget the least of it and above all, none of my present exhilarated, elated tranquility and certainty—I am going to report to you.

I had a disagreement with John. No fight but one of those vicious creeping things where very little is said and yet it is imbued by the knowledge that everything is going wrong. And I thought that we had found a good modus vivendi together! He refused an invitation by Mrs. B. to come out for Christmas dinner. Now, his reasons might perhaps be justifiable, but not his attitude. Headstrong, not considering me or the part he is reducing me to at all, not willing to give way one inch, though this would probably have meant more fun for both of us. And trying to punish me and keeping me without a word, though I was the least active part in the whole planning.

And unfortunately, I behaved exactly the way I should not: Like a young girl, incapable of overcoming my emotions of feeling neglected etc.—unhappy, rolling somewhere headlong and yet not being able to stop. I thought that I had become much more mature than acting like this.

After an afternoon of misery, Rudi came and I had to put up a show. But in the course of the conversation, after Anya had gone to bed, it stopped being a show. We talked about art and several things were clarified for me, at the same time my mind felt wonderfully relaxed, as it hardly ever did in John's company. Then we talked about politics. I probably did not make much sense, but he listened, agreed or disagreed, we both developed and enlarged—nobody lectured, there was not the feeling of having to give one's best for every word would be registered and might be played back, and that felt good.

I don't mean to say, that all of a sudden John has become quite dislikable, but he certainly has been deposed. And how I who thought to be critical, could ever have raised him to such a pedestal, is almost shameful. I was already on the point of giving up everything for him, my interests, my future, almost my ego— I know I need a man to encourage me, and yet I submitted to him who is in so many ways like my father. But I am not going to follow Freud. I know letting go for me means giving in to the current, drowning instead of swimming. Of course, one can also drown swimming against the current; but why should one not *swim with the current?*

I will go straight ahead; if he comes along, fine, if not it will be good-bye. My work is more important than he, for I don't have the certainty that he is the best for me. And if that is not the case, I may not be right for him either and one fine day be let down—then lost completely, if I have made him my aim.

My work can never let me down. I know I am good at teaching and that is something I can give without failing, and my writing—it is for myself, it will be my fulfillment, even if it is not successful. I have almost got into the track of measuring talent by success. When Rudi tonight claimed that art is to a very *small* extent communicative, but mostly a clarification, an *Auseinandersetzung* [dialogue] between the artist and his world, and when he made me see the truth of this, I began to realize how much I had already erred astray.

Now I am full of optimism and the good old fighting spirit of my first happy pioneer days in the States. How foolishly I made myself suffer this last year! I now realize that I cannot go anybody else's way, even if I love him. I can only go alongside with him if our ways are parallel. But I do have to go my way. Thanks for listening.

I find myself both embarrassed and impatient with that younger self of mine and her inability o bring the affair with John to a close. Was I just afraid of not having a boyfriend in an environment where that was almost considered a character flaw, or was I so afraid of a confrontation that I kept drawing back, I who, a few years earlier, had so glibly preached to Trude that she must break off her relationship with O? Perhaps both.

* * *

Bronxville, January 1, 1950

It is 15 minutes past twelve midnight. The new year, the second half of the twentieth century has begun.

I should have taken stock of the year before it was over, but since I did things I wished to be carried over into the New Year, I did not interrupt. I wrote, and I made some money typing. May both be successful in 1950!

In my mental state nothing much has changed. I saw "The Red Shoes," a rather sad movie about a woman dying of the dilemma between her love and her career which are incompatible. I had a rather depressed evening afterwards, took dog Kitty up on my bed to keep me company (poor thing she probably shook her head about my inconsistency!), and after a while I felt consoled. Today I am fine again, as long as I don't stir in my wound. So I only wish not to have to touch it for a long time—I hope he does not come!

Looking back, the year has not been bad at all. A scholarship to Sarah Lawrence and a successful beginning there, a trip to England and Jenny, my writing gaining strength again, and my love life richer by a great experience. Perhaps it is good that this experience ended with the year, symbolic of its temporary character, before I could have let it shape my whole life from mere fear to miss something. And yet what I would have done just then—miss life. Now I am no longer scared of not getting married. There are men everywhere, and I know how they are, so would not expect anything phantastic.

Liesl, even if it may be hard in the beginning, you must stick it through, don't get weak again and fall back just in panic you might not find a man. Rather I stay single, work how I like and where I like and am the master of my fate, however bad it may turn out. But there won't be this inevitability, doom, this knowledge that nothing can be done since I once made my choice. Therefore I have to be hard with myself and I will. May the New Year keep me away from any such deep painful entanglements, may it give me back my peace of mind, and joy in my work! I am hopeful, indeed. And may it bring us all nearer to world peace and happiness!

Amen.

• SARAH LAWRENCE (1949–1951) •

* * *

[*carbon copy*]

Dear Mr. Goldberg,   February 14, 1950

Thank you so much for your kind words. I am still not entirely convinced that the term report is as successful as you seem to interpret, but I naturally hope that you are correct. Not receiving grades is a two-edged sword, at least for me. But I will follow your idea and seek to solicit advice during the private sessions with each teacher. Or at least with Mrs. King about my writing.

I was terribly flattered that you liked my essay so much, even though reading it to your class was quite unnecessary! Is there still someone there who remembers me? But I promise that I will continue to write and improve myself, even if I need to do it piece by piece when time is too short.

I am glad that your Christmas with the family was more pleasant than you expected. I do not want to pry, but is there a serious reason for your ambivalences? If it is money, I could advance you some, for my scholarship has arrived, and I really don't need any money here. Do not hesitate letting me know.

Anya has a whole bookcase full of books. Now and then she still asks me to read to her in bed, and I became quite fascinated with American children's books. When I discovered a cobweb on top of our bathroom window and removed it, Anya began to howl. I only found out the reason when she let me read *Charlotte's Web*, so that I was truly sorry about the murder. However, a book she loves and which I have to read to her again and again I cannot understand at all. It is called *Alice in Wonderland*—perhaps you can sometimes explain to me why it is so popular.

Nothing else to report today. My very best greetings,

* * *

I found both the original of my term report and the essay I had written for Mrs. King.

"December 21, 1949

    Report on ELIZABETH WELT

        Thought and Image
        (Fitzgerald)   Good. The learning is all right on the whole,
        clear-minded and orderly. To be realized
        in writing: that in art there is a discipline of

economy and feeling, just as there is a discipline of thoroughness in study.

Psychology of Art
(Arnheim)   Elizabeth has been carrying the ball week for week. Her responses have been quick and never superficial. She has worked hard and steadily, and her excellent mastery of the material deserves every praise. Her acute criticism, which is a constant check on our work, has become thoroughly constructive and cooperative. She profits greatly and will go far.

Intermediate Writing
(King)   Elizabeth began the term with a distinctive paper, based on a striking idea. She has not quite returned to the harmony between style and subject shown here, but she has worked throughout the year with intelligent and mature interest. Her difficulty, of which she is aware, is the padded sentence and the too conventional plot. But when she limits herself to what she can handle in a genuine, natural way, she is on solid ground. She has much material and at the moment, ideas are ahead of style. A satirical one-act play, just begun, has many possibilities. In class, her contribution is outstanding for its reference to other reading, also its good sense.

Piano
(Williams)   Elizabeth is making very good progress. She works intelligently, consistently, and with great enthusiasm."

* * *

"And who are you?
I am a stranger. The stranger. One nameless being, chosen among millions to outlive them and to bear witness, by its mere existence, of their passing away.

No, I did not mean to impress upon you my being a great writer. I am just—a survivor. A grain, too tiny to be caught in the most diabolically devised net woven by man's hand, and washed ashore this happy aloof continent.

Yes, I did survive the war, as you can see! Weed does not perish, they say in my country—in the country I lived in, that is. For I have no country. I told you I was a stranger.

There is not much to be said. Or too much. And you do not really care to know it. You are all alike here: You ask, but you do not expect any answers. You are ready to pity as long as there is no need to help. And you shrink from a bitter truth for fear it might penetrate even your armor of isolation and reserve and strike wounds that you would not know how to ease.

I am sorry—I did not mean to be so bitter and so offensive. That is only because it is so hard to believe in mankind after all those years. And because I am all alone in a new world. I am afraid; I had been an undesirable stranger for too long. Why should you welcome me here? Assault is he best defense, that's why I attack.

You are very kind. But there is really not much worth mentioning. I was born in Germany, went to school in Czechoslovakia, spent the war in Austria and had Romanian citizenship. That should be sufficient to make you understand all the rest of it. I did not belong anywhere, but for this very reason I did not mind so much leaving surroundings that had become familiar, living without most of the little conveniences and comforts that amount to so much in an average life, and parting again and again from people I had grown to love. Then I did not yet realize that I would never see them again, I did not realize most of the actual happenings around myself.

Maybe that was the only way to survive and to remain sane. It was all like a nightmare, too confusing to be understood, too gruesome to be defied, too unreal to be believed. The awakening came but much later, and it was not too pleasant either.—But now I am here. Please do not ask me how I like America. I do not want to like it, for that means remaining a comparing by-stander, an eternal outsider. I want to understand it. Only then it will have become my country and I will have developed a part of it. And this is the very reason for my attending this class.

I know my English is not good enough to compete with the abundance of words that the language offers to the American-born student. But it might improve, and I am patient—what about you?

No, I have no experience at all as far as short story writing is concerned. I did work for a leading theater in Vienna for a time, but that was more criticism of plays offered to us, together with brief reviews of their contents for our files. This was the most interesting and underpaid position I ever had. I gave it up for a more lucrative job, that of an English teacher for the American Joint Distribution Committee, which still offered some opportunity for individualistic work and for interesting psychological experiments, as I love to teach.—I did some independent newspaper work too, but not in English. That's why I am so vulnerable and so aggressive. It is hard to conquer, to develop and to cherish one language and then to be forced to throw it away like a dress that, though beloved and imbued by great reminiscences, is out of style now and makes others laugh at you or even scorn you for wearing it.

I do not know. Stephan Zweig committed suicide because his language was too dear to his heart. But others succeeded, not in superceding their native tongue by another, but in subjugating this other language, making it servile to their ideas and moods and thus gaining access to another culture and life. You do live as many lives as you speak languages. I experienced it myself because I know four of them. But as far as creative work is concerned—to really master a language, every breath and sigh of it—do you think that can be accomplished?

I believe you because I want to. And I would like to beg you one favor: Will you correct every mistake I make, substitute every inexactly used expression by the fittest word, so that I may pen-etrate to its very core?

Any more questions? I am afraid you will have to ask them in person."

Even now, many years later, I am struck by the enormous contrast between this well-written and eloquent essay and the flawed diary entries and letters written at the same time. Could it all have been merely a question of self-discipline?

* * *

Dearest Truderl, April 25, 1950

Thank you for your nice letter. I am so glad that all is going well. A vacation in Salzburg sounds wonderful. It is supposed to be a beautiful city and have lots of concerts. I just hope you won't run into their *Schnürlregen* [*llit.: ribbon rain—Salzburg's notorious thin drizzle, which can continue for days at a time*].

I know I haven't been writing as often as I should have, and now, too, I will have to be short since I am in the middle of my contracts. Once school is over, I promise to write in detail, and tell you about my ambitious summer plans. To make up for the brevity of this note, I will enclose a text from our college newspaper which may amuse you. It describes the atmosphere here a little. I am sure your English is still good enough to understand it. There is no need to return it.

Have a wonderful vacation, and please send a detailed account!

Your Liesl

The following is probably the newspaper clipping in question. A note in my handwriting lists its source as "The Campus." It is not dated but sounds like an April 1st item. The format and misprints are those of the original.

"Harold Taylor Foils Gunmen

A pale, upset Harold Taylor returned to Bronxville last night after a near disasterous run-in with New York's underworld. In an exclusive campus interview this morning, Taylor, still visibly shaken, recounted his story.

'I was headed back to the college from a meeting in the city when the incident occurred. It was about ten-thirty, I guess. At the corner of Tenth Aven. and Twenty-sixth Street, I slowed down my 2nd hand Caddy for the traffic light. Another car pulled up behind but I didn't pay any attention until a voice snarled,—OK, Mac, hand over your dough!—Two men were pointing guns straight against my window. I looked to the street but it was dark and utterly deserted.

'There wasn't much else for me to do but open my window and

give them the wallet. They ripped it apart and found fifteen dollars in small change.—OK, Mac, crawl out.—The big one waved his gun at me. I got out.—Who do you think you're kiddin'?—I said I wasn't kidding anyone and explained that I was a college president.—So where are you a president, Mac?—I told him I was president of Sarah Lawrence in Bronxville. I told him about our responsibility to the individual student and American education. I told him about our experiment in learning ... our search for intellectual freedom. I also told him about the scholarship program that enables deserving girls to take part in our way of life. And I concluded,—unimportant as it seems, my car is necessary to me as president of SLC.—

'The men were silent for a minute. When the big one spoke there were tears in his eyes.—OK, Mac, we'll take your word for it. Now get going,—I did.

'Well, that's about all there is to it.' Harold Taylor leaned back in his leather-oak chair. 'I didn't call in the police because I credited my escape to philosophy and to the understanding the gunmen displayed. But, in the light of common sense, I have decided

never to go into New York again
and lose another month's salary.
Philosophy only stretches so far.'"

I often wondered what had become of Harold Taylor. Just recently the Sarah Lawrence Magazine *had a short article about him which seemed very much in line with the brash, self-assured stand described above, however teasingly, and which greatly endeared him to me in retrospect.*

It seems that in 1951, at the height of the Cold War, an American Legion magazine article accused SLC and seventeen other educational institutions of hiring or tenuring "subversive" faculty, whereupon the Westchester County American Legion's Americanism Committee began investigating SLC's hiring policies. In response, the Board of Trustees issued a revised Statement on Academic Freedom, which reaffirmed the College's commitment to freedom of thought and speech, and pledged that "teachers who meet the test of candor, honesty, and scholarly integrity may not be deprived of any rights they hold as citizens of this country, including the right to belong to any legal political organization of their own choosing."

On the very day this admirable statement was made public, the Bronxville Legion Post (so much for Westchester and Bronxville—my first impressions had not been so wrong after all!) released a series of charges to the press, alleging that SLC faculty took part in outside subversive activities. This set off a firestorm of national press coverage and much impassioned correspondence. Nor did matters end there. In the spring of 1953 eleven SLC faculty members received subpoenas to appear before the Senate Sub-Committee on Internal Security. The Legion continued its attacks through 1958.

As so happened, shortly after I read the article, its message was enhanced by a personal encounter. Lore, like me a Goldberg protégé, arrived at SLC during my second year there. After I graduated, we lost touch but, animated by my recollections of those years, I called the college to ascertain her whereabouts. I succeeded, and we met—after fifty-three years! As we reminisced, I mentioned that the best course I had at SLC was a world history course taught by Mr. Aron. Lore now confirmed what I had suspected back then: Mr. Aron had either been a member of the American Communist Party or a collaborator, and he was fired. However, my subsequent inquiry to the college yielded a significantly different perspective: President Taylor fired Mr. Aron (i.e., allowed him to resign) not because he had invoked the Fifth Amendment at the Sub-Committee hearing, but because he had not met "the test of candor" and "honesty" required by the College's statement on freedom of expression. He had not told the truth about his affiliation to the faculty and trustee committee when questioned. I now wonder how many other faculty members had been communists or sympathizers but, having owned up to the affiliation, were retained.

As Lore and I reminisced, I also learned that Mr. Arnheim, for all she knew, might still be alive, in a nursing home in Ann Arbor, Michigan. I phoned him, but he had difficulty understanding me, was coughing badly, and finally suggested that I write to him. I did. Remembering how appreciative I had been for his not only taking me seriously, but treating me as an equal in our discussions at Adda's, I described my life since leaving Sarah Lawrence, and expressed my gratitude to him for having been my teacher and mentor. The letter I received in return was dictated. It expressed pleasure at hearing from me, and suggested that our careers had been quite similar. His modesty embarrassed me, all the more when a few days later I received a paperback of 324 pages he had authored, Film als Kunst [*Film as Art*]. *Published in 1932 by its twenty-eight year old author, it was reprinted in 1978 and 2002, and hailed in the three appended essays as a unique, groundbreaking work. The footnotes contained references to quite a number of essays and reviews likewise written by Rudi.*

The barely legible dedication "To Lisa — Rudolf Arnheim" was written exactly four weeks after his one-hundredth birthday.

3.

Dearest Trude,   Lookout Mountain, Golden, Colo. [*no date*]

I am awfully sorry not to have sent you a birthday card. Everything was so hectic at the end of the school year, and with the preparations for my trip the date just slipped by me. Let me at least now wish you a very successful year, good health and great happiness with Kurt. I will try to make up to you with this letter, which you will find waiting upon your return from Salzburg.

In case you wonder about the address: picture to yourself high rocky mountains, some even with specks of snow on top, and cottages around a lodge on one of them, Lookout Mountain. It is not as high as the others and has trees, shrubs and high-alpine plants wherever you look, wonderfully cool air, a row of towering peaks on one side and a wide open plain far below on the other. Denver's matchstick-size high-rises are barely discernible in the distance. That is where I am, as a member of a two-week international student seminar of the American Friends Service Committee. It is a dream vacation, and totally free!

A notice in a newspaper invited recently arrived international students to apply; I did, and was accepted. All I had to pay for was the bus to get me here. It took almost three days. I slept on the bus, but we stopped for meals, bathrooms and to change buses. It wasn't bad at all.

It is difficult to realize how enormous this country is. One must travel across it by bus to truly experience it. Much of it is quite flat, namely the part they call the Midwest, and that can be very monotonous. Hours of driving past fields, mainly corn which is not very high now but will supposedly be six feet high by the end of the summer. That is America's "farm belt," where much of our food is grown. And what is interesting, each farm sits in the middle of its fields instead of being part of a village. There are, in fact, no villages as we know them, only small towns, usually with a wide and straight main street, which may simply be called "Main Street," and which may have one or two gas stations, a small coffee shop, perhaps a "diner," (a very inexpensive restaurant), a motel, and a few shops. Hardly any cars, no trees or grass, just the wide, dusty road, blinding sun and heat. All the towns looked similar, except for different advertising slogans on enormous billboards along the road and on flashing neon signs at night.

Chicago was impressive but much like New York, with clusters of skyscrapers. Its streets were not as orderly and straight, and now and then you could catch a glimpse of the huge Lake Michigan. Just as much traffic. We spent several hours there, but it was so hot that I stayed in the air-conditioned bus station and cannot tell you much about the city. Perhaps better that way— it is supposed to be quite unsafe.

Driving through the towns on the outskirts of Chicago was also interesting. Hardly any apartment buildings, mainly one-family homes. People here must be wealthy for everyone to own a house. However, the landscape around the towns looked terribly neglected, junkyards and construction sites with no one working, and piles of old tires. It made me think of Dickens' *Our Mutual Friend* and its dust heaps—are treasures hidden under those mounds of tires?

In Denver, Jim Morrison, our director, picked me up at the bus station. We collected several others from the train, then our van headed across the plain. (Denver is quite flat.) The Rocky Mountains appeared in front of us quite suddenly, first in a haze but then sharpening into an unbroken line of peaks, bluish gray, barren, and very majestic. It seemed as if we were driving head first into an incredibly high, impenetrable wall. Then our van began to huff up the serpentines of the Lookout Mountain road, which climbs steeply from the plain.

We eat together, cook and wash the dishes together, and clean our rooms. Shopping is taken care of by Jim and his wife, who also direct all activities. They are Quakers.

Do you know anything about the Quakers? It is a religion—and it isn't. Anyone can join, whether they have another religion or not. Even Jews. There are no priests, only silent meetings where you sit in a circle and meditate about spiritual things, or anything you want. Now and then someone will speak up and share his thoughts aloud, that's all. It is a different way of "letting one's hair down," as Mr. Goldberg would say, and it impresses me very much.

Even more impressive is the work the Quakers do. They send groups of volunteers to poor countries to help build roads, schools and hospitals, or to teach—English, house keeping, agricultural methods, whatever is needed. The idea is to work for international understanding and world peace. (And meanwhile North Korea has just invaded South Korea—will things ever get better?)

Every morning we sit in a semi-circle and listen to a speech, talk about ourselves, or discuss the assigned books and articles. The most impressive speaker so far has been a professor or writer named Milton Mayer. His first talk was especially dramatic. For a long time he sat in front of our semi-circle silently, then he raised his head, looked at each of us with a piercing stare, and suddenly shouted, pointing an accusing finger in our direction:

"It is your fault, the fault of every one of you! What have you done to help your fellowmen, your country?"

He sounded like a Savonarola, and made me feel guilty and full of good intentions. I assume that he too is a Quaker. Perhaps I can join one of their work tours once I have finished my studies.

In the afternoon we usually go on "outings." That means we are taken to scenic places like the monument of Buffalo Bill (I have no idea who he was but, judging by the statue, a famous cowboy), or up into the higher mountains. Tomorrow it is Long Lake. I will try to swim in the lake, even though it is supposed to be very cold. Anyway, it is simply breathtaking here, the air is perfect, even after Bronxville which was not as hot and humid as New York City. And the scenery is indescribable, far more dramatic than Gastein or anything else I know. Last night I even saw two deer graze quite close to our lodge.

Our group is very international. A German girl (not Jewish) kept apologizing to me for what the Germans had done to the Jews. I had to tell her to stop, that I knew it wasn't her fault. But I was afraid to ask what her parents had been doing during the war. We also have two Indians, one a Brahmin from Delhi who is extremely handsome and intelligent, and flirts a lot. But is also quite arrogant so that I am extra cautious. Besides, he has a wife at home, which he keeps forgetting. The other is from Bombay and the merchant caste, which is lower, so he is not conceited. He is not especially good-looking, short and skinny, but has a pleasant, expressive face and a warm smile. He wears glasses and looks a little like a young Gandhi. He too has a wife at home, but he does not flirt. He is interested in people and cultures (he hopes to work at the UN), and is always willing to help. He showed me a letter he had written to his two young sons, full of advice and philosophy. He asked me to correct his English. I am learning a lot about India from him, and he is good company as well.

A Czech woman, a dentist, is a bit older than the rest of us. She seems nice, and I find it a challenge to see how much Czech I still remember after more than ten years. So far, I don't know much about her, except that she flirts with the Brahmin, and does not seem to take studying very seriously. Then there is a tall, thin young man from Sweden with the teeth of a skull, also a short Mexican who always looks unshaved, and others with whom I haven't yet talked much. But it's only been five days, and we have two whole weeks.

After the seminar I will travel to Beverly Hills. Kitty Farkas (with whom I emigrated to the US) has invited me to spend two weeks with her. Her employer encouraged her to invite company for herself while he would be away.

My cousins from Berlin are now here. Their situation is very bad, but I don't want to spoil my and your mood—I will tell you their story some other time. Please let me hear how your trip turned out. I hope you had perfect weather and heard many good concerts.

All the best to everyone sends your old friend

Liesl

* * *

[*a hand-written draft, with corrections*]

Dear Mr. Goldberg,   Burbank, August 18, 1950, 9 p.m.

I hope you have received my postcard from Golden. I will try to present more details when I see you but here are a few, unfortunately hand-written since I didn't bring along my beloved Erika [my Viennese portable typewriter]. I relished the seminar greatly, and time just slided through my fingers. The last weekend we were all invited to a big party at a neighboring camp, called the Lisle Foundation. Regrettably, it was arranged very late: I would have liked to become more familiarized with their people. All in all, both groups were much more accessible than the students in my classes at SLC. (Now please don't smirk!) Perhaps it was because so many were foreigners. However, the Americans at Lisle were equally friendly.

The Lisle camp was also on top of Lookout Mountain, and only a short drive from our camp. That evening on the way back it was dreadfully foggy and one of us needed to walk before the car along the slope to show where the road was, and thereby save us from tumbling down a few thousand feet. It was scary, but we returned without crisis.

Now I am in a totally different environment—as an "au-pair" for a wealthy family in Burbank, Southern California, a suburb of Los Angeles. They are at home, so I cannot watch TV and anyway this seems a propitious moment to write to you.

At the end of this week I shall give notice, and leave the following Saturday. I can hardly wait. The job is definitely not what I expected, but it will serve its purpose: I needed a place after parting from Mrs. Farkas and before returning to Bronxville. If you were not so busy, I would have tried to come to New York first, but I don't have a place to stay there for more than a night or two, so that would not have been a good alternative.

After my stay on Lookout Mountain I spent two weeks with Kitty Farkas at the fabulous mansion in Beverly Hills where she is housekeeper. You should have seen the life of luxury we were leading! Her employer has cotton plantations in Texas and allowed her to invite me, while he was away. What a house! I felt like a movie star and not only because Hollywood was next door. An elegant manor house and a garden full of roses, with gardener and swimming pool.

Kitty and I went to Hollywood, saw Graumann's Theater and all the hand and footprints (modern dinosaur tracks!?!) on the ground. We explored museums, visited Kitty's relatives, ate in little cafés, swam and lingered around to pick roses for our rooms—of course, I had my own room—and did not even dust until the last two days, when we worked like crazy to make everything clean. It was simply terrific.

When I was looking through the newspaper ads to find a place to stay until it was time to get back to the Bozemans, one seemed just right: a family was looking for living-in help, just light housework and watering the garden. I went for an interview and it sounded good. The family, a couple with two sons and a daughter, are all grownups. Everybody works in the family business, leaves in the morning and comes home after dinner. I was to take care of the breakfast dishes, turn the sprinkler system on and off so that the garden gets watered, and iron. The rest of the time I would be free. My room (small but nice) is next to the ironing pantry. It even has its own bathroom.

Though Burbank is a long bus-ride from both Los Angeles and Beverly Hills where Kitty is, and the pay is minimal—$10 a week—the work load seemed light and since I would have free room and board, that was just what I needed. I accepted and, to be truthful, felt guilty about not telling them that I would be there only three weeks.

Now I have no guilty feelings at all. On the contrary, I can hardly wait to communicate the news. Why? The shocking awakening came on the first morning. When I entered the kitchen, finally quiet after much noise and door slamming, which implied that they had left, I was confronted with just about every dish and glass in the house stacked dirty in or next to the sink, evidence of their extensive late night snacking and equally elaborate breakfasting.

When, after cleaning up, I prepared for ironing, I discovered that the huge basket contained blouses and summer dresses of the daughter as well as several white men's shirts, something I had never had to iron before and which consumes much time. What makes it worse is the need to keep running out to turn the various sprinkler systems on and off since the garden is supposed to be watered in the morning and in the evening, when it is relatively cool. And their two canaries who have the full use of the ironing room insist on flying around me, when I am ironing, so that I have to shoo them off with one hand while ironing with the other, or they leave their signature on dresses and shirts. They have a cage in there, but try to get them back into it! Mrs. Silverman wants them to "feel free" so she lets them out in the morning.

In addition, she invariably finds other "little tasks" for me to do—like washing the grooves between the wall tiles in the kitchen and bathroom, which were probably not washed for decades.

Yesterday was the worst day until now. As I rushed to get things accomplished because I had arranged to meet Kitty in L.A., the following happened: the d... birds escaped from their little room, flew into the kitchen and from there into the living room and settled on the top of the curtain rod. After chasing them all around, without succeeding to make them fly back into their room, I finally set their cage on the dining room table and sat down, hoping that they would get hungry and give up their adventure. They did—in a fashion. Both flew down on the table, but when one hopped into the cage to eat, the other perched on top and gave an alarm the moment I moved, and the inside bird slipped back out. I begrudgingly gave them credit for their superior intelligence and, after a look at the clock, resigned myself to forego my date. As if they had read my thoughts and were now satisfied to have outsmarted me, the beasts hopped into the cage, so that I could close the door and return them to their room. When I later phoned Kitty to apologize, she sounded relieved that nothing worse had happened. She actually found my disaster funny.

To tell the truth, now that I have adjusted, I must admit that the work is really not hard, and it is nice to have house and garden to myself all day, time to read, watch TV, and relax. Except that $10 does seem stingy. Never mind. Ten more days and I will be on the bus to the East Coast.

Will you have any free time to come and see me before school starts?

4.

And so began the second, my last year at Sarah Lawrence, with few diary entries but quite a number of letters. Most focus on or revolve around the cousins from Berlin. I recall little else about the activities of that year, at least its first half, and can only assume that life at the Bozemans had settled into a comfortable groove, or that my worries about my cousins had erased all other concerns. I hardly participated in "college life," which was probably due in part to my living off-campus, in part to my considering myself more mature than my classmates and therefore making little effort to approach them, and finally, from a deep feeling of insecurity because I did not seem to belong nor knew how to try to belong.

A chance encounter with an SLC classmate during a professional meeting in Durham, North Carolina, a few years ago, sheds some light on that period. Neither of us remembered the other, but we immediately took to one another, and spent a long evening reminiscing. We had both been refugees. Gisela survived a concentration camp, and had made it her mission to visit schools and synagogues and talk about her experiences.

"I wish I had known!" I exclaimed, but she reminded me:

"Don't you know, none of us talked about those things then! All we wanted was to forget them and be like the others, blend in."

She probably did better at blending in than I had.

* * *

Hello, Liz— NY, November 13, 1950

If there's any curtness in this note—the brevity is only a result of lack of time. Fact is I do want to get this off as quickly as possible.

Did I tell you though that I thoroughly enjoyed seeing you Saturday. It was good all the way and I do hope that we shall be able to see more of each other and oftener. And I may yet convert you to Scotch! I'm of the opinion that I may have kept you out too late. Did I?

Our discussion about Lore? It was good to talk to you about her—though it never had occurred to me that we would spend so much time, if any, on the problem. But if it will enable you in any way to get a better, more compassionate understanding of the girl, then everything I said was warranted. Like you, she is a tremendously sensitive youngster. Outwardly, she may manifest a calmness that doesn't exist. Thus, knowing about her, you may in whatever way, be of some help—if only through understanding—to her.

I'm looking forward to meeting your cousin Arthur on Tuesday evening—I liked the chap at first glance. I admire his sincerity and his integrity—though I feel he is doing things the wrong way. I'm glad you felt that my presence the other night was of some help. I'm sincerely interested in helping him further. Not merely in his speech work. But we'll let that serve as the start.

Do write soon—brevity is no longer the question—just so long as I realize we're once again on the same side of the fence and that we do speak the same language. You have no idea how warming the awareness of this is.

      Regards,
      R.

* * *

Dearest Trude,   Nov. 29, 1950

I promised to brief you about my three cousins from Berlin, but first let me thank you for your beautiful birthday card. John came out for a few hours on the Saturday before, and brought me a recording of Schubert's Unfinished Symphony. The Saturday after that, Adda and Anya took me out to an expensive restaurant, and I took full advantage of that.

My cousins: it is a long and complicated story, and a very depressing situation. The worst is that I am unable to do much. Mr. Goldberg is trying to help, and that is a great relief to me. Let me recapitulate their story briefly.

The boys arrived here in November 1949. I had an unexpected telephone call from them, announcing they were in New York, and so I took a train in at the first opportunity. I had not met them before, nor known that they were coming. A Catholic refugee committee brought them over and was taking care of them. Their father was Jewish, but he had married a Catholic, except that that did not save his life. He was deported in 1941 and never returned, and the mother died at the end of the war. Arthur was about eighteen when they arrived, Michael fifteen, and Felix eight. The committee was going to find families to adopt them.

It was strange to suddenly have relatives I had never met nor known much about. I tried hard not to see them as strangers, but it was difficult. Was it because they are Catholics? Possibly, even though I have shed most of my Jewishness at Sarah Lawrence.

Felix was small, thin, very quiet, and he stammered. Michael was of medium height, solid and quite good-looking, with bright eyes, a round face and a self-assured manner. Arthur was slim but not thin, and not very tall either. But he had an informal way which was very appealing, quite grown up. He seemed disappointed that I was in college and could not really help them. He acted as if we were siblings or at least old friends, which I found a bit strange but actually nice. In view of what happened after that, his roguish smile may have been indicative of something else as well.

A few weeks later, I received a very unhappy letter from him. He wrote that Michael had been taken in by a Jewish family whom he had met on the boat, and who were planning to adopt him. Thereupon the committee quickly moved the two other boys out of town, to a school in Pennsylvania, run by nuns. It was called an agricultural and industrial school, but was, according to Arthur, more like a reform school. He claimed that he had no freedom at all, though he was grown up, that some of the children were stealing, that no one would listen to his complaints, that Felix was not getting the special care he needed, and that no attempt was being made to find a family for either of them. He also mentioned that he had sent several letters to the committee in New York, and never received an answer. In a later letter he claimed that the mail was being censored, and that he had to sneak out into the village and post his letters there, to be sure I would receive them. I did not know what to make of all that.

One day Arthur phoned me from New York to say that he had run away, and gone to the committee in person to request that they investigate the school and keep their promise to place at least his little brother in a private home so that he would get proper care. Arthur refused to return to the school. The committee promised him that Felix would be placed privately upon finishing the school year. Thereupon Arthur found a job as a messenger, worked very hard and had, by last summer, several hundred dollars in savings. He phoned me now and then, and everything seemed to be going relatively well.

In September the committee informed Arthur that they had decided Felix should spend another year at the school. When Arthur stated indignantly that they could not break their promise like that, they threw him out. That's when he decided to get justice by himself. He quit his job in order to devote all his energy to the task of helping Felix. A letter from Germany which blamed him for not having taken good care of his brother upset him terribly. After weeks of letter writing and approaching various committees, he decided that he could only prove his seriousness to the committee by going on a hunger strike.

One evening, he arrived at the Bozemans in an old, beat-up car he had bought, and asked me to give him a few blankets. I tried to talk him out of his plan and make him understand that hunger strikes might be effective in Germany, but would do no good here. I thought I had convinced him, but when I phoned the committee a few days later, I was told that he had parked himself in front of their door and, when he was still there two days later, they had him committed to Bellevue. Bellevue is a mental hospital! Now Robert Goldberg is trying to see him and get him out of there. I hope he will have a good influence on Arthur. What would I do without Robert!

Don't let me end on this depressing note, especially with Christmas coming. May it be joyful for you and your family, and may it be followed by a very good year for all of us. And may both you and Kurt pass all exams successfully!

With kisses and hugs,

Your Liesl

* * *

I have before me a blank envelope containing two letters and one two-page essay, all typed on plain white paper, with several typos. All are unsigned, and one bears the heading "Copy." They illuminate the boys' predicament far better than I could. I also found a handwritten note from the boys' grandmother, asking me to do all I could to help them. Only the essay and one letter are dated. Though thee correspondence extends over a considerable time span, all three documents are closely linked thematically. I will therefore present them together.

[*translated*]

COPY

Dear Monseigneur,

I would like to solicit your kind help and resolution with regard to the following.

I, as the grandmother of my grandson Felix, housed in an educational institution [the German term *"Erziehungsanstalt"* has overtones of a correctional facility which the English lacks], am of the conviction that his placement in that institution can only be due to an error.

My grandson is an orphan since his father perished in a concentration camp, and his mother, due to great mental anguish, died after long suffering of heart disease. Since earliest childhood, he had to live through the ominous war years as well as the equally difficult postwar years with their terrible accompaniment of hunger and misery. Through the assurances of the US Committee for the Care etc. my grandson has now been admitted into the United States, to forget the pain of those years in the protection and nurture within a family, and to live in a free, healthy and democratic country, and be able to develop as a free human being. Through the correspondence which my daughter has had with my other grandson and photographs sent to her I have unfortunately gained the conviction that the care and treatment of my grandson in the institution does not seem to meet the expectations which we have in Germany of the new and better home the poor orphans are to find in the USA.

May I perhaps add that because of the especially disastrous years of the Nazi Regime which brought his mother unbearable spiritual burdens and led to her early death, my grandson has suffered greatly both mentally and physically and therefore requires especially good personal and individual care within a family, which can hardly be accomplished in an educational institution.

As his grandmother of almost seventy-nine years I implore you sincerely, Monseigneur, to immediately see to a better arrangement for my grandson [illegible passage] … worry at my age, and to save me from having to undertake further steps.

     Deferentially,

* * *

The second letter is written in English, addressed to the boys' grandmother and dated Nov. 6, 1950. It acknowledges receipt of a letter of October 8, in which she apparently voiced concern regarding the clothing situation of grandson Felix. The writer explains that Felix's older brother is very much opposed to Felix remaining under their care and custody, and is resorting to every means to have him removed, and that he has therefore grossly misrepresented the conditions; that, as the writer had mentioned before, a deeply felt antagonism was shown by Arthur almost from the first day of his placement; though they had relaxed many regulations to favor the young man, he had failed to acquire a good attitude in his situation and was not only critical of everything, but actually acted rebelliously; that, since leaving the school, he has maintained the same attitude, and seeks to defame the committee for the evident purpose of creating sympathy for the removal of his brother.

The letter then refers to enclosed photographs that were taken of Felix on his First Communion Day, October 8, 1950, by one of the Sisters at the School, and which show him properly attired for the occasion. The sender points out that that was the way he was dressed when Arthur visited him, so that the writer cannot imagine how Arthur could have taken a picture of Felix in any other clothing. The First Communicants wore that garb throughout the day, except that Arthur, to carry out the diabolical [sic] purpose he had in mind, might have found some old discarded clothing and had Felix dress in it for the picture. The writer then asks to be sent the photo Arthur had taken, and promises to return it after seeing "just what kind of a picture it is."

Finally, the writer assures the grandmother that there is an ample supply of clothing for each boy, at least two sets, one for weekend wear and the other for weekdays, and that it was therefore not necessary to send Felix such items. However, gifts of any kind would certainly not be objected to.

There is no signature.

* * *

[*translated*]　　　　　　　　　　　　　　　　　　　　　　　　Berlin W 30, January 7, 1951

Report on the physical and mental disposition
and the life of my grandson Arthur ...

My grandson was the oldest of three children. Their father was a member of the Jewish, the mother of the Roman Catholic religious community. Any disturbances in the youthful development of Arthur were not noticed, rather he was developing as an industrious and very bright boy who, however, being a *Mischling* [*of mixed blood, i.e., a half-Jew*], was already early in his life exposed to continual animosities during the Nazi period.

When he was eleven, he saw his father put into a concentration camp and there lose his life. His now unsupported mother was thereafter exposed to constant persecutions by the agitated masses and to dire poverty with her children, age eleven, eight, five, and a one-month-old infant, without any subsidy. She even had to defend herself twice against unjustified accusations by the secret police. During the awful air attacks, which brought death and destruction with their rain of bombs, the family was not allowed to enter the air raid shelter. The explanation was that Aryans could not be expected to share the shelter with *Mischlings*.

Without any protection, the entire family was exposed to the terrible hail of bombs until half the street in which they lived was turned to rubble and ash. Arthur and his younger siblings could not obtain the sleep they needed so badly. They had to be torn from their sleep during the daily air raids. Added to that were the nutritional problems, which however I don't want to discuss further. He and his siblings were exposed to the worst threats by the hostile Hitler Youth, who ambushed them to beat them and abuse them. Under these circumstances he could not experience a cheerful, carefree youth, but had to bear much suffering, fear and anguish.

These spiritual hardships led to his mother's heart very soon beginning to fail, so that the entire burden of supporting the family fell on his young shoulders. Despite that, Arthur proved himself a brave and helpful boy even during the worst air attacks. In November 1945 he lost his dear mother and thereby a very valuable support during the worst period of suffering.

A fateful misfortune befell him in April 1946, when the drunken driver of a heavy beer truck ran over him and his ten-year-old little sister at great speed. After a few hours his little sister succumbed to her serious injuries and he himself suffered dangerous injuries. In a judicial process the guiltlessness of the children was established, and the driver punished with 2½ years jail for careless homicide and drunkenness. It lay in God's judgment that Arthur remained alive and after many months of a difficult sickbed was able to leave the hospital.

Immediately after the terrible accident Arthur and his little sister were still fully conscious, except that he complained of a bad headache, which tormented him for a long time. Mental disorders however could not be ascertained; on the contrary, as an apprentice in the electro-branch he proved himself one of the best pupils and passed his journeyman's examination with "good." Thereafter he unfortunately had another very bad misfortune in the year 1947. During a visit to a fair with some friends he had mounted an air swing [probably a Ferris wheel] and had the misfortune of falling out of the moving swing. The fall was mitigated by his falling on a woman standing below, and he only broke an arm. However, he lost consciousness for several hours after the accident. Through God's kindness Arthur soon recovered and only complained about headaches. In St. Francis Hospital he was treated by Dr. [*illegible name, with the rest of the pas-*

sage cut-off].

In July 1, 1948, through intervention by the American authorities, the children were sent to a camp for orphans, to be transferred to the USA at a given time. When, in November 1949, they undertook the voyage to New York, the local relatives on his mother's side urged him especially to take care of his little brother. They stepped on American soil with the greatest expectations, to find a new, beautiful homeland in the USA and to finally see all spiritual suffering banished. However, they were very disappointed by their transfer into a Catholic orphanage and educational institution and Arthur soon left the place again since the limits imposed on his freedom there no longer seemed acceptable to him as a twenty-year-old young man. He had to leave his by then ten-year-old brother there. In his opinion, Felix's stay in that institution does not correspond to his feelings' strong yearning for a life in a good, loving family circle, and he oriented all his endeavors toward the goal of getting Felix out of the institution. The failure of these efforts may have caused the present crisis.

May I call your attention, honored Sir, especially to this fact and ask you to investigate the conditions thoroughly in order to support your endeavors for Arthur. Moreover, it would be necessary that he regain his belief in human goodness and be convinced that everything possible will be done and they are raised to become free people in a free democratic USA, and that for his little brother only the best is intended in his education.

With great respect—

* * *

Arthur's peregrinations during that period are outlined in my subsequent correspondence with Robert Goldberg. However, before quoting it, I would like to share whatever additional information on the brothers' later lives I have.

Michael was not adopted by his foster parents, but they saw to it that he received a first-rate education, including an Ivy League college. However, after his foster mother died, her husband remarried, and Michael was on his own. He did well for himself. By the time he contacted me again, years later, he was involved in various ambitious and largely successful financial ventures, had two children in college, and owned a beautiful home. On the other hand, his efforts at maintaining a relationship with his brothers were, he said, filled with frustration and misunderstandings. He remembered his foster mother with great affection, and remained a staunch supporter of Jewish causes, though he eventually returned to Catholicism: on his deathbed, I was told, he asked for a Catholic priest.

Felix spent close to four years at the orphanage in Pennsylvania. On May 13, 1953, in response to my inquiry, I was informed that "a home has been found" for him. The couple who adopted him were school teachers, childless, and lived in California. Would I assure the relatives in Germany as well as his brother that Felix was very happy. The committee felt, however, that it was best if no contact be made with him since he was adopted. Therefore they would not disclose any details about his whereabouts. Years later, Felix obtained my address on his own, and we met. He was in his thirties then, seemed kind-hearted, always willing to help where help might be needed, but also excitable, moody and restless. When he rang my doorbell, I was startled by his uncanny resemblance to my father, though I soon realized that it was purely external. He did not want to talk about his life with his adoptive family and, to my shock, proclaimed his time at the orphanage his happiest years. If he had remained there longer, he might have become a priest. I was relieved when he eventually married a wonderful woman, and am even more relieved that today, many years later, they are still together.

According to Felix, Arthur was married and divorced more than once. He has at least two children who, however, left home as soon as they could. Though Felix and his wife made many attempts at reestablishing a cordial relationship with Arthur, they never succeeded, and are not in touch with him now.

Sadly, their nightmarish childhood seems to have left permanent scars on at least two of the three brothers.

* * *

[carbon copy]

Dear Robert,   Bronxville, December 10, 1950

    I am so very, very grateful to you for the help you have accorded me with Arthur and Felix. Without your driving me to the school, I would have never been able to visit Felix, and discussing with you afterwards helped me very much. You must have returned home extremely late and I hope did not encounter problems.

    The poor children in that orphanage or whatever the place is, they all looked so clean and neat and did not dare to open their mouth when a nun was in the vicinity—and they were always in the vicinity. So perhaps Arthur was right with his description and that they even censor outgoing mail. However I do not agree with your evaluation of him—sincerity, yes, but quite an unrealistic sincerity. To run away and ask them to turn over little Felix to his care was not going to function. Surely he may have promised his dying mother to take care of Felix, as he says, but can he really believe that with nineteen he can support and raise him? And that the committee will let Felix go with him? Of course, I did not mention to Felix that Arthur was at Bellevue.

When he appeared at my door in Bronxville and asked for blankets to go on a hunger strike in front of the committee's office, I knew that there would be trouble. Of course I could not imagine that they would send him to a mental hospital. He is upset but not crazy! I am so glad that you will see him and that he is not expected to be there long.

I did not tell you that, but after Arthur contacted me, I went to New York to the committee to establish what was really going on. The director or whatever he was assured me with a benevolent smile how well taken care the children were and that he would soon find a nice family to adopt Felix. When I mentioned that he stammers and needs a doctor, he said that that was all taken care of and I must not worry, I should instead persuade Arthur to return to the school.

In my distress I wrote a letter to Eleanor Roosevelt asking for her help. Adda didn't think much of the idea.

"Lizzy, do you really think she will take on the Catholic Church for one little refugee?"

I fear she was right. I never received a reply.

I don't know what I would do without you—you have been simply wonderful, and I am so very grateful to you. Your solicitousness is helping me very much, I cannot express it.

Write to Lore simply c/o Sarah Lawrence. I must admit that I have seen very little of her since she arrived in September. I don't even know in which dorm she lives but you don't need that to write to her.

Otherwise everything is going well. I have discovered a new "non-talent" in me: dance! Adda thought that it would be good for me to take dance, not for credit, just for the exercise (that is allowed), but I think she wanted me to become more graceful. It is actually fun, and Bessie Schoenberg, our teacher, is very encouraging and inventive. Once a week we have a guest class with José Limon, a famous dancer from New York, and then I feel totally inadequate. Luckily, he ignores me and most of the others as well, except for the best. He is tall and thin, not very young, with long black hair and the white, bony face of an American Indian. Perhaps he is one. He just soars across the hall but if I had his long legs, I would too. He is unbelievable to watch.

Three weeks ago there was a very interesting debate, and I succeeded in going to it. It was on progressive vs. classical education. I had not heard a "debate" before. There seem to be precise rules when, how long and how often one can speak and no interrupting, so that would not be anything for me, though you seem to think I am shy. The amusing part was that the three SLC girls spoke for traditional education, and the three Yale boys for progressive. I was especially impressed by Bobbie Walters whom I didn't know before because she is in none of my classes, though also a senior. She almost convinced me that classical education was better. Kurt Roesch was one of the three judges. That alone should tell you who won the debate!

Otherwise there is not much to report. This year my writing class is with Horace Gregory, a quite elderly man who drags one leg and is difficult to understand. Perhaps he had a stroke. He is a poet and translator from Greek, I think, but I have so far not explored the library about him. He is harder to impress than Mrs. King was, but I am doing my best. He also smokes a lot, one cigarette after the other, even more than you.

I am much looking forward to seeing you on Saturday. Until then, I remain most gratefully yours

* * *

Dear Liz, NY, December 20, 1950

I'm not one for greeting cards. Still, I'd like to wish you a full complement of the season's greetings. I do so hope your Christmas will be merry—that all your doubts "will thaw and resolve themselves into a dew" and that the new year will be as exciting—even as you want it to be.

We've known each other now for quite some time. Whatever the beginnings, whatever the misgivings—I know we've got something that's good. I'm glad we've come as close as we have.

Perhaps the problems of Lore and Arthur helped link us more firmly. Perhaps. I'm sure that because we're we, we've become such good friends. Knowing you all along has been a rich experience. Even after our faltering start in September—it's been richer, mellower, so much more companionable.

The knowledge that one like yourself is my good friend is a warming thought and can leave me only in a glow.

If I've never told you that I'm very fond of you, that I wish so much towards your success and happiness—what better time than now.

Your problem—and mine; your life and mine; your peace of mind and mine—certainly they are cut from separate patterns in the woof of whatever story each of us may be writing. Nonetheless, whichever way I go, whatever path my own problem takes towards its inevitable resolve—you should know, that you've but to ask and it'll be both my pleasure and my privilege to help you wherever and whenever I can. You know that—no questions asked.

Now you know what I mean when I say Merry Christmas to you and wish you a Happy New Year.
Much love,

P. S.—I talked to Dr. Trig at the hospital today. Couldn't get up to see Arthur on Tuesday. Just no way out. But Trig tells me that Arthur is coming along, was somewhat depressed at not getting visitors—and that he'll be sent to Kings Park on Friday.

I'm to see him Thursday afternoon...Dr. T will admit me even though I get there near four.

I'll get in touch with you...there's a long holiday ahead. I also want to apologize for my restlessness of Saturday night... Sometimes, even in the midst of plenty, I feel as if I'm starving—and in order not to become too droopy drawer-ish—said good night. You do understand, yes. Looking forward to seeing you—as always—

* * *

Dear Truderl, Bronxville, February 3, 1951

Thank you for your wonderful letter. I am so glad that you recovered in time for the holidays. Your romantic description of the decorated and illuminated town allowed me to stroll with you, at least in spirit, through the Graben and up the Kärntnerstraße—it made me quite nostalgic, even though I have such ambivalent feelings about Vienna. But of course not about you! Too bad that there was no snow, but the lights and the smell of roasted chestnuts must have made it festive even so.

I am really fine, don't worry. I have finally broken off my relationship with John, actually already some time ago. This time it is, I think, definite. He became very annoyed, claiming that I was spending too much time on my cousins, and we had a big argument. I finally said, "they are my family and come first." He walked out and has not called me since. I have not called him either, and am actually relieved. I am sure it is right this time, especially now that I know what he is really like. And the best thing is that it happened almost by itself.

I am very worried about Arthur. Did I write you that he is still in the hospital, though they had originally said it was only for observation, and he would soon return to the school. Robert took me to visit him once, but the situation upset me so much that he has been going alone since then. I don't know what I would do without him. He is such a wonderful, unselfish person. He says that Arthur seems all right, but is moody, angry, and difficult—who wouldn't be in that awful environment? I feel very helpless, but Robert assures me that he won't give up on Arthur and will vouch for him in case it is necessary. He also visits Felix when he can, and that is a long ride into the depths of Pennsylvania—*wo sich die Füchse gute Nacht sagen* [*where the foxes bid one another a good night—i.e., a godforsaken place*].

At home Robert's situation seems to have improved. I may not have mentioned that before, but he once told me that, were it not for his son, he would have left long ago. Of course, I ask no questions. Now they are renovating the house, so relations between him and his wife must be better. Isn't the world complicated? I no longer dare judge anyone's behavior.

Let me wish you, Kurt, and your dear mother an especially good year, which I know it will be.

Affectionately embracing you—your Liesl

This time it was indeed the end of my relationship with John. How much of a bitter aftertaste the entire affair left me with I only realized years later when, out of a clear blue sky, I received a letter in his large, pedantic handwriting. He had seen an announcement of the publication of my Holocaust memoir, had read the book with great pleasure, and wanted to congratulate me. It was a nice letter, but I tore it up and did not respond.

A few weeks later another letter arrived, likewise hand-written, on five large lined sheets of paper. He wrote that he was not blaming me for still being angry with him, and apologized for having behaved so atrociously back then. He hoped very sincerely that I could forgive him by now, for he would like to know how I was, and if he could help me publicize my book. He had already sent several copies to friends, and would gladly supply some libraries if I sent him a list. Money was no object.

He also wrote that he was a librarian until his retirement, had been very happily married, but lost his wife after a long battle with cancer. Much later he remarried, but since his second wife was working quite far away and did not want to give up her position, they had two homes, and only spent weekends together.

I did not know what to make of the letter, especially that final bit of information, but this time I did reply, briefly and formally, but I replied. A correspondence ensued, which to my surprise became so enjoyable that I began to look forward to his long hand-written letters. He reminded me of some of our pleasant or funny "adventures," he talked about music, art and philosophy, he expressed his views and asked for mine on general and personal issues, he sent me books and operatic videos—which I always returned, though unbidden—and his letters brought back the best aspects of the old days together. Had I misjudged him, or had he changed so much?

He addressed me as Elizabeth, and that felt right, too, though I could not recall if it was what I had always been for him. But when he sent a picture of himself, I recognized the old, difficult, often rigid John. My discomfort returned and expanded into resentment. All I could think of was how he had taken advantage of me way back then, had talked me into submitting to him, not by speaking of love, but by stressing that the longer I waited, the more difficult it would be, and the many agonizing weeks and months that had followed. But since neither of us mentioned the word reunion, our correspondence continued, and his stimulating letters made the imprint of his picture fade again. Also, he warned me that he had aged, and that the picture was not recent.

When, some three years later, a printed announcement, accompanied by a handwritten note from his wife, informed me that John had died of heart failure, at age eighty, the news truly saddened me. But, strangely, it also brought relief, almost a rejoicing: as if a dark, locked door deep inside me had opened and was now letting in the soothing rays of the setting sun.

5.

19. February 1951

I am reaching for you half-heartedly. I almost took a book instead but then I felt ashamed of so much escapism and cowardice. I noted when writing the date, with a smile: *Quadrat*—the exact square to my birth date! My father would say "no wonder you are depressed! The stars are against you."

I have been wasting an entire evening, writing and tearing notes to Robert. It is good I tore them, in such a mood one only hurts others or oneself by preserving it. I guess it is not so much longing for him as that feeling of loneliness that made me do it. Will this grow worse and worse as time passes on? And yet, I would not exchange it for a life with John, so I guess my state is not hopeless.

I know it is grave, though. I am on the point of losing all respect for myself. It is true, I have had a tough time, with school, being overworked with Arthur and those visits to Felix and not being able to help—I guess, it could have got depressed also others.

I don't know whether the thing with Robert was a mistake. I am inclined to think that I am only now making it into one by ascribing it undue importance. It just happened when it got too late to drive home and we took a motel room—with two beds, of course. I knew I could handle it, I had done it before. And he had after all been my teacher and was much older. We drank Scotch and talked and felt really mellow. And then he asked if I had a kiss for the guy. How could I say no? And then it turned into a dream, something I never thought possible. I had not experienced anything like it ever, and may never again. I simply floated in the air, or on a mountain top, dizzy, burning, dissolving. I didn't know what was happening with me. Or was it all due to the Scotch?

Of course, I would never want to marry him, even if he were free, not even to see too much of him. I don't want it to injure his marriage either.

Am I in love? What does it mean "in love"? I surely do not love him so that I would want to be forever together. Is "in love" just a physical infatuation for a moment after which you are "out of love"—is it just sex? That sounds cheap, not at all like that magical, extatic moment I had, which still makes me tingle. Do I want to repeat it? Yes, if he will want it, but not every day because that scares me. He can be wonderful but also moody and tense, and then I have to weigh each word, for anything I say may be interpreted wrong. Perhaps it is the flattery and attention he accords me, even though he is so much older and more educated—does not everyone like to get that? And, of course, he is a marvellous lover too, so much better than John.

All right, a certain phase has been achieved. I still can't figure out what he sees in me but he seems to see something. Did I entice him, or did he entice me? No matter, we had a wonderful moment and may have more, if I can take it when it's offered and not spend the rest of my time thinking about him. Any letters on my part can only complicate the situation, by either scaring him away or overdoing it.

I am suddenly very tired. But at least quite calm. Talking to you, diary, has helped. I should do that more often.

That diary entry brought back a memory which I had cherished for a long time and then suppressed, feeling increasingly guilty. As often before, Robert had come out to Bronxville that Sunday to pick me up for a visit with Felix and, as always, I was delighted to be with him. After a while, I noticed that we were not heading toward the City but north, and with a twinkle in his eye he told me that he had planned a surprise. Robert had often mentioned Vermont, where he would head if he wanted to "invite his soul" and leave all worries behind.

Now he wanted to show me at least one corner of his favorite state. Though the trees were still bare, even had patches of snow at their base, the hills looked serene and welcoming. Robert talked about Mt. Haystack, which he considered his very own mountain, though climbing it would have to wait for another time.

When the sun emerged from the clouds, this to me totally new environment suddenly seemed familiar. The landscape looked uncannily like the Tatra mountains of Slovakia, where as a child I had spent many happy summer vacations with aunt Paula and cousin Walter. Remembering them, who had not survived the war, was painful, but the memory was softened by the beauty of the landscape around me.

I don't recall all the places Robert took me to, only that we had lunch high above the road at a restaurant with a wonderful view. Then we headed on again. I lost all conception of time, except that we stopped briefly in a small town. While I waited in the car, Robert bought a pack of cigarettes at a drugstore.

He knew a little inn with good food. It was dark by then, but since we had often driven back from Felix's school in Pennsylvania quite late, I thought nothing of it. After dinner we had a Scotch, then another, and by the time he suggested we had better spend the night, I had no objections. A toothbrush? Who cared. But I did phone Bronxville so Adda would not worry. She asked no questions.

There were several similar outings after that, but none was as magical as that first one, and they have somehow not stayed in my memory. What I do remember is that gradually my uneasiness increased instead of diminishing, and that I began to pull back. Unfortunately, I did so before he was ready, making both of us quite miserable.

* * *

Dearest Trude, Bronxville, May 26, 1951

First of all, a very, very happy birthday and a wonderful year, both personally and professionally. May all go well with the exams and may you find an excellent job, and Kurt as well. And primarily, stay healthy!

My life is going to change once again. In September I will be going to Cornell University to study for the PhD in their German Literature department. I will be a teaching assistant in the Languages and Linguistics Department, which is separate. I was also accepted by Ohio State University and Yale, but they offered me too small a scholarship to live on. And Cornell is a very good school too. Moreover, it is in upper New York State, which is supposed to be lovely.

I have decided to become a college teacher. Perhaps I can also continue to write, but I know now that I was not meant to be a writer. How do I know? It came as a shock to me, but I guess still in time.

You know that at Sarah Lawrence we have been getting reports rather than grades. Well, this year I took a writing course with Mr. Gregory, a poet and essayist, and a much tougher critic than Mrs. King. Therefore I was especially pleased when his reports for fall and winter sounded good. He wrote:

"December 28, 1950. Miss Welt's writing has promise; it contains evidence of a genuine sensibility and a mature mind. Miss Welt is, of course, a very good student."

"April 2, 1951. Miss Welt's short essay written for the last class before spring vacation was the best piece of work she had done all year; at last her actual writing caught up with the quality of her thinking. She is a good student and she has the rare ability to go on learning."

When Cornell returned my application documents, they also enclosed a form with grades from SLC for my courses there, which I had not known existed. It should probably have been returned to the college and not to me. My grade for the Gregory course was "fair to good." None of my other grades were only "fair to good." I was shocked that I had read his reports so wrongly. Kurt Roesch offered to sound him out informally and find out what he thought of my writing. Mr. Gregory told Kurt that with a lot of hard work I might get somewhere "in ten years."

It was a rude awakening, but luckily not too late. Planning to teach is obviously much more sensible than trying to become a writer, and much safer for the future. After all, I have always enjoyed teaching, and I believe I could be good at it. When I tutored Hanna in math in the *Gymnasium*, she received an A on the final exam, despite our very tough teacher. And when I was teaching English to the JOINT-sponsored refugee group in Vienna right after the war, they loved it, and so did I.

I decided to also enroll in a Russian language course at Cornell, just in case there are no jobs in German when I finish. A lot of hostility still exists here toward Germans. Paradoxically, Russian is much in demand because everyone is afraid of the Russians, now that they may also have the bomb. Let us hope that studying Russian won't get me suspected of being a communist. That could be a real problem because now there is a Congressional Committee in Washington investigating people it suspects of being "un-American," which means communists. Actually, it started long ago, in 1948, I think, except that I was not paying much attention to politics at that time. Now there is a man in the Senate as well, McCarthy is his name. He seems much worse, and everybody is afraid of him.

In fact, it is a regular witch hunt. First they got rid of a lot of government officials, and now they are after academics, Hollywood people, even journalists. People were fired when they refused to testify or implicate others or take a loyalty oath—not necessarily because they were communists but in order to protest being unjustly suspected. In one college half the professors left rather than sign. How stupid—a communist would simply lie and sign! A while back, a high government official was accused of spying for the Russians. The accuser was a *Times* editor by the name of Whitaker Chambers, who in the Thirties had been a communist himself. (If you can believe it—he has also translated *Bambi* into English!) Alger Hiss gave a talk at SLC the year before I came, when he was still considered one of the most important American diplomats. This past January he was convicted, though many insist that he is innocent.

The Committee also interrogated Bertolt Brecht. He probably is a communist, but he told them that his plays were fiction and not necessarily his beliefs. They could not prove anything, and looked ridiculous. He went back to Europe the next day—before they realized that he had been pulling their leg. But it is ruining people's careers. Some even committed suicide.

President Taylor was also involved, as early as 1949. The House Committee on Un-American Activities asked him for the textbook and reading lists of the College. Naturally they would have found a number of suspicious texts since we study all sorts of creeds. He refused, and sent them a long letter about academic freedom. I don't know if they left him alone after that, but it is all very scary—is America just as bad as the Nazis were? And what would I do if I were asked to sign a loyalty oath? I would probably be cowardly enough to sign.

Something else I found out to my shock: even when I get my American citizenship, I will always be a second-class citizen, a little like being British but not English. I was told that if I should get arrested overseas, the United States is under no obligation to help me because I would only be "naturalized" and not a native-born citizen. It seems that, though I have adopted this country, it has not really adopted me. Is that true democracy? Or is adoption always something provisional and a little questionable? In that case, poor Felix.

Last November, they tried to assassinate President Truman; perhaps you read about it. Everything seems to be going downhill.

But let me end on something positive: I have found what looks like a very good summer job. I will be a governess for a family with two little girls, ages five and seven, and will earn some money, quite a bit, in fact. A Bronxville agency arranged it for me, with a doctor's (i.e., physician's) family. We will be somewhere near the ocean, in the state of Rhode Island, which is not too far from here. I have met Mrs. Hancher, and she seems very nice, and Adda gave me a good recommendation. I am sorry to leave the Bozemans, but I will be going to another school in the fall anyway. Somehow I think Adda is even relieved to get rid of me. When I asked her if she would take in another student, she said "Oh, no!" very spontaneously, and only then added: "Anya can by now take care of herself," as if to tone down her relief. I hope I am wrong.

Oh, I forgot to tell you that she got married again in the fall, to a Danish physician who works for the World Health Organization and travels a lot. I was an official witness. She has apparently known Arne for a long time, though he never came to the house. He is tall, blond and quiet. Really *sympathisch*, and I think he likes me. At any rate, he treats me as an adult.

That is all for today. My very best wishes to you, Kurt, and your mother,
>from your old friend
Liesl.

Adda remained my model for many years, for never before or after did I meet anyone who combined charm, poise, wit and a keen mind so seamlessly. When my daughter, ready to graduate from college, was dreaming of a career in human rights and international law, I took her, at Adda's suggestion, to Bronxville. The two had a long, intense conversation about the pros and cons of such a goal. Adda counseled against choosing so elusive a field, and my daughter went to law school instead.

Only several years later did I realize that Adda might not have been the best adviser in this matter. In one of our periodic phone conversations, my admiration for her received a sizable jolt. We were talking politics and, to my shock, she assured me that she had long ago predicted the mess Africa would be in once the colonial powers withdrew; that President Reagan had asked her to accept a posting to the UN, but she had declined, considering it far too late to remedy the situation. My daughter, I am pleased to add, practiced law for a few years but then went back to school to add a diploma in public international law, and joined Human Rights Watch as a Counsel in their International Justice Division.

* * *

[*typed carbon copy*]

Dear Robert,   Bronxville, May 31, 1951

So yesterday was the big day. To my great surprise Dr. Thierer, my cousin (second? third? who knows), arrived with his girlfriend. Though I sent him an invitation, I did not really expect him to respond—I had not heard from him for years.

Did I mention him before? When I arrived in New York, I had his name from my father and found the phone number. At first he sounded very cautious—probably afraid that I would ask for money. We met at a restaurant. He said he would wear a red carnation.

I was quite overwhelmed when he arrived: a very distinguished-looking tall gentleman in a white suit and straw hat, with a walking stick, gray temples but very black eyebrows, a black mustache and rosy cheeks. Quite young looking, with beautiful teeth, he resembled a movie star. He is a plastic surgeon and lives in a hotel, so he must be rich. He was definitely relieved when he saw that I spoke good English, had a job and did not ask for money. In fact, he seemed impressed, for he called the headwaiter to introduce to him his "little European cousin."

After the meal he insisted on taking me "shopping." We bought a very nice navy blue dotted two-piece dress which I still remember. It had a flounce (I hope this is the right word?) which went around the waist and pearl buttons in front, and it looked like silk, though it wasn't, but it made me look slim and elegant. Also a pair of shoes with very high platform heels, so I would be taller. He insisted that I should wear both right away.

Al (his name is Albert, but he asked me to call him Al) has a very nice girlfriend who didn't seem a lot older than I. We were the same height and once she arrived with a big bag of clothing for me, containing some really attractive dresses. I don't know if I should be proud or ashamed but I displayed one of them to Adda when she gave me Christmas money to buy a new dress. It fitted and looked very elegant, dark blue, gathered at the hips but narrow at the bottom, with a front slit. Adda liked it very much and did not ask for the receipt.

Once Al took me to his daughter's apartment. There was a husband and a baby, but none of them seemed very friendly or interested and I felt like an intruder, so I didn't even write down their names or address. After that I did not see Al, but I sent him an invitation to my graduation to show that I had done something worthwhile with my time. He did not reply but there he suddenly was with his girl-friend!

I must say it was nice to have something like "family" at my graduation. I wish you could have been here too. Adda was officially present, as faculty, but

Anya and Arne came as well, and Dr. Thierer invited all of us afterwards to lunch. He insisted on taking my diploma and having it "laminated" as a graduation present. I would have preferred a check but how could I say that?

The commencement speaker was Henry Steele Commager. He is apparently an eminent historian, but don't ask me what he said. I didn't absorb a word of it. All I could think of was that I was wearing high heels and must not stumble or slouch when I climb up on the podium. (Adda instructed me beforehand, which made me even more nervous.) But all went well. The whole event somehow passed by me like a dream, and when I woke after having said goodbye to the Thierers, all I could think of was that I now must get ready for my summer job in Rhode Island, and pack things to store in Adda's attic while I am gone.

The Thursday before graduation I went to a good-bye party at my don's place to which he had invited all of his donees. One was Bobbie Walters [*now known as Barbara Walters!*], whom I had heard debate some time ago and who had absolved herself so well that I was very impressed, though I never managed to talk to her. I wish I had known that we had the same don.

Sixty-nine of us received our degrees, four were veterans. Now it has finally begun to sink in that my two years at Sarah Lawrence are over. You always want appraisals, so here they are. It was unusual two years and I learned a considerable lot. Not necessarily knowledge, for I did not need to take a single science course and all I really had, if I don't count piano and creative writing, were four totally unrelated courses. Three were fascinating: "Thought and Image"; "Psychology of Art" and "Soviet Union" (officially on Russian history but in reality about the whole world, comparing developments everywhere in one particular year—1066, 1453, 1789 and 1917—a great approach!). The fourth, "Modern European Literature," was a hodgepodge with some interesting readings. It may sound strange to you but I was pleased that even here some teachers are not geniuses. This one was, to be fair, not a regular faculty member. He came out one time per week, and didn't seem to know much about good teaching. Whatever we said, he agreed to. He is an editor for an important magazine in New York so he can't be really bad.

Most of all I enjoyed to be able and encouraged to read so many interesting and different kinds of books, and be allowed to criticize them. I have always loved to read, but earlier I read only novels. Now I also learned not to be scared of such difficult works like Aristotle, St. Augustine's *Confessions* and the *Oedipus* cycle. It was like standing before a huge buffet with each dish more enticing than the other, and able to sample only a very few. I wish I could have been here for the whole four years and taken a course with Mr. Campbell, or with Kurt or Mrs. Lynd whose book *Middletown* is famous. Perhaps with Adda, too, though I am not sure that would have been a good idea. And the famous artists here I barely know by sight: Mr. Dello Joyo is a composer, Mr. Reid (very young and handsome!) a poet, Mr. Roszak a sculptor. But mostly I wish I had taken a course with Mr. Slonim since I love Dostoevsky. He was at Adda's a few times, awfully nice, with a heavy Russian accent and very funny jokes. Too late. Cinderella was at the ball but midnight came and there was no prince. Even so, what a feast it has been! I guess I have not lived as intensely as in New York but I have learned a great amount.

I am also grateful that I did not have to study science but could submerge myself in literature, which I want to continue to study. The other students? Perhaps I have underestimated them. They were surely bright and talented, except that they did not show it immediately, nor talked much about their work or interests. But when I once mentioned to another student that I live with Mrs. Bozeman, she asked, to my great surprise, if I wasn't scared of her. Should I have been? Perhaps she is very demanding as a teacher but I would not have minded. In a traditional college I might have been introduced to more areas, but I would have hated to have to take required courses whether they interest me or not, and not having exams and deadlines was great. I just hope this won't make life harder at Cornell.

About the "reports" we received instead of grades, I have mixed feelings. Some comments were definitely too general and even misleading, especially when the grades that went with them did not correspond to my interpretation of the report. Since, as I discovered by chance, they did record us grades, I wish they had not kept them a secret. It sounds good not to work for grades, but grades might have made me work harder.

I learned other valuable things too, especially at Adda's—how to behave and communicate with grownups (I mean intellectual grownups), how to disguise that I don't feel grown up at all (I wonder at what age I will?), how to carry on a conversation, and pay more attention to how I dress and stand and walk. I also learned a lot about taking care of a young girl, and I enjoyed life in a private home with a garden. Now I can even identify many flowers.

Perhaps it would have been good for me to reside in a dormitory, at least one year, and become acquainted with real Americans and their lifestyles and behaviors. It just strikes me that Adda's visitors were almost all European—though not necessarily Jewish. And that experience seemed more valuable to me than trying to approach the rich American girls at the college. (And you thought I would become a snob at Sarah Lawrence!) It somehow didn't feel right to talk about myself or about being Jewish and call attention to my being different. Perhaps I should have attempted harder to fit in and get to know them. But I was so much older and more experienced, and they were socially from such a different class. I would not have exchanged the privilege to live in Adda's house for anything.

I was lucky in something else which I did not know when I applied to Sarah Lawrence. The college has a very good reputation and as a result I was accepted by all three universities to which I applied. That is in a way unfair for, to be honest, my grades (good—excellent—good—good—good to excellent—fair to good—good to excellent—good) were not very impressive.

On Saturday I will be picked up by Mrs. Hancher to start my summer job. I have not met the two girls that will be my responsibility—they are five and seven—but taking care of Anya has given me experience, so I hope I shall succeed. There is also a cat—she asked me how I felt about cats. I didn't know what to say since I am inexperienced with cats. We had a dog when I was little, and I think I like all animals except snakes, so it should be all right.

I was so glad you were able to come here at least for a few hours last week. With my contracts all handed in, I was able to relax, which you unquestioningly noticed. I only hope we weren't too noisy since Mrs. B and Anya were at home.

Now I have to get ready for the summer. I fear we won't see each other before I leave, but I will write. Please write too, and perhaps I can come to the city on my free day and see you.

My best,

I am glad I kept a copy of that letter. Much of what it describes I had forgotten. Just recently its musings again became oddly relevant. During dinner with two women friends, both about my age, I mentioned that I felt I had lost out on college life by not living on campus. To my surprise both contradicted me emphatically. One stated that, after spending her first college year in a dormitory, she could not wait to get out, and was delighted to move to a professor's house as an au-pair. Her college was likewise in New York State, and she found the girls not only superficial and boring but arrogant and, worst of all, quite anti-Semitic. The other woman, who is not Jewish and grew up in Montana, agreed, if from an entirely different perspective: the girls at her college were incredibly prim and proper, narrow-minded and judgmental. All they could think of was how to catch a man, preferably a wealthy one. I couldn't believe that these two cases were typical, and so I took Mary MacCarthy's The Group *out of the library. Though it presumably focuses on Wellesley, it was rumored to be about Sarah Lawrence, where MacCarthy had taught. I certainly hope it wasn't. Is it a question of the glass being both half full and half empty?*

* * *

[*translated, no date*]

Awful things are happening. That man McCarthy is truly dangerous. He does not attack Jews specifically—though many of them are Jews—but he sees a communist in everybody who has ever said a critical word about the government, and nobody stops him. Don't they realize that that is how Hitler started?

I feel guilty because I have never paid much attention to politics. At Adda's, they now talk about nothing else, and have the radio turned on to the hearings all the time. It seems this has been going on for years. It is reminiscent of the Inquisition or the Nazis, except that though they may place people in jail and destroy their careers, but they don't exterminate them. Strange that the word *verraten* can mean both "reveal" and "betray" in English. And, in reverse, a "collaborator" can be a co-worker or a traitor. [*In German, the term is always negative.*] A fine line. I wonder how I would act if I feared for my life. Would I cooperate or remain firm? Just as well that I knew nothing about all that when I arrived in this country, or I might have turned around and left again. But where could I have gone?

Shame on you, Liesl! You were so involved in your own little problems that you have not noticed that the whole world is exploding and collapsing. We are embroiled in a war far away where we probably should not be, and we are working on a hydrogen bomb—that all is very frightening. Wasn't I better off when I did not know anything about politics and could admire America as a democracy? If only I could vote! But would that help?

I guess no country is perfect, and here it is still much better than in Europe. Perhaps Europe will be better again one day, and then I will have a real choice. But I am ungrateful. I survived and had a great time in New York, and now I am able to study, and am entirely free. Perhaps nothing will go wrong this time.

6.

Dearest Trude,   Watch Hill, R.I., July 18, 1951

    My summer job is a real vacation! I was very lucky to find this position, and it is good to get away from all worries. The girls are awfully cute and they try to please. And I live a life of luxury: since I don't drive, Mrs. Hancher chauffeurs the three of us to the beach, and fetches us for meals! The house is a beautiful one-story ranch, with huge windows and glass walls all around. Peggy has marvelous taste in decorating, and always sets the table with matching mats and dishes—different for each meal. The table has a glass top and is of aqua-painted wrought-iron in a leaf pattern. So are the chairs, which have aqua and pink upholstered seats in a Navajo design (Navajos are an American Indian tribe), very unusual and beautiful. It is a treat to eat in such a setting. We always have flowers on the table, even when Dr. Hancher is not here. He only joins us on weekends, and is usually tired and a bit grumpy. But he quite obviously loves the girls. He is much older than Peggy, so it may be his second marriage.

    My room is small but also very stylish, with Navajo-patterned drapes and upholstery, and a matching spread on my daybed. Indian bowls stand on the dresser and nightstand, striking with their bold geometric designs in white, rust, gray, and black. Peggy loaned me a book on the Southwest Indians: I had no idea there were so many tribes! Each has its own patterns and colors. Simple, clear and powerful lines and squares, sometimes an animal, a bird, or a snake coiled all around, but even that is pleasing and harmonious.

    A cleaning woman comes once a week, and we also have a big, round, portable dishwasher, which makes life very easy. The girls named it Irene, and every evening all four of us sing "Good night, Irene!" to it. Mrs. Hancher does the cooking and even helps afterward with the dishes.

    The girls seem to enjoy everything I do with them. We have a tent in the garden and sometimes dress like Indians and paint our faces. Once I was Mary Poppins (that's a magic governess in a children's book), with an umbrella and an old hat of Peggy's, and now the girls want me to be her all the time, even though my umbrella does not let me fly. Close to the beach is a merry-go-round, and we ride it as a special treat. The other day an unfamiliar kitty with a big tail came toward us in our yard, and we kept calling it until Peggy rushed out of the house and shouted: "Stop! It's a skunk!" Luckily, it didn't spray.

Our cat Missy is black with a white nose and belly, and two white mittens. Her big slanted yellow eyes test and evaluate you, and when she stands there looking at me and meowing, I feel embarrassed and dumb for not understanding what it is she wants. Sometimes I think Missy just tolerates us because we feed and house and pet her, but in her heart she looks down on us. You can tell that she has her own ideas, except that we can only recognize the simple ones—when she wants in or out, or food. Or petting. If Missy does something bad, she ignores our scolding completely. In fact, it offends her, and she expects us to make up to her. And even then, she may continue to sulk.

I have come to the conclusion that cats are far more interesting than dogs. A dog is like a child, always wanting you to play or be taken for a walk, whereas a cat makes her own decisions, has her own personal values and idiosyncrasies. A dog is always ready to eat, a cat has to feel like it. If a dog is naughty, he acts guilty when you scold him. A cat is as unpredictable as an adult who can be loving and lovable, but deep down remains unknowable. I think I will have a cat when I am independent.

Enough of this. Soon life will again become serious. I wonder what Cornell will be like, and how I will manage there, with deadlines, exams and all that discipline. I will write to you as soon as I am acclimated.

Meanwhile, the very best wishes to you from

Your Liesl

* * *

[carbon copy]

Dear Robert, Watch Hill, July 29

I am very sorry that you are so occupied with summer school, but I realize that it is too long a trip for a short visit, and I only have one day a week free, and not on the weekend. But at least I hear your voice now and then.

My job is a pleasure rather than work. I spend most mornings on the beach with Susi and Lawren, both cute and appreciative. While they take their afternoon nap, I read or write letters, then we snack, play in the yard, go back to the beach, or Peggy drives us somewhere, into town for ice cream or to the merry-go-round, once even to Mystic, an interesting "seaport" quite far from here.

As you see, I relish a wonderful vacation and even get paid for it, and quite a lot—$40 per week, as well as my upkeep. (By the way, when I told our friend Lore about my summer job, she said she would never work as a domestic. So she took an office job instead, works eight hours a day in the hot, humid city, and has to pay for her room and food while I can save my entire salary. That silly European pride...)

What has happened with Arthur? Is he still in the hospital or did they send him back to the school? The committee wrote to me to let me know that they have several possibilities for placing Felix, but not a word about Arthur. Do you know anything?

I hope that the summer isn't too unbearable in the city and you manage to get away, even if you can't come here. I will definitely be in New York before I leave for Cornell, and perhaps we can still take at least one short trip to Vermont. Or meet in New York State, if you are able to visit me at Cornell.

Yours, as always—

P.S. Aren't you glad I have my Erika here? Otherwise you would have to decipher my scribble!

* * *

Watch Hill, August 13

I had a very unsettling encounter yesterday. It was as if I had stepped through a mirror into a different world once again. (The image comes from an American children's book which I have been reading to the girls, *Alice through the Looking Glass*. They love it, I don't.)

It was my free day and I went by bus to Providence for the afternoon, to shop a little and explore the locality. When I climbed on the bus for the return trip, the front seat which I usually seek to occupy to avoid the possibility of becoming carsick had the driver's coat and bag on it, so I moved deeper inside the bus. The next available seat was also not very far back, and I was satisfied. A black man was sitting there, and he moved over to the window to make room for me. But as I sat down, the driver emptied the front seat and called out:

"Miss, there's an empty seat up front!"

"Thank you," I said, "I am fine."

I was certain he said it so that I would not need to sit next to a Negro. I was a bit uncomfortable, I must admit, for the man smelled of alcohol, but it did not feel right to move after this transparent invitation. Also because the other passengers were listening.

We set out and after a long pause the man next to me said:

"You know why he was offering you that seat, don't you?"

"Of course," I answered cheerfully. 'When I entered the bus, his coat was on it, but he must have noticed that I looked at that front seat."

"No," said the man. "It was so you wouldn't have to sit next to me."

"Nonsense," I said. "I am sure that wasn't it."

"Yes, it was," the man insisted. "He wouldn't have said anything if I had been white."

"Whether you are white or black doesn't make any difference to me," I retorted and considered the conversation terminated. The man looked at me carefully and then, as if he had a sudden inspiration, asked: "Are you Japanese?" I was totally puzzled.

"No, I am not. Do I look Japanese?"

"Well, a little. Perhaps you are part Japanese?" and he put his hand on my knee.

I removed his hand and said: "Look here, I am not Japanese, but you must leave me alone, otherwise I will really have to move."

He apologized and stopped talking. After a while he fell asleep. I was relieved and pretended to sleep too. When we approached Watch Hill and he saw me collecting my acquisitions, he asked: "Is that where you live?"

I nodded and he again surprised me: "Look, it's dark, would you like me to escort you?"

I declined, saying that I lived close by. Now somewhat apprehensive, I walked away fast, listening to whether he was following me. No, he did not seem to alight, and when the doors closed and the bus moved on, I took a deep breath of relief.

A lot seems to be still smoldering under the surface, even here in New England. I remember reading *Gentlemen's Agreement* long ago. I have forgotten who wrote it but it concerned a journalist who pretended to be Jewish and wanted to move to Darien, Connecticut (that name I will never forget), and he was meeting discrimination and hostility everywhere he went. Perhaps we Jews must be grateful that there are negroes in this country so that the hate gets distributed more evenly? Except that they are much worse off. We no longer have to wear the star, and even before that we could hide it. But they can't hide their color.

How unfair life is!

PART THREE

Cornell
(1952–1953)

1.

Dearest Trude,   Ithaca, September 14, 1951

You haven't written in ages! Are you all right? Was your vacation a success?

I am in Ithaca, but most definitely not in Odysseus' native land! However, even upstate New York is beautiful. Ithaca is a small unpretentious town surrounded by hills, meadows and fields, with a long lake at one end, Lake Cayuga. (I believe, that's an Indian name.) On a high plateau above the town and lake towers Cornell University, with a great many "colleges," which, in this case, are like our *Fakultäten*—of engineering, hotel management, agriculture, labor relations, humanities, etc.

Most buildings are enormous, either neo-Gothic or neo-Classical, with pillars and stone garlands; also a few modern cubes. Some buildings are of red brick, but most are gray stone with white trim, often also elaborately carved decorations over the main entrance. They look very massive and austere. We also have a tall, picturesque clock tower, which can be seen from far away. Its carillon chimes different songs three times a day. Oh yes, there is also a very ornate chapel with a revolving altar that can be adjusted for each religious service, even a Jewish one!

But what makes the campus almost unreal, like an apparition, is that this enormous, famous university is not in a major city like Vienna or Oxford but in the country, in the middle of nowhere. Perhaps a true center of learning should be like that—serene and self-sufficient, free from the pressures and temptations of city life, part of nature? An intriguing thought.

Though the buildings look like fortresses, there is a lot of space between most of them, wide lawns and grassy squares. Those are the "quads" (short for quadrangles). And from almost everywhere you can see the valley below, the hills, or the lake. "High above Cayuga's waters …" is the school's theme song.

This time it was easy to settle into my new life. Some aspects are very different from Sarah Lawrence, as was to be expected, but much is similar. First the good points: I feel at home already, am no longer an outsider. That is not just because of the attractive environment, but because we have a great many graduate students (at SLC there were only a few veterans), who not only differ in age and background, but they have come from many parts of the country, even from abroad. Some look exotic, a few behave exotically, many are very serious, others out for fun—altogether, an interesting mix. You can blend in wherever you want. Best of all, I am totally independent: I have a meaningful job, and it pays fully for my upkeep so that I need not be obligated to anyone.

The academic setup is even more different than I had expected. All languages are taught in one large department, called "Languages and Linguistics," whereas the various literature departments are in another building, across a large quadrangle. This separation may not be accidental: I have the impression that each group looks down on the other, and considers itself superior.

I teach in the linguistics building, Morrill Hall, and take my courses in Goldwyn Smith, the humanities building across the quad. Though my heart is in the humanities, in the interests of diplomacy I keep smiling, Janus-like, in both directions. Our quad, by the way, is a huge square, with majestic old trees and two statues, one of A. D. White, Cornell's first president, the other of Ezra Cornell, the school's founder (in 1868—which here means it is ancient!). On special occasions, Ezra has been decorated with a wreath, a tie or a scarf, once even a bib, I was told. And since he sits quite high up, reaching his neck must have required considerable acrobatics.

What makes the square especially attractive to me is that on non-special occasions it tends to be full of frolicking dogs. Not only are students allowed to bring their dogs to the campus (thanks to a stipulation by that same Ezra), but dogs are welcome in the classrooms as well. Now and then, you climb over a big furry thing stretched out across the threshold. I love it, though I wonder how people who don't like dogs must feel. Perhaps this, too, is considered an important part of a Cornell education? I don't want to be irreverent, but the temptation is great.

Why? Not because of the dogs but because linguistics is a big fad here. It is not philology—perish the thought!—but a very new approach to language, technical and schematic. You don't even have to speak the language well to be a linguist, to analyze and codify it. Luckily, Prof. Moulton, my chairman, is not only totally fluent in German, but his accent is so perfect that you would not believe he is an American. He is *ein großes Tier* [*a big-shot, lit.: a large animal*], if not *the* big-shot. That's because he has invented this new method of teaching languages, which is also used at Yale and at the army language school in Monterey, California. And we are stuck with it.

Why stuck? It allows us very little freedom in our teaching. Though I am called a "T.A." (pronounced Tee-Ay), that is, a teaching assistant, that description is only partially accurate; so is the less flattering unofficial designation of us as "native informants." In reality we are not allowed to inform: if anything, there is a danger of the students informing on us! Sounds weird, doesn't it?

Let me explain. We—there are four of us for German—meet the students four days a week, one hour each day. On the fifth day the linguistics professor works with them for an hour, explains the grammar and answers questions—but entirely in English. I, on the other hand, am not allowed to explain grammar at all. Heaven forbid—I might use logic instead of the proper linguistic terminology! Nor am I allowed to utter a word of English. I can only motion to the students to repeat after me, let's say, "*Guten Morgen,*" which they can of course guess, or I hold up a pencil and say "*ein Bleistift,*" motion to them to repeat, motion again while saying "*noch einmal,*" and so on. The good old Berlitz method—but at a university?

The textbooks contain silly half-page dialogues (there, at least, German and English are side by side). The students have to memorize the dialogues and recite them in class in groups of two. Some just rattle them off, a few try to put some life into them. All I am allowed to do is correct or prompt. It's very frustrating, but also an enormous challenge if one wants the class to stay awake. At times, if a smart student gets really desperate, I sneak in a short grammatical explanation. Then I hope that no one will report me, and that the student will not display his illegitimate knowledge in the grammar class.

Our training for this procedure was rather amusing. The new informants for all languages had to arrive a week early, and during that week we were introduced to elementary Serbo-Croatian. We had two hours per day with a native speaker, on the third day a grammar session with the American linguist. We, too, had to memorize and recite those silly dialogues. To my dying day I won't forget *Gde zheleznichna stanica?* (where is the railroad station) and other similarly earth-shaking phrases.

On the other hand, I can't get over Cornell's gorgeous location, and its vistas across the valley and the town of Ithaca below us. No fences or gates anywhere. A few roads cross the campus but do so unobtrusively, and its dramatic beauty is enhanced by two bridges across a deep gorge, one bridge at each end of the campus. A creek flows far below into (or out of?) Lake Cayuga. It reminds me of the mountains, lakes and rivers in the High Tatras, where I had spent many summer vacations with Aunts Paula and Erna, and Cousin Walter. Perhaps that's why it feels so much like home.

The roads and trails into town are quite steep. There is a bus, but I chose a room on top of the hill, in College Town. College Town is not at all like Bronxville, small, and much less elegant and artificial. The homes are mostly Victorian, or variations thereof, and the main street has only a couple of cafés, the "Big Red" bar which is always packed, a bookstore, and a few shops. My room is comfortable and inexpensive.

What I miss, though, is the atmosphere at the Bozemans. My landlady is from "Pennsylvania Dutch Country," which is part of rural Pennsylvania and has a lot of Germans (despite the name). They are old-time immigrants, but not Jewish. Her background, however, must really be Dutch, since her name is Van Duyne. She is a retired schoolteacher, white-haired, thin, worn and sour. I don't know if she was ever married, but she has an adopted daughter. Linda is strikingly beautiful, tall, with very white skin, long black hair, and almond-shaped dark eyes.

Linda is dreamy and moody, though now and then she and her mother argue till the walls shake, and then they outdo each other in accusations. Fortunately, when I close my door, the noise is muted. Linda is in her early twenties, and does not seem to know what to do with her life. She keeps switching majors and boyfriends, which does not make life with mother easier. Nor does she help much around the house; this too leads to conflict. At any rate, I usually eat in the college cafeteria, work in the library or the T.A. office, and try to be "at home" as little as possible. I hope the atmosphere will improve.

Next time I'll describe to you my courses and teachers. Everything is much more structured than at SLC, but interesting. Meanwhile, I want to hear about your job, what Kurt is doing, whether living with your mother-in-law is working out, and what your chances of finding an apartment are.

Please convey my best regards to her, and of course to you and Kurt go my best wishes for success and happiness.

Your Liesl

* * *

The diary entries documenting the first Cornell year are minimal. The first one is dated April 3, 1952—almost a year after my arrival. Their sparseness may appear to be a good sign, but it soon becomes clear that wisdom, or at least equanimity, was still in short supply. Among the letters for that first year are, for the first time, two from Trude, also several from Robert. Since most of my replies are missing and I can no longer fill in the gaps, the letters will have to speak for themselves. All of the diary entries are now in English.

Hello, Liz— New York, September 15, 1951

Got your letter and the check on Wednesday and would have answered immediately but...ah, but you know there'd be a but.

We got a call from Mr. Quinn of the Catholic Committee asking me for an appointment—It was made for Friday night—last night, specifically. I think it came off well. He seemed a pleasant young man and we really buttered him up aplenty... Fran and I were on our best behavior.

Of course, prior to his visit, I had been over to the local parish and had a chat with young Father Voiland and so was able to talk about the church, the big brother movement, the socials, the religious training et al—and this, of course, impressed our Mr. Quinn. We went over his case i.e., Arthur's fairly thoroughly—Felix was not even brought in. Incidentally, they have a fairly good idea of Arthur and his previous troubles. Insofar as Felix is concerned, they've had quite a number of "referrals" out on the boy—but the fact that he's ten years old lessens his chances for adoption considerably—for that matter, even placement. And they've sent referrals out all over...Said Mr. Quinn, "Institutions at best can't substitute for a home and institutions even so far as St. Michael's—good though they may be—are still weak substitutes."

At any rate, Quinn is writing to the hospital on Monday, telling them that they may proceed with the discharge procedures as soon as they want to. He mentioned that he will not be saying "a temporary spot" with us because the implication that Arthur will be with us for a longer time, will sound better. He has no doubt that Arthur will be released soon and that any further length of time he's kept there, might put him on the downgrade.

I may be wrong, but I offered a drink to Quinn—he refused it on the grounds that he already had had several beers and mixing it with Scotch wouldn't help...But he took a rain check on it and when he asked could he come to visit Arthur here at the house, he was given carte blanche...so I think it looks good for the machinery to be set in motion.

Fran also had a long chat with Mrs. Miller on the phone...That was promising too. And tomorrow, if I'm not too lazy, I'll make the trip out to Kings Park.

Your own letter sounded good—better than so many of your previous letters have in the past—The letter read as if you've landed on two feet and that you'd soon take charge of the new situation—however strange it might be...

School for me—day school is already a week old...Seem to have good classes—not too burdensome—and perhaps even interesting... Will strive to get organized and collected in the next few weeks and really give the kids a worthwhile time...Night school begins Tuesday—have a half program—Tues—Thurs—and Fridays in October and December...

Now—let's get down to some further brass tacks about Elizabeth...She's still too, too sensitive...She must try not to let the little things knock her down the way they have in the past .... Tears, idle tears I know not whence they spring—tears from the depth of some divine despair...

Your year at Cornell that you're beginning now—should be a far greater adventure and by far a greater challenge to you than ever Sarah Lawrence...The men in your classes and the fratres on the faculty should lend a certain zest to your new horizons... (With all these men around, please don't forget me-and keep away from all Jims and Marios...)

Hear the chow call right now...Must go...As before—write when the muse moves—I'll do so at this end also...Don't despair of my omissions some time...The very best of luck to you.

    Love,

    R.

Jim, a German-American, was one of the four T.A.s in the German Department. I don't recall what I had written to Robert about him, but there was not the slightest danger of a personal involvement. I don't recall any Mario.

* * *

Dearest Trude,   Ithaca, Sept. 21, 1951

I was so sorry to hear that your heart was acting up and you had to cut short your vacation to recuperate at home. When I didn't hear from you, I began to wonder if something was wrong, and I was right! You say you are fully recovered—I hope that's true? Do take it easy so that you get your strength back soon! Under the circumstances, I wonder if you want to hear more about Cornell. Feel free to skip, or skim the rest of my account.

•CORNELL (1952–1953)•

The classes I am taking are far more traditional than at Sarah Lawrence, but at least none of them are large lecture courses, though those exist as well. In some ways, this place is even more like a high school than SLC was. In addition to final examinations, we have "midterm" exams, and deadlines which, I suspect, have to be taken seriously. All that is outlined, with precise dates, topics, assignments and "reserve book lists," in a "syllabus," distributed during the first class. It looks impressive and depressing—quite inflexible. Since we had no grades at SLC, we knew that the professors would not say anything bad in their final reports, in order not to discourage us. Now it will be hard to adjust to a "normal" kind of school—provided Cornell is considered normal.

[*Vienna's University had small, highly specialized seminars as well as large lecture courses which one signed in and out of at the beginning and end of the term. Otherwise you were free to do as you pleased—until you considered yourself ready to sign up for the comprehensive examinations; for some of them you could even purchase study aids.*]

Since I didn't have a major concentration in German as an undergraduate (in fact, nothing at all to do with German), I must now catch up. The good thing is that I only have to take three courses for credit and can audit two more, which means that those receive no grade but will be listed on my report card. Also, each course lasts only one semester so that I can cover quite a range of literary periods, and fill in gaps.

I don't recall if I mentioned before that I decided to add a minor in Russian to my German major. Teaching jobs in German don't look promising because people are still very anti-everything-German. Russian, on the other hand, is much in demand. I signed up for elementary Russian, which I thought would be easy since I speak Czech. Well, it is and it isn't. I find it easy to understand, but the alphabet is a great nuisance, and the pronunciation drives me crazy. The stress jumps all over the place, whereas in Czech it was always on the first syllable so that there was no need for guessing.

The professor is a very short, slight, elderly Russian lady on high heels, Mrs. Jaryc. Her hair is still totally black and rolled into a bun on top of her head, perhaps to make her look taller. She always wears dangling earrings, uses a lot of powder, dark red lipstick on her narrow, compressed lips, and rouge on her wrinkled skin; but she wears smartly draped scarves. For her age she is quite attractive but a real task master, constantly complaining in a stern staccato voice that we don't work hard enough, don't think, don't pay attention. Her "nyet!" tends to resound along the entire corridor. I might be the only graduate student in her class. One thing is good, though: she is supposed to teach according to the Moulton method, but she breaks most of the rules. Since she has been here for many years and gets good results, no one dares interfere. Or perhaps they are as scared of her as we are, even Mr. Fairbanks, the Slavic linguist, who is a sweet, gentle man.

I also take a course on "The Social Evolution of Modern Germany" with an elderly professor, Erich Kahler, originally "von" Kahler. He began his first lecture with Adam and Eve and Lucifer, but it all somehow makes sense. He is a wonderful lecturer, and seems to have the entire range of Western civilization at his command. He has also become a mentor for me, which makes up for not having a don. Unfortunately, he is only here for half a year at a time, then at Princeton. He comes from Prague, and was considered an eminent cultural historian already before the war. As a young man, he was wooed by the poet Stefan George. But he never joined the circle around George, despite the honor. He is a real internationalist, and George, despite his impressive poetry, was a narcissistic elitist. Kahler also corresponded with Thomas Mann and other famous writers.

He is short and heavy, has a big nose, wears large, owl-like glasses, and keeps combing his few dark hairs back over his huge shiny scalp; but he is a wonderful person. Brilliant and kind, erudite, always aware of the larger picture, patient, and with a great sense of humor. "Some of these children compare a horse's mane with a donkey's tail in their papers!" he said to me with a chuckle after returning our first papers. I felt flattered that he was confiding in me.

My third course is also with Kahler and just as good—a seminar on Rilke, who is definitely my favorite German poet. His verses sing like no one else's, and yet they hide deep, complex meanings.

I also audit a course on Goethe with Professor Victor Lange. (Here we do call them Professor and not just Mr. or Mrs.) He is from Germany, very intelligent, witty, and quite a charmer. He keeps calling me *die kleine Welt* [*the little world*], which I am probably supposed to find amusing but don't. What annoys me even more is that he has the students read their research papers in class instead of lecturing himself, which makes life easy for him, but can be a waste of time for us. I don't have to write papers since I am only an auditor, but of course I have to listen. However, I am allowed to participate in class discussion, and that is challenging.

Finally, I audit a course called "Survey of Russian Literature." It is taught in English, and is a rather strange course. It will hardly be much of a survey since we seem to be spending most of the term on one Old-Russian epic, *The Song of Igor*. We are reading it line by line, in the professor's own mimeographed translation, with the Russian text next to it (otherwise I could not manage, since my Russian is still very elementary, and Czech helps only a little). He obviously adores the epic. He spends hours elucidating one little passage, or explaining to us how many shades of blue there are in the Russian language. I must admit that he makes it sound intriguing, and since I don't have to worry about exams, I don't mind. Except that the professor both amuses and annoys me.

He is a Russian immigrant, possibly of Russian nobility; his English sounds very British though he arrived here from Germany. He has apparently written several books, in Russian and German. He is tall and big, has a booming voice, a very high forehead, and arrogant eyes that look over his glasses right through or past you. Often, he paces back and forth in the room, talks about anything that comes into his head, not really to any one of us or even to us as a group, but as if he were giving a performance to an audience. Once, having mentioned Pushkin, he acted out the duel in which Pushkin was killed "by a nonentity," as he hissed disdainfully. He ran from one side of the room to the other, acting out both parts. I don't know if outrageous remarks such as "Dostoevsky was just a scribbler without any discipline," or "Freud—that charlatan," are meant to incite us into objecting, or to brainwash us. The other day, he came into the classroom and just sat there, looking down at the table with an odd grin. We waited and waited. Finally he raised his head and announced, to no one in particular: "In the European literature class this morning a girl got up and walked out on me. I couldn't believe it—she actually walked out on me!" Her impertinence seemed to have unsettled him, but I think he also admired her courage.

In his classes you never get a chance to ask questions or make comments. Or are we all too intimidated by his grand manner? Now and then he stops in mid-sentence and says: "That was good, I must write it down!" Then he pulls out a little notebook and his pen, and while he writes we sit and wait. I wonder if his own writing is any good. His name is Nabokov, Vladimir Vladimirovich (his father's name was also Vladimir) Nabokov.

His wife usually attends class as well. She is tall, slim and white-haired, with an aquiline nose and regal features, but very quiet. Shy and sbmissive. She always comes in behind him and slinks into a seat in the last row, far behind us. We forget her presence until he—and he does it quite often—requests her assistance: "Vyerochka, would you distribute these handouts!" or: "Vyerochka, would you write this poem on the blackboard!" He does not so much ask as command, and she pops up without a word and does what he requests. I find it hateful and resent him for it, although at other times he is really amusing, and sometimes brilliant. Altogether I don't know what to make of him. Is he a charlatan just showing off his ego, and is she cowed or awed by him? Or is he a real writer and she, like Tolstoy's wife, pleased to be his helpmate?

Of the three other teaching assistants in German, I have become friendly, interestingly, with the one most different from me. Not with the tall, blond German whom I find arrogant and glib; nor the very knowledgeable and actually rather pretty but stern and prudish-looking young woman from England, originally a German refugee, who does not care how she dresses (she ties her hair into a bun so that she looks twenty years older than she is); but with Jim, a mid-western former *Ami* [GI] of German background. He is a Republican, whereas I consider myself a Democrat. We have long and heated political arguments. After the first one, over lunch in the cafeteria, I was convinced that he would never talk to me again, and that I could not talk to him either. To my amazement, the next day he sat down across from me with the same big hello and friendly grin as before. That could never have happened in Europe! People seem much more tolerant here, at least with regard to politics. (The one thing that annoys them is a person with an accent criticizing American habits, such as their wasting food, dropping trash on the sidewalk, dressing too young and flashy, and so on.)

My big worry is Cousin Arthur. They moved him from Bellevue to King's Park State Hospital on Long Island, a peninsula just outside New York City. It is like Steinhof—a real mental institution and a terrible place, even to only visit. I was there only once, with Robert, and found it awful. Thank God for Robert. He has been wonderful. He tries to visit Art whenever he can, also Felix at St. Michael's in Pennsylvania, though that takes much of the day, and he has little free time. He seems to like Art and wants to help get him out of there. He feels as I do that, if Art stays in that awful place much longer, he will really crack up. But, in order to get him released, Robert has to vouch for him, let him live with them and be responsible for him until Art can find work and live on his own. Can you think of a stranger willing to do that? Fran, his wife, has apparently agreed. I don't know if she has met Art. But Robert is an unusual person, and I am not just saying it because we have a very special relationship. Young people in any kind of trouble always seek him out, and if he cannot help, he at least offers a ready ear and keeps in touch.

Now that I am too far away to see him (at least five hours by car), we write off and on. His letters are very special—sometimes very poetic, sometimes so blunt they seem coarse. Even that does not bother me. It's the way he is, always very direct, but also understanding and supportive. I don't know what I would do without him. Sometimes I feel quite guilty that he spends so much time on me and my cousins.

Enough for today. Wish me luck and that things may continue so calmly, and write!

With my very best greetings and hugs,

Your Liesl

Here are a few more recollections of Nabokov. The following fall, I was taking a course on Russian modernist poetry with him. To explain the very complicated scanning pattern of a poem by Tyutchev, he had his wife copy the entire schematic on the blackboard; then he requested that we copy and memorize it, for that was how Tyutchev's poetry had to be scanned. When I asked where I could read up on this method, he dismissed me with a wave of his hand: "You can't, it's my own system." I had almost been taken in. Or the time when, to impress on us what good writing was, he proceeded to read pages and pages from a book written by "one of the best contemporary Russian writers, by name of Sirin." I became suspicious and, after class, ran to the library to check out Sirin in the catalogue. Sure enough—it was Nabokov's pen name!

Once again I am reminded of how often first impressions can be wrong or one-sided. Recently I found a biography of Mrs. Nabokov entitled Véra. *First I read only the chapters dealing with their Cornell years, but then, with increasing fascination, the rest of the book. A very different woman emerged. Vladimir did not drive, and was not interested in things mechanical or in anything except his writing and his butterflies; therefore, throughout their long lives together, Mrs. Nabokov chauffeured him, in Ithaca, several times across the States, and in Europe. She was also his literary agent (and apparently a very tough one), his cajoling and conniving but always fiercely protective personal secretary, his public spokesperson and shrewd fiscal administrator. To my dismay, I learned that sometimes she would also teach his classes, grade his students' papers and write student recommendations, which he only signed. In fact, that docile, subdued exterior which she maintained throughout hid an unshakable determina-*

tion, *a fierce, protective loyalty, and critical assessments of other writers just as idiosyncratic and uncompromising as were her husband's. The book was an eye-opener for me.*

2.

Hello, Liz— September 26, 1951

I haven't utterly deserted you...Glad you keep writing to me despite the fact that of late I've been finding letter writing a most difficult thing to do simply because of Time—

I don't like to write letters as a matter of duty...Like to have some relaxed moments when a guy can sit down and talk and this is just such an occasion...

Your own letters sound pretty chipper and that's encouraging to me. It's good to hear that you are acclimating yourself to Cornell in as easy and facile a manner...Even your gentlemen friends sound a bit on the glowing side—but beware the jabberwock my beamish boy....and don't go getting yourself into a bit of welt-shmerz...But have fun...and get your work done...I expect big things of you—especially this year...

Yesterday was Jamie's 4th—Eheu fugaces-o tempora, o mores! He quite the young man...Invite me to your son's fourth birthday party—it gives one a good feeling...and I'd like to be present when yours becomes a person...I've no doubt that as your son, he'll be quite the young rascal—All right, all right—as you and your offspring are still somewhat in the future—and you don't even know if I'll live that long...(Well, in a pinch, I can always serve as stud and produce one for you or is the gentleman too willing?)

No news from the hospital or from Art and no news from Quinn or from Miller though Fran called Miller over a week ago and was told—well, things will take a bit of time—this cutting through red tape...and I do suppose we must bide our time...I did see Art a week ago Sunday and possibly I'll be able to manage it again this Sunday...Perhaps I'll be able to talk to Gollick once more as I did last time. He was certainly more affable...and told me that he could not do anything until he hears from the immigration people and only then can he summon Arthur before staff...I'm not sure whether I told you but it seems we'll have to undergo another investigation—this time from the hospital people...Ah me, never a dull moment...Of course, I'll let you know just as soon as anything happens...

Hey, watch out for your purse strings...Don't be like Goldberg who some times when he's flush or with money in his pocket acts like a drunken sailor...After all, if you run low—from whom am I going to borrow again? Nope—this isn't a pitch for another loan—I've made mine from the bank—Money, money, money—The new loan will enable me to pay back the 500 I already owed them and give me another couple of hundred to tie us over the next few months..And so it goes...

Oh yes—for Jamie's birthday, I built a huge toy chest in his bedroom—which he probably does not appreciate…It's a honey of a unit—modern design—and Fran at least likes it.

And now-dear lady, I'll end this note...I miss you much— and even though getting up to Cornell is something out of the question for quite a long time to come—perhaps we can find time for a get-together in Albany—in November shall we say? Save your pennies—I'll save mine.)

Much love—

R

* * *

Hi— October 24, 1951

Evidently I'm on your brown list for one reason or another...Are you perturbed that Fran answered your letter about your visit to New York some weeks ago and not myself? Are you mad that I haven't written until now?

Fact of the matter is that something must be bothering you or occupying you sufficiently...Are you in love again—in the middle of a passion flower with one of the Cornell fratres? Are you having a baby? Was the visit to New York so awful that you haven't been able to write us a word about it. Wasn't until several days afterward that Fran mentioned you had called...

Come on, Liz—give out and let us know...Ordinarily you'd have sent a card even to express your displeasure but nary a word...

Of course, you must be saying that I'm a sonovabitch and that I was to have written—and there we go being formal all over again...But until this evening—I have been busy—very busy—painting, building, constructing...getting organized in school...and I didn't want to sit down to chat with you until I had the right time...I've begun too many of my letters to you in a hurry...

And now that I have the time—I'm wondering what's with you and what you're peeved at—and wondering too whether you're going to tell me in turn that you've been busy with painting, building, constructing—getting organized in school...

Did Fran mention in her letter that the social worker from the hospital was here and (on October 11) seemed to feel that things were going smoothly and that in a matter of three weeks (from that date) Art would be with me...I'm calling her on Friday to double check and will try to get out again on Sunday...

Did you ask what I've built since...? A desk for Fran and a shadow box and cabinet bookcase for Cynthia...(the last two are my best efforts in carpentry to-date and I'm rather proud of them...But the benefits from them I believe I shall reap...I'm going to try—really try to buckle down to some assiduous labors at the typewriter—I have the time—Monday and Wednesday evenings at Cynthia's new place—a much lovelier room—in a more attractive neighborhood—and the place is inviting to work...I'm free on Mondays and Wednesdays and Cynthia is at college on those evenings and if I arrange my time properly—I can work there from five to eleven and be out before she gets in...Perhaps something will be accomplished...

Jamie is in one of his contrary moods tonight—Fran is hurrying to get on to her gin game—her usual Wednesday activity...and the t.v. set is about to go on...Do you see why Cynthia's place will be a welcome oasis and an occasional ivory tower...? And believe you me, despite the lady Lore's protestations love is not the issue...And did you see or hear from that gal on your last trip to New York...? Did she sour you on anything?

There must be a reason for your not writing as long a time as you've taken and I don't think it can be all a temper at me or your own time element...Anything wrong?

Love,

R

Yes, something was indeed wrong. I vacillated between wanting to talk to him, yearning to be with him, and yet fearing it, feeling guilty that I might be interfering with his marriage. How could I have dared preach to Trude about her relationship with O! Or was I correct then and despicable now? And what about that Cynthia? I had met her once, when she entered the cafeteria where Robert and I were having coffee. We were so engrossed in our conversation that neither of us noticed her until she stopped at our table and glared at me, or so I thought. Robert introduced us, but she would not sit down. Did I have a reason to be jealous? But what right did I have to be jealous?

What complicated things even more was that I found at Cornell the college life I had been missing at Sarah Lawrence, and as I reveled in it, my relationship with Robert lost much of its glamour. A small group of us, graduate students of both sexes, would gather regularly in Alicia's tiny apartment, likewise in College Town. She was a T.A. for Spanish, and I marveled at how she could afford that adorable, modern apartment with an open kitchen, bar counter and liquor cabinet. She always had snacks available, wine and beer, even gin and tonic, and we were welcome to drop in any evening to drink and chat till all hours—unless she had a paper due.

Pierre, a French T.A., though actually Swiss, was very stiff and proper—but only until the first drink. We all liked him and were making fun of him, which he never noticed. Eric was tall, blond and serious, but so pleasant and gentlemanly that his company was always sought out. Toby was Russian, short, pretty and voluptuous, a skillfully low-key flirt, and I admired her for that. There were others whom I no longer remember. Alicia looked like a gypsy, with long black curls, mischievous eyes, and a radiant smile. She was full of fun and energy, but also very bright and knowledgeable. Her field was political science, and I could easily imagine her as a diplomat at the United Nations some day, all male diplomats in tow.

Then there was Tony, not to be linked to the Tony of four years ago in Munich, nor part of Alicia's circle. He looked older than most of us and a little like Camus, whom I adored at the time: the same thick nose, high forehead and dark stiff hair. Or did I only think there was a resemblance because Tony considered himself an existentialist, and would treat me to lengthy philosophical expositions during our many evenings together? We would meet at our "special" place, the long, narrow cellar in town which two enterprising students had turned into a wine bar. They paid no rent but split the profits with the landlord. The place was always packed. All you could get there was white or red wine by the glass and cheese from a little cart, which one of them would roll back and forth between the two rows of small tables lining the brick walls. You paid by the slice.

Though our relationship was purely platonic, Tony's proximity made me tingle and glow, and it pushed the memory of Robert and his wife into the background. And that was why I did not know what to write to him, fearful that he would detect the false note in my communication, feeling guilty because I was letting him down, when he was doing so much for my cousins. And the more eager his letters seemed, the more uneasy I became.

* * *

Hi there, Liz—   The night of Hallow'een

Tonight's the night when the witches ride their brooms when the devil's brew is distilled in the dark of the moon...and since this is so—I am in a high mood, a good mood and I'm well nigh crocked...

Golly, the way I feel, you might think this were another Interim night....Ah, there lassie, please read that with hushed voice and proper feeling....Don't the words Interim Night (note the caps) bring to mind things that are strange and wondrous—??? What did the alchemists ever brew in their ancient bottles to match the magic of an Interim Night...Enchanted evenings are beggared...

Yes, yes, I know—such a beginning is a definite departure from the lugubrious tone of your last letter. You and your Rilke..You and your Jim...You and your Pierre...You and your damned sensitive nature...

Ah, Liz, dear girl, did anyone ever tell you that you're really a wonderful young woman...charming, intelligent and lovely.

You think I'm drunk and these words maudlin sentiments like the blown spume of a Scotch highball. Nay, a fig for such thistles.

For believe you me, I'm really not celebrating Halloween..I suppose I'm drinking because of your coming of age...

Did I ever tell you that I think you're pretty swell...

Sure, I've told that to lots of people...well, not exactly lots—but a number...

And what makes a person lifted into that rare hierarchy—that rara avis, that je ne sais quoi? I suppose it is the inner being...And that's were you shine...

Hold on, Macduff, I need a cigarette...I need a drink...And Sheridan twenty miles away (Naturally you won't get the last remark—it's from a lesser known poet in American literature—and it isn't that you don't know our lesser poets, it's simply that you know naught of Amer. Lit., you Sara Lawrencer...

Intermission—There. I have my cig... I have my drink...What was I talking about... You! all right...That's good enough for me.

But in case you think I'm really crocked, let me tell you that your actions during the past week (Not with your Pierre or your Jim) but with your Murray- have labeled you as an ineffable sonofabitch....

Nonetheless I forgive you...Big of me, aye wot?

No doubt I would have gone on and on in this vein...but a moment ago, Cynthia called (remember her, the one who doesn't quite like you as much as I do) and she's coming over for a short visit...so perforce, this letter can be delayed for hours or cut short here...And since I do want to reach you—I'm going to cut it short.

How shall I put it...Your bad moments, your mental anguish, your soul searchings of the past two months—your thoughts about Tony—puzzled me— bothered me—but I think that progress is being made—I do think my little Liz is weathering the mess in the style of the flying clippers of old...I think she's truly a wonderful wonderful person.

(And when the mind turns to thoughts of Interim—I tingle at what a wonderful gal she is-truly so.)

But—more important than my being high right now, more important than your soul-searching antics of the past few weeks—and your Dante Inferno phantasmagoria of doubts and dismal thoughts—was—your bits on Fall along old Cayuga...Liz—you old blackguard—how long, oh Cataline—your descriptions of Cornell in Autumn are precious...I'm saving that last letter of yours to read to you aloud—to show you that in moments when you aren't even trying you have ability and talent and a truly potent force—Ah yes, Liz....you've got stuff....

And—ere I quit—I saw Art last Sunday and spoke to Sollick. He said that if all the papers from Immigration are in—(and he thinks they are) Art may be going before Staff on Monday, November 5—and that on the 8th or 9th we should be notified—and in that case I pick him up on Sunday the 11th and he's home with us to stay...

Does that call for a drink...I think it does...Prosit and Salud...

So I'm high—So I think you're swell...So I miss you much...so I do want Interim nights and interim days keenly and avidly...

Much love,

R

At Sarah Lawrence, midterm vacations were called "interims." However, I have no recollection of any weekends other than that first one that could be called interims with a capital I. Had I repressed those memories, did I erase them? If so I now regret it: I think of Robert with much gratitude and affection, and with great sadness.

* * *

Hello Liz—   The day after Thanksgiving

Your letter came today. Until that minute I had given you up as a complete pain in the ass; an emotional mass and an emotional mess who couldn't take the trouble to acknowledge my own special delivery that was sent in answer to your letter the very day after it was received here at the house.

What happened to that letter; why it was never received as your letter intimates—I don't know...But there again, you go off half-cooked and insinuate that one doesn't love you anymore or that whenever an urgent letter is sent by you—you never get an answer.

In my letter I said—and it was brief I'll admit simply because I wrote it in school and wanted to get my reply to you just as fast and as urgently as your letter came to me—Thus spake Goldberg: Can't meet you either in Scranton or in Albany because I have school on Wednesday and a course as well. Thus I couldn't get to either place before eleven o'clock or midnight ...So I suggested you come in on the bus, meet me at the terminal and that I'd drive you to Bozeman's...I mentioned that since the invitation was extended, you'd probably have to spend Thursday with them—but that I was free for you all day Friday and Sunday...And I asked you to let me know as soon as you made your plans.

Naturally, I thought of you as quite the sonofabitch. I waited and waited for my letter from you. I had told Fran about your coming the day I received your letter...and so—for the past two weeks I've just refused all other plans...hoping I'd hear from you. Matter of fact, last night I said that I think you were at the Bozeman's and that you were either in another of your sensitive periods or just an ingrate completely. That's what I said—as for what I thought—well, I felt too that you had let me down.

So I said to Art—just before he turned in—your cousin is quite a stinker...

I would have made it my very first sentence, or wired you immediately about the developments and the suddenness with which we were able to cut through red tape—but I would have made that business of being so peeved at you—incidental rather than primary in doing it that way.

Yes, Art is living with us. I signed the papers Thanksgiving morning....But this you will know because now that I'm thinking more kindly of you—I've suggested to Art that we phone you tonight and let him give you the news.

Later this morning I drove him into town and with him met Nokofsky, and Quinn and Janus...and we shmaltzed them up prettily—and picked up a valise full of books—and then to his former landlady and picked up a valise full of moth-eaten, many clothes...what a shame...But since I have the permission of the Cath. Comm to go buy him some clothes and send them the bill, I'll do that first thing tomorrow...

He feels well, looks well, eats well (and how) and slept well, thank you...

As for a job...Cynthia has spoken to her boss at Combustion Engineering...He know the history and is interested...She'll talk to him again next week and perhaps Art will get an interview... At the moment there isn't any rush...

As for your coming into town...or my meeting you in Scranton ...the strain and the expense for both are more than formidable ...Let's put off until you arrive here for the Christmas holidays and we'll really make it an interim holiday... (shame on you for having lost the faith so easily)

As far as the "getting over the Tony complex" is concerned...well, you certainly seemed to have been in a muddle and I'm becoming more and more convinced that no muddles are like yours...You go in up to the ears....

But if as you say—you're over it...I'm truly glad...Truly glad that you didn't get more hurt than you did and there were letters that made it appear you were over the well known barrel and up the well-known creek...More terrifying—(sic!)—was the awareness that during that interlude you weren't close to me at all. That, however, was of your own making.

Having talked to you at this length...it implies that I'm no longer peeved with you as I have been...Waiting for your letter more or less ruined my weekend...but having Art here at the house does make up for it...

Tonight we have our Turkey dinner here....

Incidentally, Liz, should the doubts ever assail you...try to remember, you are not alone...Or do you find that so easy to forget—you sensitive bitch.

Much love—

P.S. It would be protocol to send Fran a letter now. (But don't forget mine)

* * *

Dearest Truderl, Ithaca, December 1, 1951

Thank you for your good letter and the birthday wishes. I had not told anyone that it was my birthday, and spent the day quietly, writing a little. Even if I may never become a writer, I need to keep writing; it helps, no matter whether I am in a good or a desperate mood. But far more important—I am glad that you are well again, and hope that you will stay well!

My main news is that Robert managed to get Arthur out of that hospital—it was not easy. There had to be several hearings, and even the immigration people got involved. For a while I thought that Robert's being Jewish might interfere, in case the Catholic Committee was afraid of his influence on Arthur. But luckily I was wrong. Art is now living with them, and Robert is trying to help him find a job. I am very indebted to both him and his wife.

I was in Bronxville for Thanksgiving,, which is an official holiday here. It celebrates the English pilgrims' first harvest after landing in America, somewhere in Massachusetts. The entire holiday consists of an enormous dinner eaten in the afternoon, over several hours. The traditional meal (and we did have a traditional meal) consists of a roast turkey (fairly tasteless but improved by the jellied cranberries one eats with it, and which I am beginning to like), then an odd kind of mashed very yellow and sweet potatoes (people here really seem to like sweet things with their main dishes!), and something called "stuffing" which is not stuffed inside the turkey but baked separately. It consists of spiced bread cubes, and is rather dry. Also a dish of tiny onions in a white sauce. I was surprised that Adda had not prepared a more interesting meal. However, she made a nice mixed salad, and the dessert, an open-top "pecan pie" filled with a nut-and-honey mixture, was delicious. (You can buy ready-made pies which you only need to reheat in the oven. Some of them are surprisingly good.)

Pecans are nuts which apparently grow only in the South, though I don't understand how that would qualify them for a Pilgrims' Thanksgiving. I don't think they exist in Europe—at least they are not listed in my *Langenscheidt* dictionary—but the pie was delicious. We also had wine, and afterward a wonderful coffee liqueur, which Arne produced as a surprise.

Arne, Adda's new husband, is very Scandinavian-looking, and has a nice dry humor. Even Anya has accepted him. Kitty gave me a big welcome, but that was probably because I had two dog biscuits in my pocket, which she must have smelled right away.

The only disappointment was that I was not able to see Robert. I had written to him that I was coming, but his reply got lost, and so I thought he didn't have time for me. Nor did I know that Arthur was going to be with them. Perhaps at Christmas.

That is all the news at the moment. Do I still like Cornell, now that I know it better? Yes, very much. The landscape is lovely, especially in the fall when the trees are a sea of color. Student life is easy-going, a little as it was in Vienna, and I enjoy being part of it. Perhaps also because many students have accents, and nobody pays any attention to that. Nor does it seem to matter who is Jewish and who isn't. And since graduate students are not all the same age, I don't feel different from the rest—if anything, less serious and mature than some, but even that is all right.

Enough for today. Please let me hear from you soon.

All the best to all of you for the holidays, and a good and healthy New Year!

      Your Liesl

* * *

[*January 7, 1952*]

Hello,   The night of the big storm

I'm snug inside the house rather than plowing my way home from my usual Monday evening course. Today's storm was a prize and it has upset quite a number of things in this town.

However—be that as it may. I had meant to write last week; in fact, shortly after I received your letter. I'm going to treasure it. It said so much and, begun as it was, during the old moments and carried into the new—perhaps, it presages all the good both of us have been seeking. But then again, perhaps you were aware all along that I was drinking a toast to you when the clock spun round to twelve on New Year's Eve. We were celebrating at the Claybourne menage instead of having our usual party in our house. It was cozy, charming, and thoroughly delightful. But though we drank and drank we saved the champagne for the big moment—they for the toasts and I for Interims.

Here's to them. We'll drink our toast to them next time and no doubt redefine old terms as well as add the new luster which you and I seem to have added along the way—especially during the very times—months—almost years— we've been without. Once the snows are clear from the ground and the highways more or less passable again, we'll talk of that week-end at the shore. Matter of fact, we'd better start a fund called the Shore Foundation For Interims. You and I shall be charter members. What do you say? Since it's to be a matching proposition, I'm enclosing my first contribution—We're on our way. At this rate, when do you think we might be able to make it?

Have been kept busy by the new teaching organization I have joined.

Withal I find time to spend leisure moments in the garage in my workshop—and this affords me considerable pleasure,—and proves creative as well.

However, my life is not all pure and virtuous. That would be too abrupt a transition from my old days.

It was wonderful seeing you, however briefly, and then getting your letter— written as it was...but still, I am curious enough to question—How were you released at that time? Who was then the gentleman?

   Much love,

    R

Oh yes, Claybourne. I had totally forgotten about her, and don't even recall her first name. Though I barely knew her, I liked her. Was she another one of Robert's protegés and— though I think she was married—perhaps also one of his nighttime friends? Like Lore, she

seemed quiet and in need of "letting her hair down," a challenge Robert could not resist.

The last sentence of his letter? I have no idea what that was about. Even though much resurfaces as I revisit these yellowed pages, tantalizing snippets remain afloat in the air and mock me.

3.

Dearest Trude,   Ithaca, January 24, 1952

I am sorry I let so much time pass between letters, but you surely understand since you, too, have been busy.

I think I mentioned before that Robert has succeeded in getting Arthur out of the mental hospital, actually already in late November. He is staying with them and will, I hope, not be too difficult. He still hasn't found a job. I only saw him briefly, when I was invited to their house at Christmas. He was pleasant and seemed fine.

I hope that your Christmas was wonderful, and you had a nice, long vacation. Friends gave me a ride into New York, then I took the train to Bronxville and spent five days with the Bozemans. It was a real pleasure to be with them, and it made me realize how much I miss the good conversations there.

This term I am taking German poetry from Goethe on, which is not very inspiring, even though I like poetry; then the continuation of my Russian language course; a difficult but challenging seminar on Faust; and a course on Lessing which I audit and find quite boring. I am beginning to wonder if I could switch from German to Comparative Literature, which is a new field and sounds much more creative and less confining. But I would have to change schools since Cornell doesn't have a program. At any rate, first I have to get the M.A. Incidentally, my grades for the first term were much better than at Sarah Lawrence (96 for Russian, 90 for each of the other two. That averages out to an A minus, which I probably don't deserve.)

I have two new friends, both male, and both definitely just friends. Actually only one is a real friend, Murray Salzman, American but a graduate student in German. He is in two of my courses. We often eat together, take walks and study together—it is a very relaxed and undemanding relationship, just right. And the landscape here is so beautiful that if you can't walk much because the walkways are icy, it is just as nice to look out at it from the library.

The other one is what I could even call an admirer! Jimmy is in my Russian class, an undergraduate senior. He follows me around whenever I let him. I don't have the heart to brush him off but may have to, should he become too attached to me. He has already asked if I would be willing to be his date at the "prom" (some kind of graduation party). I will have to find out more about it, but I simply couldn't say no. Now and then I still join the circle around Toby or Alicia, though there is a little too much drinking, and some of them smoke and ruin the air. But at least none of the women are trying to catch a man—it is just friendships among equals. What a relief! I am very glad that I am not serious about anybody and can concentrate on my work. It makes life so much simpler!

How is your job? Do you have nice colleagues and not too much pressure? And is Kurt also working as a lawyer? You haven't written in quite a while—I hope all is going well!

All the best to you, Kurt and your mother,

Your Liesl

Murray Salzman: a story that still haunts me. This awfully nice, modest and helpful human being, quite boyish and very idealistic, was looking forward to receiving his M.A., so that he could teach. Since, however, he was on a draft deferment, he would first have to serve his two years in the army. In the early fall of 1952 he left, luckily for Japan and not Korea. I received several enthusiastic letters from him about Japan and everything Japanese. Then I did not hear from him for a long time. Finally, a long letter arrived—signed "Brother Francis, formerly Murray Salzman"!

He described how impressed he had been by the Japanese so that, when his tour of duty ended, he decided to stay on as a civilian and teach English. He was greatly esteemed in the small town, everyone's honored mentor and treasured friend, practically a member of every family. Then one day, when they were celebrating some major festival, everybody got very drunk. And now it all came out: how much they hated and despised America and the Americans, how they wanted all of them out of their country, and on and on in that vein. Murray had a nervous breakdown and was suicidal. The local Catholic priest took him in and nursed him back to health. And that was how the Jew Salzman became Brother Francis. I was so taken aback that I did not reply nor keep the letter. Now I greatly regret it. He never wrote again.

* * *

June 10

The year is almost over, and it has been going very well, no complaints. I didn't do much writing but I think my grades will be o.k. even if I didn't work really hard and was not too excited about my classes except for *Faust*. I can hardly wait for Kahler to be back in the fall. This summer I will remain here to teach and earn extra money, and that doesn't disturb me at all—with a swimming hole in the gorge for hot days, and walking trails for cool days. Tony has left but I saw not much of him—or he of me, to speak the truth—during the last few months. Gone is also Jimmy, my undergraduate admirer. I did attend the prom with him, though it meant buying a fancy dress. I didn't want to hurt his feelings because he is not very good-looking, quite shy and has pimples, so the girls don't care for him. Also, I was curious what such a prom would be like. Now I know, and know also that I did not miss much as an undergraduate.

However, I have met somebody new, Connie. He owns a car and wants to take me to explore some of the other Finger Lakes, and also Corning which has a famous glass factory. And Connie is very good company.

The one big shadow is new trouble with Arthur. I feel very badly that I have involved Murray in this. But he seemed to genuinely like him and want to help, and that was a great relief to me. And still is. But I surmised from his phone call that matters are not going well. It seems neither of us was aware of how disturbed Arthur was. But I don't want to think of that now or my good mood will vanish.

* * *

Hello, Liz—   June 23, 1952

Alas Art…

Last Thursday—the U.S. Committee telephoned me—a Miss Block calling for Mrs. Miller…They had made arrangements for Art's committal to a private place in Katonah, New York—It is not a state hospital…More or less one of these private pavilions (one! or two?) There he'll get therapy and individual care—none of the mass situation that existed at Kings Park…

The decision was made on a Wednesday—day before her call—when after another visit to a psychiatrist, the doctor said his committal was urgent and imperative…I was told to say nothing to the Catholic Committee inasmuch as Miss Block said "their only solution was Kings Park"…and that "Mr. Stern, the legal head of the organization will act as the liaison officer—the situation between the two organizations being somewhat ticklish."

Even I am not to get in touch with Art until the U.S. Committee notifies me….But that's neither here nor there—Not only is Art recommitted but most important—he has been sent to a place where the therapy should be ideal...Without question, it's something only the very poor or the very rich can enjoy...One of those places that may cost 200 a week...Ask your cousin, Dr. Thierer, about them.

Had Art had such a place in the beginning—without doubt he'd be out of the woods by now...Perhaps, this will mark a new milestone...I hope so. It will give him a rest and give me a rest too. As I told you, I had reached the point where I felt that I was no longer of any use to him, but even began to resent him. True, the dislike I had taken to him was all a result of the manifestations of his illness—but nonetheless—since the feeling was there—what good was I.

However, I'm certain that when I'm allowed to visit him again, that feeling will have passed and I'll become his father once again—at least the good friend I'd always tried to be. Rest assured on that score, Liz, old gal and thank your stars he's in capable hands.

I appreciate your check...I'm sorry the burden has to hit you that way...I'm sorry too that I'm in the spot where I can't shrug it off either...But we can call the financial score even—Your check and something the Catholic Committee sent in to me—came in handy for another SOS that I received the very same day the U.S. Committee called.

Four more days of school and the summer work begins. I've got a fair number of kids for July and hope of half a load for August...That plus night school will make for a busy summer—but there's no question that it will also put a dent into my debts—and thereby a load will be removed...

Your own letter about your return to the campus life sounded good—seems as if the waters of Cayuga and the presence of one called Connie do you a world of good...I do hope it runs smoothly for you—and should you need the shoulder—(I hope you don't) you know I'm rooting for you as strongly and as warmly as ever...

By all means—we'll keep the letters flowing...I look forward to getting yours...and now—well—perhaps you can get back to that writing you began in that notebook of yours last Christmas.

    Love,

        R.

* * *

The following is a set of four typed pages. It is not dated but must have been written shortly after July 4, 1952.

I think I am awake now, but it is not easy to ascertain this fact beyond all doubt: it has been such a long and treacherous sleep. Long, because it had enveloped me for all the years of my growing up and rocked me into a complacent trust in this process of growing up as a passive stage, as something you allow to happen, and not something you yourself must do and act out and struggle through with tense muscles and wide open eyes and ears ... And because it kept this realization away from me, it was a treacherous sleep, treacherous in its disguise, its pretense at living, at walking while in reality I stood still with just some scenery passing by me or turning around me. But it was not deep enough to shut out all street noise. For then, as can happen in real sleep, I might have got startled at the calm, at the utter lack of anything real and alive, and I could have roused myself from my sleep. It was also not deep enough to be filled with dreams so incredible that, as in childhood nights when a malicious witch was riding through my room and threatening to attack me, I could tell myself in my sleep "this is only a dream, this *can't* really happen!" and force myself to wake up. I would reason—still in my sleep—"if I am awake I must be able to pinch myself and feel the pain." I would not be able to do it, ergo—"I am still asleep, I must try harder to open my eyes and pinch myself." And I would struggle through semi-consciousness until I succeeded in piercing it and in opening my eyes. Pinching had, of course, by then become unnecessary.

During the war all reality was a nightmare, and could only be accepted as such, so that one could preserve one's sanity. An evaluation, even just an attempt at disengagement and an individual active stand was practically out of the question. That was natural and perhaps even inevitable. But then the war had passed, then life—or what I thought was life—came back, slowly and by bits only, it is true, but it nevertheless came and expected to have me face it not only as life per se, a complex not quite determinable mosaic, but to find within that mosaic an aspect that existed merely for me, that could be seen only by me, that was my own life.

Seven years have gone by since the end of the war, seven years I had been asleep, until two little incidents penetrated the barrier I had pulled up around me, not through action but the lack of it, not through withdrawal but through the lack of curiosity, not through fear but through indifference.

The first incident was caused by an animal trap, or rather, several of them. Rectangular stainless steel traps (at least that's what they looked like to my kitchen-science-trained eye), neat and clean, with two open flaps lengthening the outlines while lifted up, thus opening the entrance into the trap. In its middle a small platform, balancing on a central axis. I had a visitor from New York, and as Bibi and I walked toward the gorge, we found the traps under many of the huge shade trees on the quadrangle. I did not at first notice them, so busy was I pointing out the beauties of the landscape and the attractions of swimming in the gorge, but Bibi stopped me.

"Look, there is a trap under the tree over there. And something is in it!"

I stopped short in surprise. The huge shady quadrangle with its old trees, sated lawns and white diagonal paths had always seemed the symbol of tranquility to me, with its calm outlines, the two statues at either end, which the legend created by student minds forced to descend from their pedestals every fall, on the first night of the term, walk across the square and shake hands if a virgin should pass ... of which feat one found traces in the form of huge chalky footsteps on the walk connecting their quarters, these footsteps sometimes meeting, some years turning back just before they would reach each other.... In this quadrangle, usually populated by dogs, pigeons, redbreasts and squirrels, and by some tolerable human forms, there was suddenly a caged animal, a sparrow, fluttering wildly and with harsh peeping calls in a shining metal cage under an old oak tree. As we approached the cage, we began to look around more attentively, and to my dismay I now realized that the shining little spots under many other trees were cages as well. So far, they were all empty.

The sparrow fluttered and humped with short spasmodic leaps from one end of the cage to the other. Every time it touched the platform in the center, it bounced down like a seesaw under his weight and gave a sharp metallic click, to swing down to its other edge the moment the sparrow released it.

"Let's open the cage for him," said Bibi. "Look, how frightened the poor thing is!"

I hesitated. The cage was marked: "Do not disturb—zool. dept." I felt that we should not encroach on university property.

"They will catch some more, I bet. And they can't need sparrows any way. And besides it is a nasty thing to do, right here, and on July fourth too!" Bibi said, with a pitying look at the little animal that would not cease in its efforts at finding the hole again that had let him pass through before.

"I don't know whether we are entitled to interfere," I said doubtfully. "Of course, they surely don't plan to catch sparrows with such big traps. But if someone sees us, we can get ourselves into trouble."

"Nonsense," said Bibi. "Isn't there a Society for the Prevention of Cruelty to Animals? I am a member."

We both laughed and stood undecided, watching the fluttering and peeping sparrow. There was no other human being on the quadrangle.

"How does that mechanism work anyway?" I asked and bent down. We both tried to lift the side flaps but were unsuccessful. Thereupon we began a closer examination of the cage and its mechanism. Finally Bibi discovered its system.

"If you lift that wire out of the hole in the flap, the flap can be lifted."

"Are you sure?" I asked as I lifted the flap. The sparrow, obviously frightened by the noise, withdrew to the other end of the cage.

"Silly thing," I said. "Why don't you come!"

Bibi opened his flap too and the sparrow fluttered out. We looked at each other with a mischievous twinkle, closed the flaps again and began to walk on toward the gorge with calm, indifferent steps, without another word.

A few yards further we saw another cage. Its flaps were down, and a squirrel was racing anxiously from one end to the other. Without a moment's hesitation we bent down, lifted the wires out of their holes, raised the flaps, and closed them again upon the empty cage. With a chuckle we marched on.

The third cage was empty, but we were too exuberant by then to let it go untouched. With one finger I reached through the meshing, touched the little platform, tipping it to one side, upon which the flaps bounced down with a loud noise, so loud that it shook the cage and made it resound. With a stealthy look around us we walked on toward the gorge.

"Did you notice," I said about ten minutes later, "how long we were in deciding what to do in front of the first cage, and how quickly we acted afterwards?"

"Yes," Bibi grinned. "Only the first step toward crime is difficult. Then everything slides on by itself." And he began to talk about something else. I bit my lip not to blurt out my thoughts: You were in hiding for five years in Vienna, in a tiny room. Is that why you could not stand the sight of a caged animal? I was freer than you but afraid, differently afraid. Brainwashed into obeying orders. But now there is really no need to be afraid. No, that's not it. One should never be a coward, especially when confronted by suffering. It had taken me too long to remember that.

In the evening, as we approached the quad on our way home, he said:

"Any more rescue work for us to do?" But all cages were empty and open—even those whose flaps we had closed.

"They are too efficient for us," he said, and I could not tell if irony, bitterness or resignation tinged his voice.

I could not forget his words about the first step only being difficult. They gave the matter a much wider frame, turned it from the question of releasing a little sparrow from another man's cage to the problem about one's right to interfere in general. It brought back memories of the war, of the problems one had been faced with then, whether to become guilty through action or inaction. The whole complex, monstrous problem of guilt arose, and I felt that I had never really solved its dilemma for myself, had never battled through to a firm stand of my own. Even now, with this little sparrow incident, I did not feel at ease, did not know what stand to take.

On the one hand, I definitely had no right to interfere in an experiment conducted by the university, all the more since I had no justifiable suspicion of the zoology department's criminal or even just detrimental intentions. On the other hand, I had seen an animal suffer, an animal that had no power to defend itself; could I shake off this sight by merely looking away, avoiding any connection with it, could I dismiss it from my mind once I had been forced to witness it, was I allowed to do that? Though perhaps legally, even rationally wrong, was I not compelled to follow my emotional and perhaps ethical objections, was I not forced to react to the challenge in a personal way, simply because I had seen the situation as a challenge? Wasn't that what was needed to wake up? Was I now waking up?

The next day my landlady announced to me: "I have as good as rented Linda's room for the fall."

This did not come as a surprise. Linda had finished college and left town several weeks before to accept a job in Hartford, Connecticut. I had expected her room to be rented out. But her mother added proudly:

"We are going to get a German girl in."

"Oh?" I asked, somewhat taken aback, not so much by the prospect of the German girl as by her emphasis on that prospect.

Mrs. van Duyne is a very stern looking woman, who will rarely smile and if she does, she reminds you of an openmouthed fish or an irate gorilla rather than a smiling human. Perhaps a specimen of such a smile can be found in the dictionary under the classification of "landlady's mirth."

Now Mrs. v. D. pulled such a smile and said with visible self-satisfaction:

"I am broadminded, not like so many people around here! I don't mind one bit taking a foreign girl in—as long as she is not colored."

"Oh!" I said again, at a loss for a better response, but she swept my comment away with a wave of her hand.

"You know, the foreign student adviser called me up and asked whether I would be willing to take a German girl in. They come here for a year as exchange students, usually don't speak good English and so they have a lot of difficulties finding rooms. Of course I said it was all right with me, I would be glad to help her with her English, after all, I taught school for, let me see, how many years? I started teaching in 1908, I think, no wait a minute, it must have been later for when the war came I had been teaching—well, anyway, I know how to teach people something, after all, I have helped you along with your English too, haven't I? So I told him, it was all right with me, and at least the girl would have a chance to live with real Americans, though of course you would be here too, but then, your English is pretty good, except for some expressions you use, such as healthy instead of healthful or—"

"I know," I managed to get in. "When is the girl supposed to arrive?"

"Let me finish! I am on the point of telling you anyway!" she said with all the dignity of forty years of teaching. "She won't come before September. But at least I will have enough time to straighten the room out. I don't want anybody for the summer anyway!" And there followed a long description of the state of Linda's room, of the suddenness of Linda's departure, which was no news to me since it had cost me several nights'" sleep while listening to Linda's agonizing, and of the disadvantages of having strangers stay in the apartment during the summer in general, which I did not know whether to relate to myself or not. I preferred not to, and began to dust my room, the only occupation commensurate with that lecture.

Slowly the news sank in and worked itself into my thoughts and all around them. A German girl—again a figure out of the past which I had dismissed and which I had thought dismissed for good. Coming to America I had felt was enough of a break from the experiences of the war, and life here, entirely different and much more satisfactory than anything I had known before, became for me—after a not unusual initial disillusionment and feelings of superiority—the accepted modus vivendi, within which I had to shape my future. The past had been dismissed, so entirely as if it had not been my own at any time but a story read in a novel or seen on the screen. And the present was so full, the pageant so colorful, that I did not even feel impoverished by this absence of a past, by this lack of continuity. Sometimes, when I read some old letters of mine or those written to me, which in a sentimental moment I had kept, or when I glanced at the troubled writing in my old diaries, I would be amazed to find the same anxieties and problems there come up now, the same sort of uneasy love, of halfhearted hate, of fear and hope—the whole gamut of emotions I had ever run through, was still running through. And then I felt that I had not changed at all, not matured at all, and since I did not know whether to be uneasy or glad about this, I just dismissed it from my thoughts.

At other times, I would read these old confessions and marvel at them like at a strange and incomprehensible writing, for they would seem centuries away, and they might move me the way an awkward but sincere child's drawing can move one, or they would bore me the way this same drawing can bore one during a closed moment. And I would feel completely disassociated from anything there, I would feel that this really belonged to me as little as if it had never been mine, and again I would dismiss it quickly and turn toward my pageant.

And now this past keeps coming back at me, with its people and problems, for the second time in a few days, and it has hit me, very low, where I cannot ward off the blow, where it makes me wince. But perhaps this wincing too was needed to wake me up.

I suddenly realized that I did not want this German girl here, that I did not want to have to face her, reveal myself, take a stand, perhaps even try to like her. I had dismissed all Germans from my mind as part of that past that I had slid out of like a crumpled, ugly, rigid skin. I had developed an attitude of aloof superiority which seemed more dignified than actual hatred, and less vulnerable.

But I also realized that this attitude had been an easy escape, that it too belonged to my role as spectator, had lulled me into this long, stagnant sleep which prevented my facing issues, my growing up. And I began to tense my muscles, to force my eyes open and turn my ears toward the sounds, force myself to the surface of my sleep. Perhaps I can already pinch myself and feel it.

It seems as if the past had been waiting around the corner all along, waiting possibly together with that own life of mine which I had neglected, being so preoccupied with the bright colors of the present. I have not caught a clear glimpse of this life of mine yet, but I have seen it flit by, shadowy but existing, and I know that it is hiding behind the past and that I have to approach that first, so that I might then, possibly, if I am fortunate, find behind it that life of mine which I had scorned for seven years. And the past is already all around me. It came to me in these two incidents, it also emerged in Salomon's book *Der Fragebogen* [*The Questionnaire, in which an interrogator elicits a detailed exposition of an individual's life during the Nazi period*], which Kahler had recommended to me, and in Anne Frank's diary, and in my relationship to the Polish, non-Jewish Connie. It can only be coped with within the chain of past relationships and experiences if it is not to submerge me into a new, heavier and more harmful sleep.

4.

Dearest Truderl, [*undated*]

The summer is almost over, and I am thinking of you and your trip. Did all go well, and did you have a good time? Tell me about it as soon as you catch your breath. I hope you didn't have a similar bad spell as last summer, when you had to shorten your vacation and return home to see the doctor.

I did not forget your birthday, though my congratulations are terribly late. A small package will follow, but I have not had time to mail it. I hope you will like that little bit of luxury, especially since I know you are saving every penny for the house. Don't be discouraged if that will take a long time—at least you have the plot on which to build. I am sure that some day the house will be up, and I will get to see it!

My summer was quiet but nice. I taught summer school here since I was very short of money. It was actually fun. In my group were two Chinese students whose English pronunciation was quite a challenge. One was totally unable to pronounce the English "w" properly, always saying "h" instead. No matter how hard I tried, and he tried, it was as if that sound did not exist for him. The other did much better. Both worked hard and were immensely appreciative for my help. At the end each gave me a little present! Nothing embarrassing, just a small decorated cardboard box from one, a fan inside from the other. No one had ever done anything like that, and though I am not sure whether I am allowed to accept presents from students, I did. It would have offended them, had I refused.

I also had quite a bit of company. One weekend Robert came up with his wife, Fran. I like her a lot. Attractive and easygoing. She still seems to be in love with him, even though he probably is not. Sad. Meeting her confirmed me in my resolution to stay away from him completely from now on. Though she acted cheerful and happy, I am convinced she suffers from his spending so much time with his students and who knows whom else.

On another weekend, an old friend from Vienna visited me (we were in the *Matura* class together). Bibi lives in New Jersey and works for Dupont as an engineer. I had the feeling that he was interested in me, but I could not reciprocate, even though he is very nice. His Aunt Anni still lives in Vienna. She and Paul (that's his real name, but we always called him Bibi) were both in hiding during the war. Actually, only he was hidden; she was mostly on the run and had a much tougher time. They survived, though none of their other family members did. Eventually, she married Uncle Max—that was after he gave up hope that Aunt Olga might still be alive and return from Italy. I was in the States by then. I have always liked Anni, and I know she would be pleased if I married Bibi. Unfortunately, I can't. The weekend was very hot, but below the Cornell hill a little river runs at the bottom of a deep gorge, and under a rocky dam there is a wonderful swimming hole. We spent most of our two days together there, swimming and eating water melon (see the enclosed picture).

Recently, I have become friends with another graduate student, Connie, who is in the philosophy department. We take long walks and never run out of conversation topics, even though we are very different. Connie looks quite a bit older than the rest, though he may not be. Just very serious and mature. And gentle, almost fatherly, so that one has the feeling he would take care of you in any situation, and that you can rely on him.

It occurs to me that most of my friends are men—but believe me, I am not looking for an involvement. I am very happy to be on an even keel, with no ups and downs, just enjoying my studies and books, and company whenever I want it. To find someone with whom you harmonize completely is very rare, and if that does not happen, it is better to remain alone. It took me a long time to realize this. Now, finally, no one is pushing me to get married or compete in popularity, and my experience with John was enough to cure me forever.

I hope that you will have a very good year, that working for the government isn't too strenuous or dull, and that Kurt's import problems will soon be resolved. And you need not apologize for not writing more often. I know how busy you are, and I don't write as frequently as I would like to either.

Remain healthy and think of me often!

Your old friend Liesl

Despite the cheerful tone of the letter, Robert's and his wife's visit seriously shook my much-touted equilibrium. The memory of that visit kept haunting me—the pleasant walk in the gorge with Fran, the exuberant picnic with beer and pizza (a photo I found includes, besides Robert and Fran, two fellow students, though I now only recognize one, Eric), and especially how impressed I was by Fran, how much I liked her. How could he be unfaithful to such an attractive, vivacious and affectionate wife! I was determined to withdraw completely, but how do it without hurting his feelings? Life was once again becoming very complicated.

*   *   *

[*carbon copy*]

Dear Robert, Ithaca, Sept. 23, 1952

This morning I registered, and tomorrow classes are starting. But before I begin, I want to thank you for your letter and check. Receiving it at this time made me wonder if you were trying to reemphasize the break. But apparently that was not the case, if I read your letter correctly and, though I think that speaking of "the evening ending on a sour note" is a bit of an understatement, your note made me want to answer before the year starts, and re-discuss the whole matter, for better or worse.

I must admit that I was shocked and hurt by your reaction that Tuesday night. Perhaps I had put too much trust in your understanding, more than any second person asked to follow the meandering pilgrimage of one's own thoughts could ever have. Perhaps I had also not made myself clear or rather not expressed what I had to say, the way I felt it should be said. It has happened to me before that I could not live up to immediate critical situations and their challenge, and I felt afterwards that I had been on the right track but somehow muddled it all up hopelessly. And this I do want to stress—I felt and feel myself on the right track. Perhaps a written explanation of my ideas will be somewhat clearer than my groping sermon that night—or perhaps that can be of no interest whatsoever. I'll try anyway, if only to draw the balance for myself.

This summer was not a very good one for myself. Feeling that I was living only at the surface of things, I fled into the desert, disregarding that the desert may not prove a stimulating surrounding to everybody alike. Some see the stars above it, some only the sand all around them ... I tried to see the stars, but perhaps I tried too hard. Possibly they are only there, and reassuringly there, if you don't try at all. At any rate, instead of rising above it, I sank into the sand and let it all but cover me. I realized this fully at the Bozemans last week. That one evening offered me more of a mental challenge and stimulation than I had met all summer long. And now I know that the desert is not for me.

But possibly for the very reason that I had been thrown back onto my own resources, had analyzed every thought and trait of mine I could discern, I did again become conscious of a few basic realities concerning me, which had been shoved aside or disregarded during the rush of the school year. I did become conscious of my lack at asserting my own judgment, of making my own decisions when upon calm thought they would seem imperative. In my half-dazed state of emotional stress and the mental inertia caused thereby, most of my decisions were haphazardly made and capriciously executed. I could no longer discern any firm pattern in them, hardly even a trend kept consistently. In other words, I could not find much of any individuality, not even of sound rationality.

And so, while I did not manage to see the stars above me, at least I began to search again for the world within me.

When now I searched for that ethical and moral system I had believed to have set up for myself—I found nothing but hollow or ambiguous phrases and, all the worse, I did not find a single deed to support them. Upon honest scrutiny it appeared that for a long time my decisions had been motivated by expediency or selfishness, or momentary relief, or by a half conscious half unrecognized sophistry. Furthermore, and this applies especially to my relations with you through the last few months, that where I had dimly become aware of a need for reevaluation and decision, I had tried to delay or overlook it as long as possible, using excuses and even creating obvious misunderstandings, so that now, when I finally did make a try at coming out clearly and openly—however confusing a try it may have been—there was already this high wall heaped up of those excuses and misunderstandings which rendered straight communication extremely difficult—possibly even impossible. That I don't know yet.

My critical self-evaluation has told me that a relationship such as ours has been in the past, cannot be accepted by me with a clear conscience. Whatever else I may have said in the past—and I have thought it as well!—was self-deceit influenced by your own standards (which are however somewhat different from mine. Being based on a different type of character they needs must be!) and by my own desires and self-complacency. I don't know whether it has actually impaired any other relationships of yours or mine, but the mere possibility of this—and I feel it is by no means very remote!—forbids me to pretend that no harm can be done. And I don't believe in the possibility of achieving good ends with bad means.

Where this leaves us, I don't know. You sneered at me when I said that I would not want to forget any of our common past. If pressed for a self-justifiable stand on this—I ought to wish it undone. I don't even say I do, for I don't. For one, I am no saint, and then there is no sense in discussing the possibility of turning the wheel back if it can't be turned back—no use crying over spilt milk, as you might put it. Even less do I wish to forget it, for it meant very much to me, at least as much as to you. And therefore I must admit that I resented your whimsical comparisons about borrowing money from people etc. They seemed not only unkind, but a bit unjust as well. I just want to state this, not argue about it—for if the wall between us is still up, and it probably is—I can't see what is going on on its other side, and I can't even expect my description of the activities on this side of it to be accepted. But I shall still try to describe ...

So, on the danger of being repetitious, what now—I don't know, and I have no suggestions to make except for trying honestly and sincerely to communicate, possibly with new words, possibly in a new language, but one that both of us understand and will learn to like.

Good luck for the year.

* * *

Hello— N.Y. October 13, 1952

Yes, I know it's quite some time since I received your letter....But I too had to think things out after that talk we had that night...You explained yourself well—there was no argument against it and I tried to explain on the spur of the moment my own feelings.

Then your long letter arrived in answer to my note with the check. Again you stated the case ably, clearly and effectively....

So much so that I had to take all this time to find a moment to answer—not your arguments—but rather all the things that had been reacting in me ever since our talk...

I believed I got something that will serve to explain my reactions to your own decision as to which way our relationship should plot its course—when I climbed Haystack Mountain on another one of my weekends to Vermont—just a week ago.

This time four of us went up—Claybourne, Sid, Fran and I. Had a hunch that the color parade would be at its peak during that first week-end in October and I've never seen it more glorious. It was at peak tide....And if you recall a story I did some time back, you may remember the first line—"High on the hilltops they burn, the blood red spumes of the maples..." It was such a week-end.

We started at one in the morning, drove all night and reached Hogback Mountain at 6:30. Then to the Haystack Cabins for breakfast and a wash and at 10 we began our climb. I had to go slowly—my knee, you know—but regardless of the many times I had been up there in the past—this was the most stirring...It was a tremendous physical and psychical experience...The view from the top—absorbing and tingling to the very roots of one's being...

Perhaps then I knew the real reason I always had climbed it and what I was constantly returning to find. It didn't fail me...

And even though the mountain is far away from my ordinary everyday humdrum routine, it is the knowledge that the mountain there in Vermont can give me that blend of the physical and psychical that it has always loomed so all important to me—always been a sort of purge and renascence at the same time....Perhaps this last time I recognized it as a true catharsis.

So with you—Our relationship though distant—loomed—as I tried to express it to you on our last talk—as a personal and intimate sort of merging the likes of which is given to some people...and as the years went by, it came to mean more and more—Ethics were not involved—Morals were not involved—Codes were not for the mountaintops...

Perhaps our visits were all too infrequent...To be sure—at moments when you felt you needed me—(does it matter which way) I couldn't be there....But there were times when we did have the opportunities of being together and perhaps Interims like the mountain tops made up for so many things...

Any relationship like any flower in my garden must be watered, nurtured, pruned. True some wildflowers grow like greenbay trees but the flowers that have been handnursed so to speak—can they be matched for delicate fragrance, for beauty for tenderness.

What then has happened to ours? Whether your words hadn't been uttered that night; whether you had never thought them at all, we still would have had but few—all too infrequent intervals—for seeing each other—for comparing the notes, the high ones and the lows, the sharps and the flats of the many things that had happened each unto each...And we would have been able to do these things as we had in the past because there is always that intangible essence between us.

There is no question but that we can still be friends..."Yes, I know a gal at Cornell....."...and what of such a thing...The threads of such a relationship wear thin after a time—and life is made up of whole woof and warps of such thin-worn threads...

Since our cords were not woven of such evanescent things as affairs between man and woman, nor of such things as physical love—I was quite sure that our relationship would grow and that such things as Interims could weather the test of a lifetime.

For interims have come to mean to me what the top of Haystack has meant for such a long time. Interims have —I think I have said enough.

How then can we proceed with your ethics—your codes—??? Shall I greet you hence and look at you and say—This was my mountain top but alas this too crumbled?

With all my heart I offer you all the help I shall ever be able to give you—mental, physical, financial—no strings attached and no questions asked. Should you ever find it so—stamp out pride or whatever foolish thing may prevent your coming, writing, or calling.

But I'm a guy—crazy to be sure—who looks to the mountain. I seek out my mountain tops with people too. I've been constant to my mountain from halfway across the world. I try to be that way with people too. Since mountain tops seldom crumble in the lifespan of an individual, I can see them in all weathers— They loom large, different, but true...and one can muse not on what they have looked like or what they have given us—but on what is and what will be.

You have told me that the mountain that was our Interim has caved in—irrevocably....I would rather think that the mountain top is momentarily bleak—its gorgeous foliage gone for the time—but I would like to think of what was, what is and of what will be.

If I am seeking something in you which I am unable to find, or which you are seeking in me and also unable to grasp—then the two of us will take our own turns in the road.

I hope, sincerely, that we can still climb the same road, still seek our same Interims....

Write to me whenever you think that we can walk the same road again....wherever you are and whatever you are doing...

Haystack is a lovely mountain. You're quite wonderful yourself...

Someday, perhaps, we can both take the high road.

        Love,

           R.

* * *

Hello—   October 28, 1952

Apropos of your opening quotation that people only see projected images of themselves in others...may one also remind you of another tale that "beauty is in the eye of the beholder."

But your letter—or your thesis—gave me no clue whatsoever as to where we stand...I read it carefully—Your groping, your weltshmerz (sp?) is highly articulate—and quite polished—but unfortunately it was not revelatory...That inward eye you turned upon yourself or upon my lengthy exposition of my case—yes, my case for your—or, put another way, our need for each other—was in no wise answered—or if it were, the answer escaped me—and I read and re-read seeking for your answer not only between the lines but between every word.

Perhaps the companion you seem to seek—or are fortunate enough to share a moment with—I seem to have found in you. Again, that is what Interim had come to mean to me...I felt for some time that it meant much the same to you...

How else, could one have sensed the change in you so long ago...unless one were so strongly attuned to your moods, your reactions. But I am repeating my last letter.

Do we hold on to what we had—to what we have—? Can you and I walk along—mute or conversant—each on our own and leaning to the other whenever and however and wherever...? Or do you insist on divergent paths?

Stronger than ever, I still give you Interims.

One hopes that like bread cast upon the waters......

                                                Love,

                                                    R

* * *

[*diary entry, undated*]

I am depressed. Stevenson lost—the only intellectual we have had in a long time, and a truly outstanding man. Eleanor, Dave and I were drinking beer all evening while we waited for the results. When they began to trickle in, it got worse and worse: Ike got almost every state! And both Houses are Republican as well, though the Senate almost made it. Once we finally have someone who has the right kind of experience (he is governor of Illinois), who is educated and brilliant, and they all vote for the uniform!

I did help a little and that did me good because it distracted me but I was ashamed before the Billmyers, for they were so much more active. I am glad I have met them, and met them now when I need someone sane so badly. Eleanor has a very interesting face, with her black pageboy and dangling earrings. She also has a lot of style, different from Mrs. B but just as effective. Her voice is so quiet that I sometimes have trouble understanding her. She barely moves her lips when she speaks, but there is a chuckle in her voice and she can be very witty. I don't know if she is older than I but she seems so much more grownup.

Dave likewise is very quiet, but he has a sparkle in his eyes. They both are very American but in a good sense. Clean. Straight forward. I am so glad that they seem to like me. Somehow they are real people, genuine and solid. The only other real person I know here is Kahler and, though he has no idea what chaos I have inside me, I can tell that he is and always will be there for me.

Eleanor works for the university, writing articles and press releases. Dave is in ILR (the School of Industrial and Labor Relations) as a researcher on labor unions, I believe. Both have what is called integrity while I am all over the place. They shamed me by being so much better informed and able to judge what was going on, so I tried my best to inform myself. Of course I cannot yet vote but at least I was able to work for the election. Much good that did but if you live in a democracy that's what you should do, not just live your own private life, especially if like mine, it is always a mess. Right?

5.

November 19

On my birthday I am sitting in my new room, in a good chair at a lovely walnut desk, dark and comforting, and a few trees with bits of golden foliage looking in on me from behind the house. A good setting for recording a nightmare so that it can be forgotten.

I must have mentioned Connie before, the graduate student in philosophy with whom I became friends. He is a bit older than most of my friends, a bit on the short side and not really good looking, with glasses and thinning dark hair, but very gentle and solicitous, with a kind face, a low, melodious voice and compassionate eyes. He comes from Poland, though I never asked him anything about his background. All I know is that he is Catholic which initially held me back. In fact, it gave me a few sleepless nights, for it was like treason to get close to him. I don't want to go into all the reasons, good and bad ones, but they should be obvious.

Of course, I told him that I was Jewish. He did not seem to mind, which may have swayed me, and also that he began to court me, truly court me as no one had before, gently, patiently, with delicious home-cooked suppers in his cozy and neat apartment, with wine and candlelight, and good conversations on long walks. When, after quite some time elapsing, he asked for permission to kiss me, I was ready. It all felt so comfortable that I dismissed my doubts about our totally different background and character, and how I could even think of going with a Catholic.

We had a wonderful summer and fall together. Neither of us went out with anyone else or felt it necessary, and I began seriously to consider marrying him if he should ask me, and I knew he was going to, though we never talked about it. It felt so comfortable, there were no ecstasies or letdowns, just a calm, totally natural pleasure—a real homecoming.

And then he went to a conference in Texas and came back glowing: he had met someone there he had known before and knew immediately that this was it! "You understand, don't you? But let us stay friends."

It was like a slap in the face, and it toppled me completely. In class, I managed to do my work mechanically but once outside, I did not know how to go on. I could not face "home" with the two women shouting at each other (Linda is back and pregnant but that is another story). There was no one to talk to.

The Cornell campus has a bridge over a deep gorge, and almost every year someone jumps. I felt very tempted to let it be me this year. The thought wouldn't leave but became more and more urgent and liberating, till one evening when I decided to do it. After my last class which ended at four. Was it providence, luck or a quirk of fate that kept me from it? I'll never know.

The new home environment helps greatly, especially the daily walk up the hill to the campus, toward the open sky. Betsy is even-tempered and friendly, and the fact that she knows nothing helps too. She is not around much and when she is, I am usually in my room studying. The other day she informed me, with a big grin, that the neighbors across the street had asked who that was living with her now and always drawing the living room curtains in the evening…

"But it's quite all right," she quickly added, "they don't have to be so nosy."

At school I am fine as long as I work. I wish I had someone with whom I could confide. My friends are only casual, but it still helps to be with them, especially Eleanor and Dave. I can of course also drop in at any time on Alicia or on Toby who is in my Nabokov class. I have tried that but the effort to appear cheerful was almost unbearable. And now Eric seems to have developed a crush on me, just like Jimmy before. Why does one always fall in love with people who are in love with someone else? Like in Heine's poem about the young man who loves a girl who has chosen another man who loves another girl and marries her, whereupon the first girl takes the first man who runs across her path— "it is an old story yet it always remains new—*und wem es just passieret, dem bricht das Herz entzwei*" [and to whom it has just happened, his heart will break in two]. Is that the way of the world?

But by now it's over, and I am almost fine.

No, everything was not over, and I was far from fine, as subsequent diary entries will show.

* * *

My dear Liesl,   Vienna, November 24, 1952

Please don't scold me for congratulating you only today on your birthday. I wish you all the more sincerely the very best, and much success in your studies. I know it is insolent of me to write so late, but I can only beg you not to be angry, and to give me another chance. I started three letters, and have not managed to finish one.

Before all else, I want to thank you for your truly delightful letter, which I read several times and answered even more often—to be sure, only in my mind—as well as for your sweet offer to send me some fabric for a dress or suit. That, I think, makes little sense for we can by now get everything we need, and on gifts the duty is about 40%, so it wouldn't be worth it. At any rate I want to thank you for your nice offer, and would like in return to make one to you. Is there anything (I am thinking mainly of art or science books, perhaps good handicraft etc.) which you would like and can't get there, or only at great expense, and which I could send you? Perhaps your customs duties are lower (I would suggest you inquire) and, in that case, I would have the opportunity to send a nice gift. Please think about it.

But now I still need to report briefly on what has happened here since I have written. To be sure, I don't remember when that was, but will begin with the vacation. We remained in Austria this year, spent a few days at the Attersee, then in Salzburg, finally in Fieberbrunn in Tyrol. We were very satisfied both with the weather and everything else, and kept saying "da capo, next year!" Unfortunately, the final week was spoiled by my having heart problems, it was so-called "fibrillations." I have had them several times before, and within a day or two they always disappeared, after I strengthened the heart through rest and strong medication. This time, however, they were more stubborn, and ruined my last vacation week. They could only be got rid of after ten days of intensive treatment. What is unpleasant is that then one can barely walk a few steps; besides it is rather dangerous (one can easily get water on the heart, and it can also lead to sudden cardiac arrest). Therefore the trip home was not very pleasant. Even less pleasant was the fact that the same thing happened once more a few weeks later, and that not even two weeks of intensive treatments could take care of it.

You will imagine my emotional state—I could already see myself spending the rest of my life in a wheelchair. I could barely leave my bed. When Primarius Scharff (my old cardiologist, you may remember) returned from vacation, I went to see him immediately in my despair, and once again he helped me. He explained that such attacks happen with old heart defects, they become more and more frequent and last longer. The only help is to switch the heart to a new activity; that is, the outer chamber has to be completely bypassed, and the inner chamber takes on all the work. That takes a few weeks. Naturally, it has to be done in the hospital under constant electro-cardiographic control and, in fact, immediately.

The next day I was in the hospital, where I spent four weeks, then two more at home. My heart was rerouted, and now I feel almost as well as before. The only thing which one feels constantly is the irregular heartbeat. Of course, the heart is not as strong; also, blood clots can develop easily and could lead to embolisms—some not very pleasant disadvantages in contrast to my previous state of health—but I don't think of that. Instead, I am glad to be a useful human being again. If one were to think of all possibilities all the time, one could no longer enjoy life. Kurt wanted me to stay at home (since I must not exert myself at all), but Prof. Scharff was against that, both for psychological reasons and because he thought that once I felt better, I would do too much at home, and office work is less strenuous than housework. So for a week now I have been working again. In the evening, when I come home, I still lie down—fortunately, *Mutti* helps me greatly with the domestic chores—and in one to two months I hope to be able to live as before. At worst I will have to give up walks.

Kurt too has experienced some tense weeks, professionally. I believe that now all is again moving in the right direction. His business is thriving, only he had considerable difficulties with import permits. The day before yesterday he returned from Stuttgart with the permit to manufacture in Austria, which will secure our financial existence for some time. Now he has the difficult task of starting production here, but it will surely work out. I think the double "downer" (my being ill, he seriously endangered by the new import restrictions) is now behind us.

I hope that my letter hasn't been a mere whining and sounds at least somewhat positive. I beg you again, don't be angry that I am writing only today, and don't punish me by keeping me waiting in turn. I would be so sorry if our correspondence were to peter out. Every letter from you brings me much joy, and I don't want to lose touch with you under any circumstances!

Once more many good wishes for your birthday!

Your Trude

* * *

Dear Liz——   December 14, 1952

It's weeks since I received your answer to my birthday note for you...and though there have been many occasions when I would have liked to have written—I did find myself blocked... Whether I am all to blame for the hurdle or whether your words of last September still are the overpowering obstacle or perhaps—even a combination of both—is an unimportant factor in itself...That a barrier exists where none existed before is of vital significance. I for one would like to remove it—blast it irrevocably out of the way...How you feel—is for you to decide and to let me know.

A year ago Christmas—we celebrated the event in New York—even more—here at the house ...You had a notebook—You read. You poured out

•CORNELL (1952–1953)• 199

yourself in a torrent of words that revealed emotional depth, maturity and more than anything else—more sustained power than you had shown....ever. Of course, still unorganized, still too undisciplined—but definite promise of that ability you revealed years and years ago when you were writing for me in class.

And we celebrated ourselves...Whether the interim that came merely was an outgrowth of the bond between us or simply a manifestation of the bond itself—The Interim was there...The bond between us was sealed again.

And this has been my contention through these months... Whether I myself have gone astray or whether I have been pushed out of your sphere and scheme of things or whether I have made too much of a matter that you may feel irrelevant and immaterial is for you to tell me.

Of course, one would like to hear from you...of you...One would still like to come to you...

I would have answered your note of several weeks ago in this same vein—much earlier...I was snowed under in a tentative business venture that gave promise of becoming something big—which fizzled after weeks of preparation into a dud—and which only now begins to show signs of reviving. But the pressure is off...And I do have time—and this my first Sunday in months and months with the time to write—and with the obstacles somehow overcome—I'm writing to you.

Do I wish you well? That would be stupid to reply to. What is it then? I think we have the potential of recreating a relationship that was strong as it was intimate—but whose strength ebbed on an outgoing tide...But this is the time of the year when the tides are strongest—and who knows but that the flood may bring us together again.

Whichever way we go—let me say now that I do hope your Christmas is a merry one—that the New Year brings you all the things you want. I do hope too—that we shall begin writing again—no holds barred and no barrier existing...and I do hope too that someday I'll get a letter that may once again be signed with an Interim—with a special reference to the capital I.

Until then—
Love-

No, I don't remember the "Interim" of the year before, nor is there a reference to it in any diary entry or letter. And since I am determined not to embellish or fabricate, the question mark will have to remain. Have I eradicated that memory, and perhaps others that were part of this strange, exhilarating and tormenting relationship?

* * *

Dearest Liesl! December 28, 1952

How thrilled I was to receive your Christmas card—which by the way was very beautiful and stood the entire time under our tree. I know you must have been very busy, or you would have enclosed a letter. Why did you move? And is the new place more restful than the old one?

Many, many thanks for your wonderful package. It arrived last week and gave me great pleasure. Don't apologize for sending it so late, this way I put it under the tree for Christmas Eve. I have been wearing the nightgown for several days now. Kurt is thrilled with it; he finds that no color has ever suited me so well, and wants me to buy more underwear in that color from now on—not always the "dull white and pink," as he puts it.

Dearest Liesl, I would like to please you with something as well, but I don't dare guess your wishes and your taste as well as you did mine. Besides, I think that with clothing I could hardly please you as much, since over there ready-made apparel is so much better than here. But I remember your writing about an art book you bought at the museum. What would interest you? Please, let me know, and I will look around. Or anything else. Don't forget to let me know.

As for my health, I feel much better. Don't worry, and don't think that I am depressed. My circulation seems to have adjusted well to the new heart rhythm, and I feel quite normal. Besides, this year I have not yet had the flu, despite the advanced season—thus I have every reason to be cheerful and feel well. I now know that I have to avoid exertion even more, and I am watching it—I don't try to do all I would like to do. The rest I leave up to fate.

Otherwise—thank God—there is not much news. We had a lovely Christmas, an enjoyable New Year's Eve, and are arranging our weekends as beautifully as possible with interesting books and records. (Kurt gave me Bruckner's Fifth for Christmas, which is also the fourth anniversary of our engagement.) We now have a television set since there are finally sensible TV program (without advertising). We see each week at least one transmission from a Viennese theater (one of the good ones), or a studio production and other interesting programs. However much I objected to television before, now I am enthusiastic if one uses it sensibly, as we do, and does not watch everything.

Dearest Liesl, I must quit now and would be very happy to receive a letter from you soon, preferably with a wish list.

Many greetings and hugs from
Your Trude

6.

I found only two letters from Robert for 1953 (though he refers to others), and a very minimal correspondence with Trude. However, there is also a new diary, entitled "Dedicated to the Search ... (1953-55)." Quite a few of its entries predate the arrival at Yale, and especially the early ones show how difficult it had been to come to terms with the Connie episode.

Jan. 2, 1953

Humbly I search, humbly and painfully stumbling as awkwardly as a child that has not yet accepted its legs, bruising against objects that don't belong and yet stand firmer and more stubbornly than I ... No, no longer stubbornly, there can be no stubborn force where there is a search and clear will.

There is no fear, and no impatience now, but much bewilderment. Why did I not know that it is not the knowledge of one's limbs, of one's mind, of others' minds that teaches one how to live. Why have I tried to live other people's lives for so long instead of searching for my own, why did I look for "the" world, everybody's world, in which I had to get lost, because it was not my own world? No, I don't want to question, nor accuse myself. Even this blindness has come out of me, was in me and had to be overcome.

I don't know how many people manage to live their own lives. Trude is one of them, and Hanna seems to have found it as well. She is wise and cautious, and so the reigns don't slip from her fingers too frequently. Only from hints did I realize that they sometimes do, and I admire her all the more for it. Her husband is good-looking, selfish and moody. He is also very fond of her, and probably would not want anybody else to be the mother of his children. There are none, so far, for every time they had saved a little money to afford the necessary silver spoon, he surprised her by a sudden purchase, once a car, then again a television set. So she dismisses thoughts of walks and hikes together with a faint yearning for her gay childhood days in Ostrau and the Carpathian mountains, so she buys a few classical records for herself which she can play every Tuesday night when he is at a meeting and not watching television, and she continues working in his office eight hours a day and saving money.

She is not unhappy, not even very disappointed, for the "big boy ought to have his toy if it means so much to him" and some day they are going to have the baby too. While her husband watches television, she sews her own drapes and bedspreads and is glad that he is at home and not spending his time and money somewhere without her. For he is attractive to women and she is never quite sure of him.

He is in the reserves and once a month she stays alone for a day or two. She fears these days, not for what they may do to him but for what they do to her. They make her lonely and dissatisfied, and leave her empty and perhaps even bitter. But when he comes back, she knows she would not want to live a different life.

Hanna: After many years without contact, I recalled that her daughter had moved to Israel. Since I was planning a trip there, I checked the New York telephone directory, just in case Hanna was still listed. Yes, indeed, there was the familiar address, but it had her son's name! I phoned, worried that she might have died, and ready to explain who I was; but there was Hanna's voice, unmistakable, cheerful and bubbling as ever. She was delighted to hear from me, and in a long conversation we tried to bridge the span of many years. She was living alone. Her husband had died in 1974 of a heart attack. She managed his import business for several more years but was now retired, her days filled with hiking, folk dancing, painting and traveling—to folk dance festivals, to her son and his family in Los Angeles, to her daughter in Israel. In fact, every year she would sign up for a short-term stint in the Israeli army, which paid for her flight and gave her free weekends. "Don't you have to be a citizen to do that?"—"No, they are glad to get people to do menial jobs like kitchen duty or painting the barracks. And it is just for four weeks at a time. I love doing it." I was impressed.

When I met her daughter Judy in Rehovot, I liked her immensely. Full of vitality and energy, just like her mother. She was working as a midwife, was a dedicated environmentalist, deeply involved in community affairs, and a wonderful mother to her three little girls. She was raising them by herself, divorced from their father, who had returned to the States. No, she did not intend to go back. Judy wanted to know everything I could remember about her mother's childhood. "My father's death must have hit her very hard," she said. "She never remarried."

When I quoted Judy's words to her mother, Hanna protested emphatically: "Baloney!" she laughed. "Don't you believe it! I tried very hard to find someone, though by now I have just about given up. I simply never met anyone I could see myself living with, and when I did, he wasn't free." But she still seemed to be taking life in her stride.

* * *

Jan. 6

Language: We all sin against you, we trespass in you and abuse you who are ever willing and generous! You are the path, but we obstruct it with weeds stones and shrubs, and we cut painful furrows into it and cover them with treacherous dissipated sand.

When I first began to use the English language, I was humble enough. I wondered whether I could ever master it, own its every shade and melody, the way it must be owned if it is not to remain a stranger, unknown and abused. And what have I done during four long years? I have snatched it toward me, clasped what I could hold with my two hands, and carried it triumphantly forward. Not confronting it any longer, not seeing how I was only clasping and mutilating shreds, and loosing pieces all along the way which did not even lead somewhere. Small wonder I was deluded and thought I could write, and no wonder that what I rashly presented as my creation, was mercilessly rejected.

I stand outside the fortress and its walls seem harsh and unstructured, sometimes of an unforgivable functionlessness without the excuse of artistic extravagance, then again so boringly even and simple that the slightest complication would seem a blessing.

Of course, I know that my judgment is only so bitter because I am outside the wall at the moment, defeated and humiliated.

And already I know that the path of my search must lead through the fortress and that I have to pass through other people's gates and go on searching inside, so that I may one day find my own gate out again, the only gate that will really lead farther ... I must not think at this time of the horrible vision that I may be spending all my life in front of that gate, waiting without ever getting through it ...Or perhaps I should keep in mind even that possibility, for only the chosen are strong enough to go through and on, yet there is no way around the fortress. Would Peer Gynt have been to go around?

P.S. I feel I must stop—and yet I do it without satisfaction and relief: I have not said half the things that I felt in me and I have not said what I did say the way I felt it wanted, needed be said. I shall still have to discover my own method: is it better for me to write and write and then weed and file, or ought I to be more disciplined and relentless from the start, with every word and sound? And do I write about myself, does one have to write about oneself, no matter how disguised? Or is this solipsism, self-indulgence, Narcissus drowning instead of turning away from the pond, either toward the world or toward the heavens?

Oh, how many obstacles, how difficult to really learn to walk!

* * *

Jan. 11

Twice recently my eyes were open, quite unexpectedly, and nature came and sank into me strong and personal.

The first time it happened on a subway ride in New York, on the BMT, Manhattan-bound. The subway was half empty, with a few stale faces subdued by chewing-gum. The windows were blindly withdrawn from the tunnel's darkness, and they seemed to swallow up the dull yellow light inside, till it reflected its own poverty without much conviction. I was a figure next to others, reflected like they in the windows across, dully and lifelessly. And then we emerged onto the bridge and the outside swept the shadows off the panes. It was shortly before six, and already quite dark outside. But the skyline was dotted, no, suffused with lights, for the workday had not yet ended, and every window contributed its spark of light. None of the people in my subway car looked up, and I felt an impulse to call out to them and tell them to look, shake them to make them not only look but see what I was seeing.

For I saw New York, not as a giant monster, not as simply a big busy city, but a city that was put together and rendered a whole by subways, however dim and dirty, and by the river, and by huge houses which really "housed" people and gave them work and words and community. Why had one ever invented the word "skyscraper" for them? This word has belied their existence, has falsified it, even hidden it, until all humanity was sucked out and they remained drained and dried up skeletons, seemingly erected only for publicity and display. But that moment I saw them alive, for the first time alive—my New York!

One other time I saw, a few days ago, again as dusk fell. But it was still earlier, the time of deepening shadow and of darkening outlines. And as I perceived the trees from my window, my hand on the window shade, I could not pull the shade down, so powerful and intensive was the view. Snow covered the street, and the garden patches in front of the houses had assumed a violet whiteness, through which the gray emerged in mere patches. The trees had drawn violent lines across the snow, engraved themselves into it, the way they do in a painting by Van Gogh. The intensity of the contrast was enormous. It breathed such tension, such unsolved and insoluble violence that my breath turned hot. It emanated such concentrated power, that I could not escape its threat. And then, within moments, the shadows lost their violet tinge and relapsed into gray, the outlines of the trees dissolved into dark patches, and I left the window awed by what nature had allowed me to see before it withdrew.

* * *

Jan. 12

It is quite surprising that the preceding pages live as they do, if I think of the painful process which led to them! As always, I read the last pages I had written before leaving school so that on my way home I might think about them. I did and felt I had something important to say ... And yet at home I was joyless and my mind unwilling and dull. I took some sewing—for I could not study—and hoped my fingers would appease my mind. I listened to music, took up an anthology of verse—but they hardly left an imprint. Only my good old Frost's matter-of-factness calmed me a bit. I read a few pages of Thomas Wolfe, and they fitted in with the trend of my thoughts. I hardly spoke at dinner, then I wandered round and round in my room, smoked three of Betsy's cigarettes, I who never smokes, until I finally could sit down and write!

* * *

Jan. 21

There was a long barren pause up to this moment when I take the pen again, a pause of reluctance before an especially difficult insight.

When I was a child, I saw very poorly and tried to hide this shortcoming for fear of laughter or pity. Therefore I did not look at things carefully so that I might not be expected to see what I really did not see. Later, when glasses had finally been forced upon me and usually were not quite strong enough (I think that corresponded to the theories of the day), I again refrained from focusing my eyes on any far object or person, so that I might not give the impression of having seen something that demanded a reaction.

Only now I realize how deep-rooted that fear was and how it kept me from learning to see altogether. I supplied emotions instead, emotions not based on sensations but on my own yearnings and insecurities. And so in the end I did not meet people, I only met my qualities in them, and their reactions to me!

All I want to do now is to begin seeing and see what it was that has kept me from it in the past for so long, and if possible, find any beginnings I might have already touched or anticipated.

One person has almost succeeded in making me see. Robert has done all that could be done by an outsider. He has revealed to me the mission of waiting, of patient listening and watching, quite passive, just all eye and ear and one great willingness. But he has become so penetrated by this willingness of his that it has taken his own life into it and transformed it until it has become part of all these other lives that live in his ear and his eye. In the beginning I could only see that gap where his own life should have been and I could not understand why all these other lives should be allowed to crowd around and cling and make demands.

By now I have begun to understand him. Little by little, with many misconceptions intruding and many whimsical emotions interfering. But the realization of my own failure to just listen and look and accept without questioning has led me towards more understanding, just because I know now it must remain a limited understanding.

Now that the block has been surmounted, I begin to see a stretch of road again, perhaps not yet my own road, it is true, but one lined by people and things all of which are looking at me ...

* * *

[*this undated copy of a letter to Robert might belong here*]

Hello -   Saturday, 8:40 p.m.

This then is the moment we may have both been waiting for—the moment that wants to be used for a long letter to you. A letter to you, and somehow also a letter to myself, an attempt at reaching myself via letter at least since all other approaches seem to have caved in or are lost in a maze of steps.

In your good long letter you made a remark, rather harshly and cholerically, but still different from all other remarks. At least it must have been, since it penetrated so deeply into me and is still spreading and growing there. You just said, probably in utmost disgust, something like—"if you will consider every word you say to somebody as leaning on that person, I'll mark you nuts in my books ..." Yes, perhaps this desperate attempt to withdraw into myself, though it had sprung from a genuine desire to have time and freedom to set my own house in order—this attempt, instead of leading me to a firm basis, was dragging me into a whirlpool.

I am coming back, or perhaps not back, for there is never a coming back, only a going forward, or a standing still. I am going forward then, again, to our friendship, whatever and however it will be. I also don't yet know what if anything I will be able to contribute to it, except for the yearning for it. I bring an experience along that has pulled and torn me to the last tenable moment. Nothing dramatic, only an uncanny sleepwalker's march toward the precipice of utter inner dissolution—and to the very brink of it, now in its most direct physical sense. It was a narrow escape, all the more so because it came about not by my own strength but by the lucky streak of outside interference. All this may sound unintelligible, but I prefer to leave it so and have your intuition extract what it can. I repeat, don't search for facts, this terrible dying off and dissolving within me was brought about, it is true, by an outward disappointment, but surpassing it by far. I have tried to trace this development in writing, more as a means to retain an experience as terrifying as this so that it might not have been had in vain—but those pages are still too raw to really exist, even for me. I tried to re-read them last night, but they can't be read. Perhaps they can be made to live some time, their own independent life, but the moment is not yet.

But it is the moment to write you. I feel it and therefore I also know that you will understand, not with your mind, but with all of you that knows me. Or rather knew me, for at the moment there are only loose ends that I am gathering up again where I find them, trying to dust or wash them and put ointment to the ones sorely bruised. But I may not have found the right ointment so far, or perhaps there is no miracle-working ointment. And many of those loose ends I haven't found yet. But I have patience now, and that is the strongest sign that I am breathing again.

This is an awful letter—but something makes me write it, that is not me, and perhaps that same something will enable you to read it.

To go crazy cannot really be a sickness—it is just that utmost degree of loneliness that the body will bear though the mind has been torn out of cohesion by it. Is it perhaps true that the mind can only bear it if it transforms it into an existence, a being of its own, a *creation*, and if it cannot succeed at that—then there is no way out, or rather no way of staying. No, I won't continue in this vein, I am not even truthful, for at other times—in stronger moments than this one—I have been grateful for having been allowed and able to go through this depth, and even if no enriching may be visible immediately, it may already be in my blood, it may have merged and fused with its substance and raised its bitterness into something much stronger and richer.

Don't misunderstand my tone—I am getting well. This is only a slight reverberation of the other great loneliness of the past—but it is only caused by the silent apartment and the melancholy drip of the bathroom faucet, it is no longer inside me.

I don't know where and how we two can start—this will all have to be given to the moment's mercy. I am not yet strong enough for any concrete expectations or suggestions, and perhaps this is all to the good. Somehow the knowledge that you are still there, after all this, that you have somehow, even if not consciously, gone along, up on the rim perhaps while I was down below, but walking in the same direction and *seeing* me, so that now that I emerge, you are there and turned towards my ascent—somehow all this must make something quite new and unimaginable out of our Interims, so don't start spelling them with a small I, if you can in any way help it.

Let me say hello now and thank you—for being here.

* * *

Hello. Liz— February 7, 1953

I hope your exams have been concluded in the successful fashion you had hoped for rather than feared. Perhaps with these bugbears out of the way, you might sit down and write me a real letter—(Provided your tale of Liz Welt in the slough of despond doesn't make you feel as if you're leaning on somebody for support, salvation, solution, solace, security, and sympathy.)

Two things in your letter is prompting this reply—One—your salutation began with a simple Hello (something your last note sadly lacked) The second—may I quote—"And don't start spelling Interims with a small i—if you can in any way help it."

That last sentence even made me feel that you are no longer a consummate idiot, but just a plain ignorant bastard. Where I can't tolerate morons, I do have a soft spot in my heart for the second....

But first things first. Of Arthur...His depressive mood has worn itself into a state of enthusiasm for his day school at a radio-tee-vee institute (tuition for which is being paid for by the rehabilitation committee). He works at Nedicks on 1st Avenue and 23rd from 4 to 10, earning 22 bucks a week, and lives in some rat-hole on E. 56 Street—(it can't be palatial—he pays but 5 a week). As I said, there was a good chance of his getting connected with a friend of mine in the electrical business—but Art's lapse cost him that...Now he's tied up in other schemes and we'll have to wait to see what comes of it. I manage to see him for a few brief minutes over at Nedicks at least once a week—

My own new term is running its course...Since the chores at night school are usually the same—the only difference in the classes I teach, result from the make-up of the groups themselves. Last term, the work was interesting—the groups were pleasant personable and capable. Too early to tell about this crop.

Did you really mean Interims could be capitalized again?

If so, then it's high time you sat down and wrote to me. If you are going to proceed in the false interpretation that talking to someone is the same as leaning on that person, you will be marked nuts in my book.

Once last September I walked out on you simply because you were becoming all screwed up about standing on your own feet, new ethics, new ideas and lots of other things. I was annoyed. Bothered. And hurt. Regardless of your shennanigans at that time—you gave me the feeling you were far, far away—in another country and speaking another tongue...Even Interims wouldn't have reached you then (and those too you threw out) but what was the most unkindest cut of all was the fact that you even ruled out the idea that through understanding, empathy and compassion—one might spell things with a Capital I again.

Think it over...This is February. Interims were first capitalized two years ago. Even letters can be written in caps.

Much love,

R.

* * *

March 2

Two days ago I finished reading Sartre's *Nausea*. I don't think anyone can read this unchallenged, and so I woke up again, at least into a semi-slumber, one of those states of drowsiness, during which you can hear and understand words about you, and can even comment on them in your mind, but somehow vaguely, lazily, without being able to undertake the effort of actually opening your eyes, or speaking, or even moving.

But when today I walked out onto the road, towards the fields and snow and trees and sunny hills, along a deserted country road, I suddenly found myself wide awake—no, more than awake, full of this four-dimensional clarity which comes upon us only sometimes and very unpredictably. For as I walked uphill, on a wet empty and uneven road with glistening snowy patches, without a sidewalk, just lined by bare emaciated trees, a few garden patches w. name plates which pointed to the houses further back, and long white horse-smelling fields, I saw a figure before me, a man's, walking fast into the horizon so that I could not tell whether there was an aim before it or not in this lifeless wintry hillscape. But I saw this figure before me for a long time, in the middle of the road, head and shoulders dark against the light gray sky, flanked by the black twisted lines of trees left and right. And then it reached the peak of the road and began to sink into it, until it immerged totally, while the trees still stretched their branches upward, one right, one left.

And then I suddenly saw that other figure that was myself, saw it walk along an empty road, uphill, shaded with motionless trees, I saw the road lead across the hill in a motionless countryside of many such hills under a grayish white sky, I saw an enormous curved expansion of such hills under the sky, I saw or rather I felt, for it transcended seeing, an enormous ball under this same sky, not moving, for the tranquility around rendered it impossible to imagine rapid giddying motion, no, simply a huge inert ball with one figure on a hill road on top of the ball, moving and permeated by all this, and a part of it, and yet by its acceptance and knowledge transcending it, beyond mere existence, the way Sartre has arrived at it. And I suddenly knew that I could decline Sartre's existentialism for myself, that existence was the beginning but not the end, and that there was something fuller, more powerful in us that could lead us from existence to life, to our own life, if we were only open and patient and eager enough to seek for it. And I felt that I was on the right path towards it, that one had to return and begin at the very beginning, that one had to break with everything until existence became clear and bare again, as Sartre had done it, but that then, with this new consciousness which is the first letter in everyone's alphabet—and how few people today can still write or even read ... that then one had to go on beyond existence, towards one's own life. Sartre, too, speaks of an involvement, but it is a haphazard involvement, willed by oneself perhaps, but planless, planlessly committing. But this cannot be all—man can do more than that!

There are two missions for man, and for man alone for he can discern: He is an individual, a unique, mysterious and powerful individual, and he can shape his own unique, powerful, mysterious life and thus actualize himself. Thus and only thus he really lives up to humanhood. But he is also a part of a whole, a part of nature and of mankind, and he has to find his own place therein, his own relationship thereto, again unique, mysterious and powerful, and thus fulfill his function within the world. This function may consist of incredibly small and simple relations which contribute strands to the web, or of a definite color pattern within this web, or even of one of the underlying main tissues.

The web in its totality cannot be seen by one of its particles, nor the presence or absence of a plan or a maker discerned, but a failure to take one's place within it by one's very existence, even before it, and shirking it now would equal a tearing away and destroying or mutilating a whole section.

What difference, then, can it make to such a piece of thread whether the web is woven by a machine according to technical rules (for even there the thread can tear and thus change the whole pattern or at least cause local irregularity!) or whether a weaver has predesigned its development (again with the variant of tearability!) or whether forces are constantly at interplay with the development of the web, shaping it and being led by it to further shaping.

And thus existence should not, as Sartre seems to see it, be the only stable denominator in a chaotic world, to be forgotten in the very attempt at transcending it creatively, but it should be the first letter for an inscription.

I wish I could talk to someone besides you, diary, about all this, share these insights. But to whom? Robert? No, he wouldn't understand, either smile indulgently and hug me, or perhaps get irritated by all that talk, not realizing how much more important all this is than drinking Scotch until the only thing that matters is physical ecstasy. Trude? No, I am too embarrassed to let her see the chaos inside me, while she thinks I am doing so well, am so sane and have such a good sense of humor. So I can only hint at things to her.

But perhaps that is as it should be, must be—being alone as a first step to self-reliance, to self-realization. Let it be so.

* * *

Thursday

It has descended like crows and covered my soul by its shroud,
Warm and heavy, making it ready for sleep. The great tormented sleep.
But a ray must have pierced it, the sigh of a falling leaf
And given it movement and given a chill and a speck of life.
Not for rebellion—the shroud is thick, it strangles passion before it is born.
But to wince and to stir and cry out against sound, and to stretch
And reach and force a crack in the shroud
And see light and hear laughter once more.
But the crack is not wide and it is closing again.
Hold on, my soul, breathe deep at the chink, hold fast, my soul,
And perhaps at last some ear will catch your moan and some eye your tear
And will reach out through fear and will touch you and bless.
And my soul is too weak even to hear its own fear:

Come soon, bless soon, I am in distress…

7.

Dearest Trudekind,   Ithaca, March 21, 1953

Congratulations on your moped, which seems to be a true flying carpet. If it could only carry you to me! This must mean you are feeling better, perhaps totally "normal" again?

Yes, you sensed correctly that something was wrong, and I apologize for not writing in such a long time. I have, actually for the first time in my life, tasted utter loneliness to the bitterest sediment, but can only now talk about it. Connie broke off our relationship (that was about four months ago), and it hit me really hard; somehow I couldn't get over the episode. I lost myself more and more within myself, till contact to the outside seemed meaningless and an inner resolution totally impossible. I lost my individuality completely, really completely. Since I acted and talked normally toward the outside, half mechanically, half dissembling (perhaps from a self-preservation drive?), no one noticed how miserable I was. That made it even worse, for I did not find a single outstretched hand, and my will was too paralyzed for me to stretch out a hand myself. I survived by a miracle, a simple logical miracle: I reached the point when I could not go on, literally, and at that last moment accidental, unsuspecting friends grasped me and pulled me away from the cliff…

Now it is finally going better, very slowly, for I gather my dispersed and torn pieces only painfully and singly together, and feel far from complete. However, I have at least some will power back, and thereby also a future. All that probably sounds very confused, but I can't formulate it more clearly. It began with my disappointment about C. and the ensuing self-criticism, but grew so uncannily and confusingly beyond all real events that it cannot be put into concrete words.

In brief, it was a bad, bad year, and at times it seems to me that, since I survived that, I can survive anything. However, it is disquieting that months of that awful helplessness and loneliness haven't brought me a step further, that I experienced all that totally negatively and destructively, without growing. For now C. is back and, as if that entire year had not happened, I was again totally ready for him, totally available, though I hated myself for it. And as before, he made me understand (even more clearly) that the beauty of our relationship lay precisely in its being totally in the present, its absolute, unchangeable lack of a future (!). But perhaps the year was not wasted, and perhaps the pain I felt was only a sign of my undiminished affection. For now I am at least capable of affirming the present the way he wants me to, if not with a light heart. And I also know that when this is over, when I can bring about a drastic change (a trip, moving to a different place—perhaps not even that is needed since he is leaving in June), I will be able to go on.

At any rate, this so very painful experience—and please don't be appalled by the big words—taught me one thing: emotionally I am still very immature and allow myself far too much to be dominated, perhaps because nothing is stable around me, no regular job, no obligations, no truly close friends. Perhaps all that only came about because of that overwhelming aloneness which I cannot yet cope with.

This is not turning into a cheerful nor a lucid letter, Truderl, and I don't know how much sense it will make to you. But I hope that you will somehow understand me, intuitively more than logically. And, if that's not too immodest to ask, do write soon. If I had not been so passive and thereby forgone all claims to a letter, you might have perhaps been able to help me a little.

I am not sure if I mentioned to you that I had also stopped all contact with Robert. That was during the stage of my great withdrawal into myself, which was supposed to bring me closer to the stars but instead dropped me in the desert. Robert must have empathized: at least I recently received a few letters from him that were so warm and heartfelt that I realized how wrong I had been, and how hurtful to myself and to my true friends my rejection had been. There are no black and white positions. I knew that once, and had only forgotten in my sweeping interior house cleaning that these delicate, rare links of true human relations have to be nurtured and protected, not swept or washed away. Now I am slowly beginning to collect and nourish them again. Still with little strength, but with much patience.

I want you to know that your letters are always so full of warmth that they strengthen me for days. If this were not so impossible—and also immodest—I would wish to be allowed to be near the two of you for a few days. I know there would be enough warmth for me as well. But that is all nonsense. And I would only depress you.

My plans are still entirely uncertain. At times I am so tired that I would just as soon end my studies in June when I receive my Master's (hopefully!), and accept a quiet, undemanding job somewhere. But then again I think that I couldn't stand that for long, and that I do want to teach. Which means another two to three years to the PhD. I have applied to Yale, but at the moment all I want is to give myself a long summer, teach summer school, and travel before and after, to California, perhaps even to Mexico if my savings hold out.

Yes, I have moved, and I now have a large, attractive room in a three-room apartment. It is not in College Town but at the bottom of the hill. In good weather the walk to the campus is beautiful. For bad weather there is a bus. On top of everything else, in my old place the mood had become nightmarish after the daughter returned home from three months' work elsewhere married, pregnant and talking of divorce! A configuration of the most unfortunate circumstances, which depressed me all the more since I could not help in any way. Betsy, who owns this apartment, works and isn't home much, but she is quiet and pleasant, and very grown up.

This is a confusing letter, but now that I seem again able to communicate, a more cheerful letter will follow soon. And please write that you are with me, and say so often, often! And I am keeping my fingers crossed that you continue to be well.

Affectionately, I am your old friend—whether a friend or not, but old, for sure, old and worn—even if it is not noticeable—and also childishly young, stupid and unteachable—

        Liesl

* * *

[*carbon copy*]

Dear Robert,   Ithaca, June 3, 1953

So I have made it, on all counts, and yet it feels more like a defeat than a victory. But I will go to Yale in the fall, and that will, I hope be more interesting and less anguished than Cornell was. I was lucky to get in and get a fellowship, mainly I think because Comparative Literature is a new program so they may not have many applicants, especially women. And the chairman is Czech, like me.

I have my M.A. but it was touch and go. When I handed the thesis in, Mr. Lange returned it saying that it was good but needed some rewriting. That I was too influenced by Rilke, whom I was writing about, and therefore not objective enough. Each chapter should have an introduction and a conclusion. I was horrified. I pointed out that there is a detailed introduction at the beginning and an extensive conclusion, and that I would be repeating myself. But he insisted, that pedant. All right, I said resigned, in that case I will have to spend another semester here.—"Oh no," he said, "you have a whole week! You can manage it."

I practically killed myself rewriting, engaged a typist who literally was sitting next to me and typing as I handed her each page. And when I took it to Lange, a week later, he reached for the form and signed it without even looking at the thesis! Was I mad!!!

No, Cornell was not a good experience, though it began so well. The courses at Sarah Lawrence were far more stimulating, even if they were not systematic and I may not be able to use what I learned there in my teaching. Except for Kahler whose courses I loved and who has urged me to stay in touch. Perhaps I was too much an outsider at Sarah Lawrence, but here I became too much an insider, I guess, and that was worse. You used to say I needed to let my hair down. I did and that was a great mistake. I began to float, drift and then to sink, and was submerged for a long time. I know you sensed it even though I could not talk about it. But please don't give up on me yet—I am on my way back to the surface. Only it may still take a while.

I will be in Middlebury for six weeks studying Russian.

    Be well—

*   *   *

Dearest Truderl,   June 15, 1953

The year is over, and, after a very difficult two weeks with much last-minute rewriting, my thesis was accepted, and I can now call myself Magister Artium, whatever that means. And more good news—Yale has accepted me, and is giving me a decent fellowship. When I applied, I told them that I had to refuse before because Cornell had offered me a teaching assistantship on which I could live, whereas on their offer I could not; but that I would definitely prefer to continue my studies at Yale and, if possible, in their new Comparative Literature Department. That must have done it. I just hope I will be up to it. It means that I had to back out of teaching summer school at Cornell (Prof. White was very angry!), because Yale requires three modern foreign languages, and my Russian is weak. I have signed up for a six-week intensive Russian course in

Middlebury, Vermont.

At Yale I will be a PhD candidate, and live at the International House. I will probably have to share a room, but it is quite inexpensive, and I hope to be able to concentrate fully on my studies, and not have to take on additional work.

This is just a short note, but it will keep you informed. I still have a lot to take care of before leaving. Oh, yes—you keep reminding me to tell you what you could send me—there is no need to send anything! I know you are saving every penny for the new house, and I have everything I need. But if you insist—perhaps a small sketch of some pretty corner of Vienna, so that I can remember it and you, whenever I look at it? But please don't spend much money!!

I hope everything is going well? I haven't heard from you in a long time!

With hugs and kisses, and sending my very best wishes to your mother and Kurt,

    Your Liesl

* * *

June 23

Here I am, after a very long pause. It was again a time of submerged existence, of muffled unreal reality, and only now the pain has subsided, was first followed by a dull ache—but when I listened to Brahms' piano concerto, it sank into me and cooled and comforted me. Perhaps it has to be like that, perhaps this is my life, this constant, desperate struggle for balance, while I myself am made that way that every impression from the outside sinks into me tumultuously and painfully, disturbing that balance. Perhaps I need this constant gripping with challenges to feel alive, and so, whenever my environment does not provide them, I create them on my own, talk myself into complications, and unbalance myself out of my own doing. And all the while there is this underlying need for balance, this tenacious desire to find my way through the chaos to clarity—and to a new chaos.

If this is I—why? Why this painful, painful way of experiencing? Does all sensitivity have to be paid for by such an unalleviated, tormenting struggle? Or is it up to me to turn this struggle into creative channels? I don't know but I must try, as long as I can keep my head above water—and even if I could never do more than keep it just there!

What if one had one free wish and wished not to be able to fall in love, and not to miss that inability? Wouldn't life on an even keel be easier? But wouldn't it also be devoid of hope, of excitement, of expectation? Perhaps that is the way one feels if one is old, but it sounds so sad. There must be an in-between, a growing up, a maturity which keeps feelings within the right proportions. Will I ever reach it?

* * *

July 21, Middlebury

Just a few lines so that I can read them, should I get depressed again. Middlebury is a real release, I have left everything that happened in Ithaca far behind. Perhaps this is a cowardly solution, and it will all catch up with me again, but I am sure all that soul-searching just got me enmeshed more and more in my own dark corners instead of showing a way out. And I am not simply escaping—I am doing something useful for my future career, and really acquiring knowledge as well. And I begin to look forward to Yale.

* * *

July 26

This day must be noted down, for it was again one of those days on which a walk, "my walk" became memorable for an insight it revealed.

It was nothing new, really, and yet overwhelmingly important. After weeks of unhappiness, insecurity and nervous restlessness I finally started out this last week on "my" walk, towards the sky and the wide open spaces of the hillside. It was evening, shortly before sunset, clear and warm, with crickets chirping, birds still singing and some man-directed machine clattering across the fields quite far in the distance. Behind the turn to the cemetery was a cattle exhibition. One could not see it from my skyway, but the voice through the loudspeaker reached me, and so did an occasional lowing of the cows and heifers.

And suddenly I knew not only that I must write but how I must write and what, what my problem was and always would be, and that it was a problem wider than I and valid. It was the conflict between mind and emotions, the desire at harmony between the two and yet the inability to always achieve it, the pain of blundering, always as intense as before since every situation is really new and emotions just don't react rationally.

Every individual has to fight this fight, always has had and probably always will have to. There are those to whom the fight is easy, or unimportant, and those who have no strength or desire to fight at all and succumb to one of the two aspects. But the fight is hardest for those who see it clearly yet know that they can only win battles but never the war, that they have to fight from day to day in order not to succumb, though they will never win a final victory as long as life stirs in them.

*   *   *

My dearest Liesl,   Vienna, July 28, 1953

It's been a while since your dear letter arrived, but I ungrateful soul only manage to answer today. I am delighted to finally know a wish of yours. I am sure I will find something suitable, except that it will take time. At any rate, I will try to meet your taste and hope that I will succeed.

Now I want to give you a short overview over the last half year. I almost think that you have not heard from me since winter. I would like to say first—so you won't have a shock—that I am healthy at the moment, and as happy as a lark. I only hope that I will cause fewer worries to my poor Kurt in the future. In March I acquired a thorough pneumonia, which did not react to either sulfanomides or penicillin. Only streptomycin produced the desired result. Unfortunately, it gave me a very bad rash.

I had hardly recovered (some four weeks later), when I caught an insignificant cold and awoke one night spitting blood for several hours. I had a high fever, and my heart was behaving very badly. To top it all, the next day was a holiday (Ascension Day), and every physician I knew was unreachable. Of course I caused Kurt a sleepless night—I myself was far too exhausted to do or want anything—but thanks to his care I was in the hospital at nine in the morning, and at 9:30 Dr. Scharff was at my bedside. It was again pneumonia, this time on both sides and much more serious, caused by my heart, which is not able to pump the blood properly out of the lungs. Because of that, the lungs are constantly congested and inclined to become inflamed.

In June that too was finally over. I recovered relatively quickly by lying in our garden every day, sometimes 10-14 hours. The peacefulness and good air were so good for me that I see only now how marvelous such a community garden is. Kurt wanted me to give up my job right away, but we have now reached a compromise—to wait two more years. On the one hand, he is undoubtedly right; I cannot simply skip work just because I don't feel well or have a slight cold. On the other hand, I am restless in the small apartment, and would hate to be at home the entire day doing nothing. That will of course change immediately when our house is built because then I will have quite a range of activities.

If everything remains as is, we hope to begin building next spring, and move in a year later. Until then, my income will come in handy (even if it is not much). Also, I will by then have the years needed to be eligible for a small pension. That is only important because you never know what may come—after all, Kurt is not quite well either, and I cannot wholly rely on him. Also, we would then like to adopt a child (possibly a second one later on), and that way I will have plenty of work at home. Perhaps I can also take on some pupils so that I have mental stimulation, or I could limit myself to accompanying Kurt on his business trips.

These are my plans for the next few years. What do you think of them? You probably cannot imagine staying at home altogether, and being just a housewife and mother, can you? But I must say that I am relieved to know that my professional life will end in two years. I used to be ambitious, I wanted to achieve something, and was always angry when I became ill at the decisive moment. Just when I had all threads in hand, I had to let others who knew much less than I take over, only because at the appropriate time they weren't sick. I probably went to the office too often with a cold, hoping that it would simply disappear. Now that I know I will leave in two years, I have no ambition to attain certain goals, but can limit myself—as I have promised to Kurt—to watching my health.

I never thought I would be so resigned, but the fact that there is a person who needs me, and for whom I must be well, helps greatly. You will probably think that I will have even more work with a house and a child, but I have thought it all through. The house will be designed in such a way that there will be minimal work (gas central heating, a fully automatic washing machine, etc.), and for the heavy work I'll have a cleaning woman. *Mutti* who, thank God, continues to be totally healthy, will join us, and have her own two rooms. She has promised me her full support, both with the house and the child; and at least while the child is small, she will still be physically able to do that. Also, I can ration my work, won't have to do much on days I don't feel well, and can lie down for an hour after lunch, when the body has to work at digesting—something very important for me, and impossible at the office.

Aside from these plans, which we worked out during the recent weeks, we also had a short but very nice vacation, spent in part in the lovely Stubai valley, in part in Fieberbrunn in Tyrol. No sooner were we back in Vienna, when we had to face business problems, intrigues etc., which caused us sleepless nights. Thank God, they have by now been at least partially resolved, and last Saturday we were able to celebrate our wedding anniversary—with somewhat frayed nerves but otherwise happy and satisfied. The entire family was invited. The atmosphere was splendid, and I was almost speechless with surprise at Kurt's regal gifts to me: a magnificent Persian lamb coat and a pearl necklace! And what is especially great—he did not take the money from his salary (and thereby from our funds for the house), but he saved it, schilling by schilling, by only smoking on Sundays, drinking a mocha only rarely, and living very frugally on his business trips. That makes his presents doubly valuable to me.

If I begin to consider how happy and fulfilled I really am, then I simply tell myself that one has to pay for everything in life—in my case it happens to be my health. There are worse things in the world than an ailing heart, and spending a few weeks in the hospital.

But now I have really rambled on long enough about myself. If you can find a little time, tell me about yourself, your plans, joys and concerns. Yesterday I accidentally found your letter of January 24, 1952, and enjoyed reading it again. I hope you can rest up properly; your activities at the university will probably be just as hectic as ours. Kurt is in his office from five in the morning, and when he comes home at six in the evening, all he wants is to eat and lie down. Even the weekends are busy. On Sundays we are quite happy to drive to our garden, where we either rest up alone or with friends, spend the entire day in bathing suits, hose each other down, and are glad not to hear or smell a car.

But now I must definitely end. I am very much looking forward to hearing from you—please don't keep me waiting too long. And good luck at Yale!

      Best wishes and greetings
            from your old Trude

8.

[*a diary insert on two sheets of paper, written in pencil, and by hand*]

There are two ways of finding oneself—by seeking one's self out in the world, and by seeking it in one's own depths. Both ways are fraught with dangers, for the self can be lost in the profusion that is outside and it can be atomized in the confusion that is inside. No other way exists, for those who seek not yet or no longer do not really exist.

Which will it be? Which danger seems more formidable? And which is the path? Whose thread turns the image into a map? Whose thread dare I invoke?

"I?"—but what else can this be called which is as much a mystery as the sacred letters which bear no sound? No, *He* was so formidable because he could not be placed into reality, into any, even the most precarious existence. I however cast a shadow. By their shadow you can recognize them. The shadow controls light and darkness, it is the password into existence.

Or only a password toward probation. Free access to the trial. And the trial lights the shadow and dissolves it. Light and darkness will merge into the original chaos, once more and again and again, inexorable, futile movement, unless you can separate them anew, recreate the world, thy world, thou, the creator.

Is it eternal loneliness then—myriads of worlds around myriads of selves in different realities? Terrible freedom in emptiness? Is this the punishment for rebellion? For Eve's sin over and over again?

Eve?

Sin?

Where ... when ... what ... who who who?

Who am I. The same old question, after all these years. No, not a question, for questions presuppose answers. A path. In and out. Go around, the invisible one said. Around it will be.

A pebble washed ashore by the Deluge, battered and smoothed. An insect thrust through the meshes of the net by the Whirlwind, intact even if bruised. A life spared whimsically by the Conflagration. Worthier than others? Unworthier? Neither applies. Survival is a heavy weight, the darkness of memory, the flame of memory. Darkness and flame are one—are the world. Where is the self that can give them voice? Go around.

A child in a monsoon world. Bright with sulfuric sunshine. School, friends, a first kiss, a first love, a first cigarette, a first agony—and a home to flee into, past the bookstore, through the passageway, two flights up, door on the left, two short rings, it is me, it is me, Anna, it is me, it is me, Grandma, I want to stay, hold me tight, I am glad now ... is it true, that if someone kisses you, you will have a baby? ... no, nobody, I knew it could not be true ...I am glad now ... hold me tight ... I had a bad dream ...

And then the wind came and tore us apart, thrust me far into the wilderness where sinners do penance, thrust them into death, every one of them. Why, why?

Go around, child, and do not look back.

Child? No longer. A strange in-between creature, bewildered, pained, fearful and foolhardy at once.

A long ride, a long walk past forbidden doors, past forbidden gates, for the sake of his hot hand in mine, his dark eyes in mine, his hard lips on mine. The happiness of stealthy glances, of walking by each other's house, on each other's path, the ecstasy of being near each other and exchanging flippant cool words before curious, envious eyes. First love, full of a new cruelty. Did I have a right to woo where she had been before, hampered by her star and grateful for my confidence? Did I have a right to kiss? On the cemetery, the only place where the gates were open to us, to him, at a time when death and destruction sent messages every hour. Safe among the dead.

The dead were still and we felt at home with them. The stones held us, sheltered and hid us in a bower of timeless bliss. On Sunday afternoon, until sundown, we were alone. We, the world ... we, the time ... we, the power ...

But around us the whip was cracking. One after another our friends were marked by it. Nightly knocks on the door ... a black uniform ... roundup ... get ready! ... Yes, sir, we are ready, sir, we have our suitcases all packed...not even one, sir? But mother is sick, at least a blanket ...Thank you, sir, I will never forget your kindness.

Sign? What? Where? Anything, of course; we don't have any jewels anyway, and all the rest, certainly, take it ... could we at least all go together, sir? You see, mother needs me, she is sick...No, mother, I would not leave you even if I could still sneak out ... I know I meant to, but forget it ... how could I let you be deported alone ... you are sick, I can at least nurse you and do your work for you. If we are lucky, they will ship us to the Theresienstadt camp and there even Red Cross packages are received ... and if worst comes to worse, it will be a work camp in Poland ... I will work for both of us. Don't you worry, they are bound to have a hospital for the sick. Just rely on me, I will get you in there ... Don't even mention my disappearing—we are going together wherever it will be.

They went together. Who knows how far? The witnesses went with them too, all together.

If strength lies in being alone, I must have been very strong. The bliss was three months long. Ninety days of glances, little notes, little smiles, and long kisses among the dead. Then the knock came for him too. But it can't be true...he worked at the hospital and was supposed to be protected ... They found someone hiding in their apartment. A fugitive. Why did his father let him hide there? He had no right, no right. He could have been safe and remain here, with me among the dead...now he will join them ... I know it, I know it, I feel it...I don't care if it is to the good camp ... they die there too, the packages remain undelivered ... why this to me, when I have never before been happy, why, why?

I must learn to accept, repeat to myself that ninety days in one lifetime is a great deal.

* * *

Sept. 9

I have been awake, gathering forces, perhaps even growing. Growth sometimes comes like that, stealthily, against your expectations and almost against your will, and it penetrates you slowly, persuasively until suddenly you are all taut and imbued by something new, incomprehensible, which almost makes you burst but does not allow for a definition, not even a description...And then, when the pressure is almost unbearable, you open up, from one moment to the next, like the bud of a cactus, and suddenly there is this new flower that has risen from darkness to light but has risen within you.

Something like that happened to me while reading *The Brothers Karamazov*. As I read on, I thought this strange tense feeling of personal involvement was merely called forth by the thrill of a fascinating book; that my uneasy surrender, mixed with uneasier resistance, was caused by Dostoevsky's magic wand, by the concern he asks for his heroes, and the attention for their thoughts and non-thoughts. But that was not the reason at all. As I read on, my admiration for the author grew, but something else with it, an infatuation with the written words, with this whole world that lived between those sheets, on those pages, an enthrallment with the treasures of this world, its exuberance and suffering, a reality which was altogether unreal but complete, round, so that it could turn before my eyes and show them all its surfaces as well as all depths.

Life a dream? What nonsense. If anything, life is a trail that curves and bifurcates, goes up and down hills, with signposts but not when you need them, with fallen and falling trees, flowers and leaves, sun, rain and snow, little piles of dug up earth to sound a memento mori but with wonderful vistas, bird song and breezes. And no matter how many detours, the path before me is entirely my path and it is dearer to me than any other and has given me more happiness than any wide vistas or romantic alleys. I know also that I must make sure the path remains wide and wide open, that it lead right through the world, accessible to its influences but not caving in under them, and that it is the written word that will be me and will transcend me, that will give me mastery over a world of my own.

I think I am ready to start.

* * *

Sept. 16—New York

I cannot tell whether it was a victory or a defeat. Perhaps both, though, judging by the tranquility within me, more of a victory. Of course, my tranquility may simply be exhaustion after nine hours in the car without much of a breathing spell except for this evening's conversation, which cannot be truly called a breathing spell either.

I will simply recapitulate what took place and leave the evaluation to a moment of wider perspective.

Truthfully, I had worried a lot about the rencontre w. Robert, yet I had surely not planned to have it out with him, though I had realized that under certain circumstances, which would demand an outright refusal, such a crisis might become inevitable. I had also wondered for a while whether to postpone it by simply pretending nothing had changed between us, but that thought did not last long. It must also be admitted that my decision to end our relationship, or at least keep it from being as intensive as before, had partly stemmed from my newly won appreciation and admiration for Fran, and from my realization of her love for Robert. Partly also, this decision was to prove to me my return to positive values, after I had vacillated in a valueless nonselective acceptance of, actually submittance to any influence reaching me.

To some extent, and I am fully aware of this, my own physical satiety—if what amounts to a compilation of quantity may be called so!—must have contributed to my steadfastness. I am not at all sure whether I would have acted as proud and independent, had I not had such a full summer, and had I not on the other hand feared that a return to the old raptures might leave me more disappointed and unsatisfied than before. The thought did crop up that it might cure me from my unhappy yearning for Connie, but such playing with fire seemed too dangerous, and in view of the other reasons against it I rejected it.

My conversation with Robert on the way here from Ithaca was artificial and he must have felt it too. But though I was painfully aware of this, it did not touch me too much. How often in the past had he seemed distant and I had practically prostrated myself before him to have him move closer again. He called me moody but so was he. I had to be so careful, for our togethers could either sparkle and glow or be full of pauses and his reaching for cigarettes ... Sometimes he seemed like a big, willful kid who had to be humored and have his way. How often had I talked myself into a maudlin self-accusation, which had appealed to his protector and hero impulses and made him come to save me! How I had worn myself out in this one great desire to please him and go on pleasing him, not to speak of the first two years of our acquaintance when I had resisted my need for him and transformed it into self-lacerating inferiority.

It is true, he gave me wonderful memorable hours and was near and patient whenever I needed him, whenever the yearning for a friendly soul almost drove me to insanity. And thus, from his standpoint it is true, that I have let him down: Suddenly I had changed, spoke of my new value-consciousness, of my not being able to act as if there were no one concerned but us. Yes, to him this must have come as a bitter accusation from my part, after for a long time I had accepted all these very same factors without a word or a thought. And so in the end, while I was trying to bridge over this new gap, to rescue some parts of our old friendship—though not knowing how or what for!—he rushed out without a word and left me here. And it does not even hurt—it just leaves a dull dissatisfaction and a slight shame at this unsuccessful ending. Was I right, was I wrong?

But these conjectures do not contribute anything to clarifying the situation—on the contrary, they involve me in the very contradictions I wanted to avoid by giving an objective picture of what actually happened.

On the road I inquired about our mutual friends, mentioned my writing, my summer diversions (getting a little tangled up in my lie when I told him about having N.Y. company on Labor Day weekend which he had wanted me to spend with him in the country)—I don't think he noticed it, though.

Here I at first began to defend myself against a remark made by him earlier that I had not used my potential fully. I told him all I had done and had had to do, and my record seemed to impress him. I mentioned the C. affair and admitted that it had got me deeply involved but that that was only natural—for the first time in my life had I really wanted to marry someone and could not get him.

"Yes, but you have been re-bouncing ever since."

"No, I have not. I have gone out a lot, had good times, but that had never gone deep, had never changed anything in my feelings towards Connie."

And then I burst out saying that I must be getting old or what, but that never had I had such an intense desire for roots, for belongingness.

"You always have, that has nothing to do with getting old. You were even willing to embrace a farm in Arkansas, for all that!"

"No, I was always doubtful about that, I never felt the way I do now."

And then somehow he came over and asked whether I had a kiss for the guy. And I said yes, but I could not guarantee how much of a kiss it would be, for I had changed.

There was not too much heart in my kiss, but there was warmth and for a while everything seemed alright, and I said it was wonderful to have him and have him be so patient, and he said, I had certainly gone through a fog in June.

"Yes, but people cannot always go together, sometimes they must wait and meet again."

And we said very little and just sat there, till I felt the need to speak and said:

"Yes, but let's quit talking about myself—tell me a bit about yourself!"

"Some other time, when we have much time and a few drinks, not just such few hasty minutes."

"We have a little time, don't we?"

"Then let's use it for something better!"—and he touched my skirt.

"No," I said quietly, and he immediately stopped.

"Then let me get a cigarette."

"All right."

And he sat down in the chair across from me and the crisis began. I could not tell who started it, but he said I had become a stranger, and he had already known it in June and then when I refused to come along to Vermont, and that now too my mind was still at Cornell and not here. I said no, I could assure him, it was not there but here, and whatever the reasons for my actions then and now were he should trust me without questioning, they were valid ones. He said, he could not follow at all and that all I apparently wanted was to turn the clock back one and a half years and start from there. Instead of saying yes then, I declined indignantly that I would not want to lose any of the past. He expressed his doubts. I felt I had to prove my honesty and began to tell him the whole truth.

"I don't know whether by telling you this, I don't do more harm than good, but I do feel I must show you that I am at least sincere and not speaking merely from a whim."

And then I told him that I felt Fran was involved too and that now I could not pass that over, I felt it would mean hurting her.

He sat long without answering. I felt ashamed, for then and there I realized that I should have never said that, that it would not change his attitude towards me but might harm it towards Fran. Finally, trying to make amends, I got up, walked by him to the window, putting my hand on his shoulder in passing:

"Is there not one word you want to say to me?"

After a pause and another cigarette: "I don't know what to say to myself."

I went back to the sofa. Then he began speaking of the lovely times we had had together, recalling one evening after another in detail, until I called out:

"Stop, don't go on!"

"You asked me to say what I felt and now you don't want me to go on. So what do you want?"

"I did want you to tell me, and now I can't hear it. I am not so strong. I am afraid for my decision. I have played a few times with the idea of pushing it aside—"

"That would not have been the right thing. There would not have been any honesty between us."

Then after a long pause, he said:

"Remember, in the beginning you also distrusted me?"

"Do you think I distrust you now?"

No answer.

I repeated my question.

He shrugged his shoulders.

"I guess I had better go. It might have been a redeeming justice if I had let you stay at Lore's mother!" he added with a light grin.

"So you are trying to get back at me this way!"

"What way?"

"By being sarcastic."

"Who is being sarcastic? You asked me what I felt, didn't you?"

He got up.

"Don't go yet," I said.

"Why not?"

"Not like this. I am trying so hard to find a bridge to you, help me, don't let all of our friendship be destroyed. What did it consist of for you, anyway, this friendship? Just physical closeness?"

"No, some blind trust, some physical attraction—yes, perhaps that was inextricably linked to it, because all our interims made me feel so completely relaxed, no violent love affairs, we were "without shoes": God, how long it is that I used that phrase, three years! Well, and some real affection, and the feeling of being close however far we might be."

"And that is gone now,' I said discouraged, "all of it."

"All but the affection perhaps."

But I am getting my reminiscences mixed up. That was said earlier in the evening, before I told him about my new concern for Fran's happiness. He made a nasty crack then, saying that in my talks with Fran ... when two women get together ... I assured him that we had not talked about him in any personal way, but he did not believe me, I saw that. And as I was trying to make him stay, the phone rang and while I reached for the receiver, he mumbled something and left.

And now, strangely, I am calm. Relieved. As if all the outer layers of this charmed flower had been peeled off, and the core is there, pure, strong, ready to open. I am entering my new life unencumbered, free. And now that I have written all this down, I can shake it off without analyzing, dissecting. I just must remember not to become what is the word—recidivistic?

PART FOUR

Yale
(1953–1956)

1.

[*a greeting card on airmail stationery; the front displays a bunch of red and white carnations, and birthday wishes in large gold lettering*]

My dear Liesl!   Vienna, November 7, 1953

For your birthday I wish you the very best with all my heart. Stay healthy and successful as before and never lose your zest and drive!

It's been very long that I have heard from you (you probably feel the same as I do—you often think of writing and only get down to it weeks later). I have not been very prompt either, and you are probably busier than I am. I hope, at any rate, that nothing disturbing has happened and you are only "busy," as always. But I would like to know what you are doing, and what your plans are.

I have nothing negative to report this time. I have recovered well from both bouts of pneumonia, and my heart has switched over to the new rhythm surprisingly well—Primarius Scharff is very satisfied with me. You can't imagine how happy one is when one feels truly well!! May it only stay this way—I don't wish for more. I am even so immodest as to think of having my own child. I have talked about it with Scharff, and after a four-hour heart examination (which was done in the hospital) he agreed, on condition that it is born via Caesarian. Who knows, perhaps next Christmas I will have a little screamer. Wouldn't that be great!

I am anxiously waiting to hear from you, and wish you again all the best.
           Your Trude

* * *

Dearest Trude,   New Haven, Dec. 5, 1953

I am so glad that you are feeling well—may it stay that way!

Please forgive me for writing so late, but once again I had to adjust to a totally new environment. Yale University is very impressive—it looks almost like a stage set from another century, with imposing Gothic cathedrals and English mansions (all of them contain classrooms and offices), but also with a few huge but simpler buildings, some quite modern—a real mixture of styles. Some border on the "town common," a big grassy square cut in half by a street, on it two typically New England white clapboard and red-brick churches with tall steeples. They are used for concerts as well as church services. However, in contrast to SLC and Cornell, Yale has no real "campus." The buildings line city streets, though some have lawns, or courtyards with tall old trees. For a change, it feels like a real university, except that the school does not have only one enormous main building as Vienna's does, but it is spread out over several blocks and cut through by city traffic—a city within a city.

The streets of the campus, if one can call it that, have various college-related stores (clothing, books, stationery etc.) and several eating places. And then there is "Mory's", a famous pub, dark, cozy, smoke-filled, with a very English atmosphere. Students sit there for hours, nurse a beer and debate or argue. So far I have met there a young Irish poet, two friendly English instructors working on their PhD., also a very erudite Jesuit priest. He seems a bit older, and is surprisingly liberal so that one can have real discussions with him. However, in contrast to Ithaca, a real gulf exists between the town's inhabitants and us, in fact, almost hostility. If I can believe what I am told, there have even been occasional break-ins into the dorms.

The International House, my current home, looks like a small English country manor, with a wide, semi-circular driveway. It is a twenty-minute walk from the university, on Prospect Street, which climbs a fairly steep hill. The big buildings on lower Prospect Street are still part of the university.

The International House is run by a young, pleasant and easy-going couple. They tend to stay in the background, unless there is a problem with the house, or with people who forgot to clean up after themselves. (We all use the kitchen on our own.) Everybody is at least twenty-two, some quite a bit older, and several are from overseas. My room is linked by a bathroom to the next room where Poppy and Lieva live. Poppy is from California, nice but a bit "spaced out," mainly because she tends to drink too much beer, which she shouldn't because she is a diabetic. It may be even worse in her case, for her eyesight isn't good—and she paints. Her paintings look very professional, have strong lines and colors. One would not expect that from someone so vague and dreamy. Markets, boats, the seashore—vivid, semi-abstract landscapes. That's what the southern California landscape must look like, sunny and vibrant. I predict that Poppy will become a successful painter—provided her eyes and health hold out. Lieva and I worry about her, but she won't listen.

Lieva is from Belgium, very pretty, and the exact opposite. Practical, sure of herself, and always full of energy. She seems to have boyfriends on the outside, and we don't see much of her.

A very different type is José, a dentist from Spain. He must be quite a bit older than the rest of us, but he has flirtatious black eyes. I will have to be careful not to fall for him. Oh yes, and Stella from Holland, who is my roommate and quite an original. She is stocky, with short, light brown, frizzled hair, permanently red cheeks, a huge smile, a slightly British accent, and a lot of enthusiasm. You can somehow see her milk cows and take care of a slew of small children. And indeed, she is studying nursery school teaching, at the Gesell Behavioral Institute in town, which is separate from Yale. She also practices the recorder with great energy and endurance. I don't feel close to her, but she is fun. And the interesting thing is that the daughter of Dr. Ilg, the director of Stella's Institute, is an almost constant visitor at the International House, and living proof of the success of her mother's progressive educational theories. She looks and acts so grown-up that no one would guess that she is only fourteen. She seems to parry José's flirting, which worries me, but Stella thinks she is too sensible to fall for him. I hope she is right.

[*How wrong both of us were! Years later, when Stella and her husband visited me in Amherst, I asked about Dr. Ilg, and expressed my admiration for the way she had brought up Chris. "Nonsense," said Stella, "at one point Chris wanted to marry someone whom Dr. Ilg did not approve of, and they had long battles. "—"Who won?"—"Dr. Ilg, but only after she threatened to jump out of the window."*

Stella is the only one of that group that I am still in touch with. I have always admired her factual but upbeat attitude which prevailed even when she lost a daughter, and now that her husband has Parkinson's.]

My courses—and here too we meet in small classrooms and seminar rooms rather than the large lecture halls—are surprisingly easy. They run the entire year, just as at Sarah Lawrence, but each of the four meets only once a week, for two hours. You do the reading, and in class there is either discussion (some students never open their mouth, and then it's like pulling teeth), or the professor lectures. In one of my courses there are no tests at all, and we will most likely be graded entirely on the term paper. To my relief, not all students seem brighter than I, even though this is Yale. I think I will be all right.

I am taking "Dostoevsky and Tolstoy in their European Setting" with Mr. Wellek. He is Czech and a very eminent scholar. He has written a basic text on literary criticism called *Theory of Literature,* which was translated into many languages and has apparently revolutionized modern literary criticism. He is also the chairman of the Comparative Literature Department, and I think I was accepted and got a fellowship mainly because it is a new department and needs women, perhaps also because of my Czech background. Incidentally, I had to pass reading exams for German and French. Both were easy—except that I couldn't for the world of me figure out what "pot-au-feu" meant! It turns out to be *Suppenfleisch* [*boiled beef*]—how could one guess that! But I passed anyway. here was also a Latin exam, which I had dreaded since I had just a few weeks of Latin in that make-up course in Vienna years ago, and now a few weeks of cramming at the end of the summer. Fortunately, it was medieval Latin and amazingly simple. My Russian was not tested.

Mr. Wellek is quite elderly but an awfully nice man, kind and gentle, though disappointing as a teacher. He simply reads from his lecture notes which, I suspect, are the draft for a book. There is no discussion at all; we merely take notes. Luckily, the novels we read are great. Now and then he looks up from his paper, his eyes light up and a grin spreads over his face. Then we know he has thought of something funny. His jokes are not like anyone else's jokes. With a chuckle he will say: "Little Leo [*i.e.: Tolstoy*] loved especially their housekeeper—you know, they had a house full of servants—but he never forgave her that she once gave him an enema which was meant for his brother!" Or: "Already early on, Turgenev, who later became Dostoevsky's bitter enemy, was publicly comparing him to Don Quixote, the Knight of the Sorrowful Countenance, and telling everybody of his distasteful amorous escapades. But he didn't say a word about the many rumors circulating about Dostoevsky's wife, and she was anything but an angel!" Here Mr. Wellek winks, implying that Turgenev, too, may have been susceptible to her charms. That may not seem very funny to you, except that when Mr. Wellek says it, his eyes sparkle mischievously behind his glasses, and his gleeful chuckle is totally disarming. Since he is so serious and scholarly the rest of the time, it is doubly funny.

So now you have met Mr. Wellek (we don't call him or anyone else here "Professor," no matter how prominent or elderly). I like him very much, and not only because he is Czech. He is so totally straightforward—he treats us as if we were his colleagues and not just ignorant students.

His other course is "Literary Criticism in England, France, Germany and Italy: The Middle of the 19th Century." Here, too, he reads, this time definitely from chapters of a book he is working on, and I am bored stiff. I just hope I can manage a meaningful paper. But I have learned something valuable in that class. One day, one of the undergraduates raised his hand and asked:

"Mr. Wellek, why do we need to study all this? What relevance can it have for us?"

I gasped. The tension in the room was palpable, but Mr. Wellek did not explode. On the contrary, patiently and not at all condescendingly, he explained at great length why literary theory was important. I must admit that he didn't entirely convince me, but I was immensely impressed by his taking the trouble to respond at such length to even so disrespectful, almost sacrilegious a question.

In "German Drama since 1880" with Mr. Weigand, on the other hand, we read very interesting German plays, also a lot of Ibsen, whose plays I like even better. Why Ibsen? No one would dare question Weigand's including the Dane, for has written a book about Ibsen's plays. Mr. Weigand is totally different from Mr. Wellek, and we are all intimidated by him. He has a sharp, biting irony, and can drive you to tears if he thinks a remark you have made is stupid, or that you have not read the assigned play. Our group is small so that he can glare at us across the large rectangular table. Even so, I really like his class, mainly because he does not insist on our reading lots of boring secondary literature, but stresses close analysis of the text. He also encourages, almost demands that we express our own ideas. He and I often argue about our interpretations, and he does not seem to mind that at all—on the contrary, we try to outwit each other with our arguments. He seems to like being challenged, and of course he always wins because he knows so much more than I do. He has a phenomenal memory, and can quote entire passages from a play in support of his interpretation. On one paper of mine (he requires several papers) he wrote: "Well argued, though you haven't convinced me." I felt very proud.

Then I take "Russian Readings" for which my Russian is definitely still weak, though it is improving. The instructor is fairly young, pleasant, and very forgiving.

You know, by now I love my studies and am more and more certain that I want to teach literature. In fact, I am at the moment absolutely happy. Even the Connie episode has receded into the background. I believe I can now also handle Robert the right way, so that neither of us will get hurt. After all, I owe him a great deal.

All this must sound strange to you who finished her studies so long ago and lives in the real world and in a happy relationship. But I hope, it conveys a little of my present life. Please reciprocate and write a long letter about your activities and thoughts. Also let me know how the plans for the house are progressing.

All my love,

   Your finally a bit wiser old friend

      Liesl.

Wellek vs. Weigand—a complicated chapter, as was the battle then being waged at Yale between the traditional "old" criticism, with its emphasis on biographical, historical, sociological, psychoanalytical, philosophical and religious influences, and the "New Critics." They insisted on pure "explication de textes": only the work itself mattered, and it had to be analyzed into its deepest linguistic and symbolic recesses. I don't know if Mr. Weigand considered himself a New Critic, and to what extent his textual emphasis was influenced by his poor eyesight, compensated for by an excellent memory for detail. All I knew was that I loved his approach to literature, and that eventually my students, too, found it stimulating as well as challenging.

From Mr. Wellek, on the other hand, I acquired an easily understandable and fairly comprehensive theoretical underpinning for such textual analysis. He called it the "intrinsic approach" to the study of literature. It succeeded, at least in my view, in linking the two hostile camps, was both more organic and more open than either, and avoided losing the text in a tangle of extraneous or, as he would call it, "extrinsic" speculations. I have never forgotten his telling us, with his usual disarming grin, that it made no sense to look for the part of the picture that was hidden behind the frame; or that one should not paint chaotically in order to depict chaos; finally, that it was senseless to speculate on how many children Lady Macbeth had! (By chance I discovered the target of this last example: a footnote in his *Theory of Literature* refers to an article called "How many Children had Lady Macbeth?" by L. C. Knight. It was published in 1933 and has thirty-nine pages!)

Mr. Wellek's theorem was quite simple. He drew a set of "concentric circle," on the blackboard and explained that the innermost circle was the work itself; the next circle, subdivided into segments, showed the various ways a work could be analyzed and interpreted; the next larger circle contained the literary tradition the work was part of, both within national boundaries and outside them—since writers did, after all, read other writers, at times even (chuckle) in the original language! Then, separated by a thicker outline, came the biographical circle, which might or might not be interesting, but which was not really relevant to the work; finally, behind a heavy double line, were the various "extrinsic" circles that traditional criticism indulged in, and that were best left alone unless you had run out of topics (chuckle) for your dissertation.

This seemed so simple and reasonable that I could not reconcile it with his immensely erudite (and dull) theoretical lectures, which eventually yielded an impressive eight-volume History of Literary Criticism. Many years later, when I visited Mr. Wellek in a New Haven nursing home, he was, though bedridden, surrounded by stacks of papers and books, and in the process of dictating the final chapters of the final volume of that history.

* * *

My dear Liesl,   December 7, 1953

Before anything else, I wish you with all my heart a beautiful and cheerful Christmas and a happy New Year. By the same mail I am sending you a small etching of the Belvedere. I hope you will like it.

The choice of theme was not easy, for it was not only supposed to remind you of Vienna but also represent Vienna to others there—so I thought that since the Belvedere Palace is linked to several historical events (beginning with Prince Eugene), it can speak even to those who had never been to Austria. At any rate, please accept it as a little reminder of our (unfortunately not very beautiful) time together in Vienna. I believe it was the low-point in both our lives, but it is all the more meaningful to remember that time later, when things are going better. And difficult times spent and overcome jointly tie one together more tightly than the good ones.

Perhaps you will manage to report to me during the holidays what you are doing, how your studies are going, and what your holidays look like. Is it customary to put up Christmas trees? If so, do you do it?

I am looking forward to Christmas immensely. The day before yesterday we walked through the city to buy presents. The Graben was already decorated, everywhere little wrought iron lamps are swinging, which give the city a very intimate appearance. Add the cold, gray weather—the only thing lacking is snow. What a pleasure then to search jointly for gifts for parents, friends and children (my sister-in-law's). The *Christkindlmarkt* is already open (now it is in front of the *Messepalast*), and Mariahilf Street is adorned with Christmas bells and light garlands.

I am just noticing that my letter has turned into a real Christmas letter. I had not intended that. I hope you received my birthday letter at least more or less on time; this one will surely do better. You can't put it on the fireplace mantel, but it will reach you early.

Liesl baby, I also still want to tell you how unbelievably happy I am that I am feeling so well at the moment, and have not yet caught the flu or pneumonia. Likewise, the prospect that in a year I might already have a child makes me ecstatic. Day after tomorrow I see Prof. Antoine (you may recall—he runs the First Gynecological Clinic at the university), for Dr. Scharff would like to have him as the surgeon. It will cost a fortune, but we will gladly pay if only all goes well. There one must not economize. Then at least you have your own child.

Now I am very curious how you are doing. Has your father's wife arrived? And does your father want to follow as well? Wonderful holidays to you and, above all, much happiness and success in the new year.

Your Trude.

Mutti and Kurt are likewise sending greetings and good wishes for the holidays.

Oh yes, my father's wife. I had totally forgotten that Angela planned to visit me at that time but then postponed the trip. During the war, she had supplied us with butter, eggs, coffee, soap—whatever she could get hold of on the black market. "She is very good to her mother, so how can I go wrong?" my father wrote when he informed me of the marriage, and I was glad that he now had someone to take care of him. However, judging from my own experience with him, I wondered how much attention he would pay to her, and I felt sorry for her. Yet, when I visited them in Vienna in 1956, it seemed to me that both were caught in their own snares.

Angela's mother was living with them at the time and, to be sure, Angela pampered and fussed over the querulous old woman who kept "hearing voices" and felt persecuted by a certain "he" whom she never identified. Her daughter was much younger than my father, blond and very pretty. She looked like the typical "süße Mädel" of Arthur Schnitzler's tales and plays about the amorous exploits of Vienna's pre-war young dandies. Except that Angela, though simple, was neither sweet nor innocent. According to Jenny whom she visited, Angela let slip out that Father married her because she was pregnant. "And?" Jenny inquired.—"Dös hob i mir natürlich nehma lossn!" ["Of course, I got rid of it!"] was her answer.

To be sure, Angela was a good cook, perhaps also a good lover. And she did all her own sewing. In fact, I had to acknowledge her excellent taste when she presented me with a fashion show of her outfits. She insisted, despite my protests, on making an evening dress for me, and I still have the picture of the two of us in elegant long gowns—hers a brilliant blue, mine off-white—and with elbow-length white gloves. The backdrop was, characteristically, our living room: Angela had little chance to show off her finery elsewhere. She could look stunning, but all was well only until she opened her mouth. In her heavy and rather crude Viennese brogue she would expound publicly and at great length on such topics as her delicate stomach, her problematic bowel movements, or the day's arguments with the concierge or the neighbors.

Father must have realized fairly soon that he had made a big mistake. With his usual equanimity, he adjusted. When Angela complained to me that he never took her out, not even to the Kaffeehaus where he spent most of his afternoons and evenings, conducting business or playing bridge, I felt sorry for her, but understood his reasons only too well.

After her mother died, Angela did come to the States. She visited both her sister in Detroit and me in Pittsburgh. She was a difficult guest, and not just to listen to. Her delicate stomach could only handle the choicest cuts of veal simmered in butter, and she insisted on doing her own shopping and cooking. Our sightseeing ventures were similarly frustrating, since she showed little interest in anything I showed her. After a moment's glance, she would pull me away: "Hab scho g'sehn!" [*"Yes, I have seen it!"*] Her three-day stay seemed endless, and it drove my husband crazy.

After Father died, I instructed his lawyer to transfer my share of the cash to Jenny. It was only a few hundred dollars, but they enabled her to put a down-payment on the house she lived in, and she was in seventh heaven. The furniture and oriental rugs, which were to be mine after Angela's death, I had the lawyer put at her immediate disposal—in case she needed money. She never acknowledged the gift, nor did she write. Eventually, I learned from the concierge that she gradually became so difficult and aggressive that she had to be committed. The woman did not remember when or where, and I did not inquire further.

Father's plans to come to America never materialized, and he may have been better off for it. His applications, even for a mere visitor's permit, kept being rejected, no reason given. Finally he was advised to have me check into the matter in this country, through my congressional representative. Dutifully, though apprehensively, I wrote from Ithaca to Senator Lehman. A few months later, I received the following information: my father had been rejected because anyone, and this may not have been the exact wording, "who is or has been friendly with any government that is or has been hostile to the United States" (my wording) could be kept out. Those were the years of the un-American Activities Committee and the McCarran Act. To be sure, right after the war Father had been writing articles urging cooperation with the Soviet Union which had, after all, liberated us ...

* * *

January 18

I have learned a lot about myself lately, and perhaps writing it down and turning to it at least once a month—if I can space my distress periods so far apart—might help. For I know that I can't retain them just because I have once found them, these maxims, that I have to be reminded of them. That in itself is one of my new insights.

Nothing can make me profoundly happy, and nothing profoundly unhappy—except for my desire that it be so: for by nature I easily switch from unhappiness to happiness, and I cannot endure too much of either. But I can change the strain, unless I talk myself into breaking under it. And from that follows that it does not make one bit of a difference whether I am married or single, do this or that: I will always find aspects about my state that will please me, and always some that will make me suffer extremely.

But even now I am accepting all this much too superficially, floating somewhere on the surface, in a mild wave of excitement, and pretending that the depths underneath don't concern me at all, that they cannot make me sink—and that they do not carry me! And yet they are my riches.

My will power has become such an illtreated, humbled annex—what have I only done to it? In your school days, remember how impressed you were with Socrates' stoicism? And how you practiced self-discipline, carrying your term report home unopened, not opening a letter right away, or deciding when and at what speed you would do some very urgent and desirable act? And now?

Now I am drifting and it is *eros* and not even *amor* that determines my moves, my speed, my urgency. And I know it and cannot—no, do not muster enough strength to resist it but I let it drift me on, voluptuously, guided only by the most immediate common sense, by a purely hedonistic caution.

I no longer recall what these erotic effusions refer to. For all I remember, my life at the International House was productive but uneventful, except for a few parties with too many drinks and too much noise. Since we did not take our meals together, and everybody was pursuing a different goal (except for Stella I don't even recall what anyone was studying), my life began to focus far more on my studies than it had at Cornell. Oh yes, there was one minor, embarrassing episode, a brief get-together with José during an opportune moment, but it remained meaningless and did not invite repetition.

Robert visited now and then, usually on Sunday afternoons. His visits were quite neutral, not only because I limited them to coffee in the International House lounge, but also because I took care not to let the conversation become too intimate, especially after I had to listen to his long, angry but obviously well-meant lecture upon my mentioning the José episode.

2.

My dear Liesl! June 9, 1954

Finally I manage to write to you (I won't even try to apologize), and to thank you for the note you sent upon receipt of the picture. I am very pleased that you like the little etching of the Belvedere and that it gives you pleasure. Should there be something else which might please you (and which I could somehow get for you), then please let me know.

Several months have passed since my last letter. Our child project has been somewhat derailed, at least in terms of timing. At the end of April I had a miscarriage (however, already after two months), and so my dream to have something small lie under the Christmas tree won't be fulfilled. I was a little sad (but I think after five or six months it would have been worse), and now I console myself that next spring I might be successful, God willing. Perhaps this has its advantages: the house will be finished by next summer and, that way, I will have the inconvenience of the small apartment for only a few months.

The house seems to be progressing well. While we are on vacation, the basement is being excavated, by the end of June we hope to settle the mortgage, and by fall the shell should be up. Next spring it will be finished, and in the summer we can move in.

Health-wise, I am fine at the moment (I survived the winter without pneumonia, and my heart, is, according to Scharff, in what for me is the best possible condition. If there is to be a child at all, then now.

That, in brief, is all I can report. I would very much like to hear from you soon. Listen, you are not angry that I take a bit long at times, are you? I think of you often and if I manage to find time, I'll write again. I wish you a great vacation and am sending my warmest greetings.

Your old Trude

* * *

August 1954

I must recapitulate. It was a good summer, and it has revived me, allowed Antæus to gather new strength by touching the ground. Not that I really needed reviving. The year had gone surprisingly well, without any great crises, so that I had little to report to Robert whenever he drove over for a snack and a few drinks, "to keep an eye on me," as he put it. He seems amorously engaged elsewhere, I suspect with Cynthia, but I asked no questions and he volunteered no information. Perhaps we have finally found a mutually acceptable modus vivendi, and I am relieved that I did not have to break off with him completely.

Academically, too, things have been going well—almost too well. I was feeling somewhat guilty at the "honors" I received for each of my courses and which I was not at all sure I deserved. I worked hard, to be sure, but not that hard, my memory was good but not that good, and I did not at all feel that I "mastered" the subjects I had studied. I was also well aware that among my colleagues some knew an awful lot more than I (in fact, one of them, Peter Demetz, already has one PhD—from Prague University—and is working on a second!), while others were definitely weaker—or perhaps only less skillful at assessing the professor's mindset. On the other hand, I was pleased not to have disappointed Mr. Wellek who has after all brought me here, and who is again providing me with a fellowship for next year.

This time I will live at "Roachdale," a cooperative house. It is likewise on Prospect Street but closer to the university, in an old, rundown building. The inmates do everything themselves, eat together, finance food from a common kitty—perhaps a little like the Quaker seminar long ago but without supervision and, I assume, without educational programs. I will again have to share a room, but since I found it easy to live with Stella, this too should go well. Besides, my roommate is planning to be in New York most weekends.

Later.

I looked up Roachdale in the Encyclopedia and it turns out that it is spelled Rochdale, which was a great relief. Let's hope the roaches know that too. Looking at the place from the outside, I had been quite worried. The original Rochdale Cooperative Association was founded over a hundred years ago in England and has been imitated all over. Except that its concept was much more comprehensive, with a pooling of resources, paying of dividends to the members, conducting classes and lectures, and much else. A real Socialist undertaking. Ours is only based on the democratic principle of making joint decisions, keeping house together and not discriminating on religious or racial grounds, but that's really all I want. And a low rent.

* * *

Next day

Back to the summer. Mr. and Mrs. Sparks, with whom I have corresponded ever since meeting them on the boat returning from England, invited me to join them in Salt Lake City for a fishing trip to Yellowstone by trailer—for them—and tent for me. Then Stella decided that she wanted to see America before going back to Holland, so she invited Lieva and me to help her drive. The Sparkses who live in San José, California, promised to eventually put me on the train back to New Haven. So I was all set.

Stella bought an old Ford coupe for $50, put a supply of motor oil cans in the trunk as well as an air pressure gage, a "tarp" and four wooden poles, then she made Lieva and me get sleeping bags and drivers' licenses. I had infinite confidence in Stella's expertise, especially since the car looked only a little beat up but otherwise fine, and I didn't give much thought to the distances before us. I was, to be sure, worried about the driving test. I had tried it once before, in Ithaca, and flunked. I was told that New York is much tougher than Connecticut. Be that as it may, this time I passed.

The first day was quite nerve-wracking, with Route 6 windy and slow, but the car behaved despite the heat and we made it all the way to the Sandusky peninsula. On a sandy area right by the water we pitched our tent under Stella's supervision. We were looking forward to a swim but gave up very quickly when we saw the sky turning darker and darker. Stella kept urging us to hurry and that was a good thing. In fact, we were glad we bought sandwiches earlier, for we had barely crawled under our tent when a tremendous thunderstorm broke loose. The edges around us got wet, even though we had a floor tarp, but our sleeping bags remained fairly dry and, once it quieted down outside, we managed to relax. I briefly wondered what kind of animals might be around—snakes? skunks? anything wilder?—then I fell asleep.

It was my first camping experience ever and I was not sure I liked it, waking up stiff and very unwashed. How would I manage to sleep in the Sparks' tent for several weeks? Perhaps it had not been so smart to accept their invitation. Sure, he was a retired teacher and very nice and friendly, but she was a bit of a sourpuss. I wondered if he had to talk her into agreeing to let me join them. Perhaps he had done it for his own wellbeing. Too late now ...

The next night was much more civilized, though it began under a worrisome omen. We had reservations at the Chicago International House. When we arrived in the early afternoon and reached the address after some nervewracking driving—Lieva was the victim this time—we were lucky and found a parking spot right across from the entrance. But when the woman at the desk heard that our car was unattended, even across the street, she insisted that one of us rush out and stay with it until we had emptied it. It was not a safe neighborhood, she said, not even in daylight. That was worse than New Haven! We gave up all sightseeing plans and went to bed early, and it felt great to have a real bed and be again clean.

In Salt Lake City I wished the girls a good trip. (They had it, despite two flat tires and quite a lot of oil, with the car overheating repeatedly across the Rockies. They made it all the way to California. And what impressed me even more, back in New Haven Stella sold the car for $50 before leaving for Holland!)

Before meeting Mr. and Mrs. Sparks, I had time for some sightseeing. The tabernacle was very impressive, like a cathedral. I suppose that's what it is, though the thought of the Mormons makes me quite uncomfortable, despite the wonderful Sunday morning radio hour by their choir which I listen to regularly. I sure would not want to be one of four wives, even if it is probably not nearly as bad as Pearl Buck describes it for China. When I lived at Betsy's house in Ithaca, a car once stopped on our dead-end street while I was sitting in the living room. Four young men got out and each headed toward a different house. Like in a gangster film. Our doorbell rang, and there was one of them. He did look civilized, wearing a white shirt, dark jacket and tie, and holding a booklet in his hand. He began to talk to me about the Church of Latter Day Saints, and how it could save me. I thought it would be rude to interrupt him, so I took the booklet he offered me, "The Watchtower" it was called, thanked him and said I would read it. It was an act of cowardice. I should have said that I was Jewish and did not believe in Christ. But I only realized that later.

To my surprise, living in a trailer is not bad at all. It is like an oversize dollhouse, with two sofa-like beds, a folding table, a kitchen corner, even a real toilet. Of course, there was no tub but you could wash yourself in the kitchen sink, and the campgrounds usually had public showers.

We first stopped briefly at Jackson Hole, which faces an enormous meadow and behind it, a whole range of mountains, Not as high and austere as the Rockies but bluish gray, white-capped and quite mysterious, mirrored in a very picturesque lake. In front of the inn where we ate was an enormous pile of antlers. And then we saw them—a whole herd of huge elks, munching grass without paying the slightest attention to our car and trailer which pulled up quite close to the fence. I know their German name, *Elch*, but I had never seen one in real life. They were awe-inspiring and truly beautiful. I would have liked to stay longer but we had to head on to Yellowstone to find a campsite and settle, because tomorrow was the opening of the fishing season and we must not miss it.

My tent was a great relief. It was not a tarp on the ground you had to crawl into, but a real big tent in which you could stand up. It had a cot, a nightstand and even a lamp. The height of luxury, right in the wilderness.

There were wild animals, so all the food had to be inside the trailer not to attract the bears. Yes, we saw bears, right by the road. They came up to the car windows, begging and looking very cute, like huge toy animals. But it was forbidden to feed them and even open the windows, though some people did if the bear was not too close, or even left their car to take photos. I would have too, but Mr. Sparks was very strict about that.

That first morning they woke me very early so that I would be at the lake with them for the opening of the fishing season. What a disappointment! When we got to the large bridge, it was just about filled with people, all in a row like sardines, both men and women. Every one was holding a fishing line above the water, ready to lower it the moment the whistle announced the opening of the season. I too had a rod in my hand and was told that there was nothing to it, I just had to throw the line as far as I could and wait.

There was no need to wait. The moment the line hit the water, a trout snapped at the bait and was hooked. Mr. Sparks took over and pulled it out, baited the rod again and made me throw it in. Within fifteen minutes or less each of us had the permitted daily catch of three, nine total. Those poor fish. I didn't have the courage to protest or to refuse to eat them. It seems that the lake had been stocked with rainbow trout, and they were totally naïve on that first day. Later they became a bit smarter and took longer to catch, but we never failed to get our nine daily trouts, and they were large. Trout for breakfast, trout for lunch, trout for dinner, fried, steamed, souped, pancaked, chopped, marinated—I could not wait for the four days to be over, even though they included fascinating sights. There was Old Faithful, the tall geyser which erupts more or less on the hour, then a huge waterfall at the far end of a deep wooded valley, and my favorite, a transparent aqua-blue pool, with a whisp of steam hovering above it. Even the sulphur smell did not diminish its weird beauty. Gone was my hesitation about having come, tent and trout notwithstanding. To be allowed to see this richness of nature's wonders—I was truly privileged.

We drove on to "apple country"—the state of Washington where, in a small town, the Sparkses have old friends. It was a funny visit. A pleasant woman, quite pretty and young looking except that she was very fat, served us tea and coffee and an enormous platter of homemade cookies and cakes. Mrs. Sparks inquired if her mother was still alive. "Oh, she is fine, she just got married again. For the fourth time."—"How old is she now?"—"Eighty-four, and as fit as ever. I think she feeds those poor men to death. Would you like to walk over to her place?" We did.

The mother was equally cheerful and round and did not look that much older than her daughter. She seemed remarkably energetic for her age. She too immediately presented a tray with cookies and cake. She wore glasses but her hearing was fine. Her new husband was there as well, sitting in a rocking chair in the corner, thin and taciturn.

"He can't hear much, the poor thing. His hearing is almost gone. But I take good care of him, and he will soon fill out a bit. You know, I just don't like being alone. So when Bert died, bless his soul, I waited half a year, then I looked around the senior center to see who could use some home cooking. I told him he could move into my place and I would take good care of him. Of course, I made it clear right away—no monkey business at our age, and I wanted us to get married first. I am a decent woman. How could he say no? I will soon have him looking fit again."

I could not believe my ears. It seemed like acting out a weird comedy. But the Sparkses stayed completely serious and seemed to think this a very normal situation. So was this how life was handled in America? I would never fit in.

After that detour—forget trout, now we were eating apples all day!—we headed into northern California, to the Trinity Alps. That was to be my reward: Frank, my stepmother's nephew, and his wife lived on a ranch somewhere near Tarzana, and Mr. Sparks had agreed to drive there so I could meet them.

[*Frank Kozel's father, Hans Eduard Kozel, born in Vienna in 1875, had been a well-known painter, eventually a member of the Munich Secession group. When I visited my father in Vienna in 1956, Angela let me choose several of his canvasses to take with me. I liked Kozel's work very much and, though I did not have space or money to have them framed just then, by now they are part of my "art collection."*]

The ride up and around the steep mountain curves was hair-raising. ("My God, you drove across the mountains with that big trailer? There is a highway you should have taken!") When we finally reached the valley and the ranch, it turned out to be a very modest farmhouse, with a small vegetable garden along one side and a real junkyard in the back, full of old vehicles and machine parts.

Frank and Margaret were obviously living very modestly. Though they did not know any of us, here too we were given a friendly, warm welcome, offered cake and coffee, and eventually a simple but tasty dinner. We had our trailer and tent for sleeping, but they insisted that I at least sleep inside, on their living room couch. On the walls hung quite a few of Frank's father's paintings which he was visibly proud of, though they were poorly lit and in dingy frames. Unfortunately, I didn't have time for a closer look because Frank insisted on driving us to a nearby summer camp: It had an Austrian counselor whom he was sure I would enjoy meeting.

Off we went, along an endless overgrown track toward what seemed like the end of the world. There is nothing like this anywhere in Europe, I was thinking; I am finally seeing the real America, not that glittering, frantic New York which in Europe we consider the epitome of the Promised Land, not the arty, experimental but also snobbish, pseudo-aristocratic Sarah Lawrence campus, not the lowkey display of a benevolently detached scholarly pursuit at Cornell in its parklike setting high on a hill, nor Yale's earnest attempt at replicating and reliving the pretense of centuries-old European ivory-tower scholarship—no, this here was the land of pioneers and Indians, the home of proud Winnetou and Old Shatterhand [*the heroes of an immensely popular juvenile book series on the "Wild West" by the German author Karl May*], the land of buffalos like the herd we had seen grazing in Wyoming, the land where settlers still lived the way their ancestors had lived, from hand to mouth. I wanted to ask my hosts when and how they had arrived here, and what their life had been like over the decades, but it didn't seem right to pry, especially not when others were present.

We arrived at a cluster of small buildings in the middle of nowhere. "Hey, boy," Frank called out to a youngster appearing in a doorway. "Could you find that Austrian counselor of yours? There's someone here who would like to meet him."

The boy took off and after a while a figure appeared from behind one of the buildings. He must have made out my features at the same time I made out his, for we called out in unison:

"Heinz!"

"Liesl!"

Frank just stared, and it was really hard to believe: here, at the far end of another continent, in the middle of nowhere, I had run into an old friend from Vienna! Perhaps not quite a friend but at any rate a friend of Harry's in whose company we had met several times right after the war. We hugged, then sat down on a bench and, with Frank patiently waiting, briefed each other about our peregrinations since leaving Vienna.

The rest of the trip was uneventful, except for one other interesting experience. Frank, it turned out, was working in Hollywood as a technician for a major movie studio. He would be back at work in two weeks, he said, and if I would like him to show me around the studio some time after that, he could arrange it. Mr. Sparks immediately offered his help: once he had found their house in San José in good order, he or both of them could drive me down to Southern California and show me some of the sights, and it would be easy to include a stop in Hollywood. It sounded very exciting.

On that trip we visited the Huntington Library and paid a visit to its famous "Boy in Blue," then we drove up to the Palomar Observatory which crouches massive and immobile on top of a wide open hill. I probably didn't do justice to either because I could hardly wait to get to the studio.

"You have arrived just in time," Frank welcomed us. "They are shooting a scene with Jimmy Stewart right now, and we can watch."

And so we watched. Frank pushed me to the front until I stood right next to a few men surrounding a platform. On it was a chair and a small table with a telephone. At the right end of the platform was a curved set of stairs, leading up to a little landing with a door. There did not seem to be a room behind that door. At one point a voice said "go!" The phone started ringing and Jimmy Stewart appeared at the top of the stairs, raced down, picked up the receiver and said "hello." Then he turned around and, at normal speed, walked back up and closed the door behind him. The phone rang again and again Jimmy Stewart appeared, raced down, said "hello" and disappeared upstairs. And again. And again. Then someone said "that will do," and people began to disperse.

Though Frank took the Sparkses and me around the lot and showed us assorted stage sets, among them an entire village street, I barely took any of it in. I could not get over that two-minute scene which was being shot over and over, and each time seemed exactly the same, a mindless rerun. Was that how films were made? The best, or simply one of ever so many identical piecelets glued together? Could that create a coherent story, not to speak of honest acting, of an actor immersing himself in his role, in the character? Was all of Hollywood like that, pure make-believe, no, not even make-believe but simply pretense, a paid job like any other, prescribed gestures that were assembled into an artificial entity? Live theater offered at least a reflection of a coherent reality, and had genuine, personal acting. I was sure I would never be able to enjoy a film the same way as before.

The Sparkses' house was a modest ranch on a quiet street of similar ranches. Altogether, San José seemed quite a bit like Bronxville, perhaps less affluent but also a toy town of clean streets, except that they were wider and intersected at right angles. In fact, whenever you reached a corner, all four cars would stop and wait for you to decide which way to cross. It was almost embarrassing, especially if you were just going for a walk. The weather was invariably sunny and warm, the lawns were neat, the window boxes overflowing with flowers. And for a cool rest you could always retreat to the public library—a good excuse if you wanted to be by yourself. The three weeks in San José seemed just a little too long and, when the time came to board the eastbound train, I was quite ready.

The ride back was long and not too comfortable (I slept on the train) but it again brought back to me the hugeness of this country. How little I know of it, how small I am and how unimportant all my poeticizing, agonizing and self-lacerating! I am determined to focus on studying, not for grades but to learn as much as I can of this big land, and of the world it is in, and then try to put this knowledge to the best use I can manage.

What good intentions. Alas, they were soon if not forgotten then at least pushed aside and under, and the mental and emotional peregrinations resumed, if somewhat less melodramatically than before.

* * *

August 21, 1954

A long stretch of road has been covered, the deep woods have gradually opened up onto the plains, and slowly the road has begun to lead uphill again, in a few wide curves until I reached the peak and saw the sun rise over the wide open spaces in front ...

I came back to my studies with new zest, and every day strengthened my feeling of achievement. So that when I finally got restless it was not from boredom but from a desire to accomplish more, get back into my old and yet new life. This new attitude has also made me more conscious of myself. "Learn to live with yourself," Erich Kahler had said. I wondered if that might not be dangerous by leading to too much emphasis on the self. Now I realize that it can also mean "learn to live with others and without others"—and that is a better wording for me.

I had pitched all my emotions too high, not because I could not help it, but because I did not try to curb them. I realized that my early attitude towards life, that of striving very consciously for a balance, had been the correct and most satisfying one, even though my friends would say "let your hair down"—"relax"—"don't think so much about everything." Of course, then this attitude was not natural yet, for my personality had not stabilized sufficiently to make such balance a natural one. But I should have stayed with it anyway, instead of "letting my hair down" into a whirlpool of emotional extremes, from which, after almost drowning, I have come back to my first maxim of balance. Though I am not sorry, for these depths had to be explored, painful as they were, in order to balance my first overconfident intellectual period from age eighteen to twenty-two when I could solve all the world's problems with the greatest ease.

So now I am back, confident yet cautious, knowing that I bruise easily, but also knowing something about the antidotes: the first one is change of scenery, whenever I get bogged down, any kind of interesting activity, anything but a preoccupation with my sores. How simple and matter of fact all that sounds, and how long it took me to realize it! It's quite humiliating.

The second antidote is people. Not too many (that makes it worse) but a few really good friends that make me feel appreciated and keep me from plunging into the first pair of open arms I find.

The third antidote and perhaps it really should rate first in importance, though it will have to rate last in efficacy, is my work and the enjoyment it supplies me. It is worth putting all forces to the task of reaching that moment yet no effort will do unless I have by means of antidotes one and two pulled through the worst of it.

Another thing I have realized: I can't push things. I can help them along a little, but I am just not the type of person who can set her mind on something and get it achieved no matter what the obstacles. I have tried to do that about marriage when I thought I had found the right partner, and thus I took my failure as the most obvious proof of my inability. Here too I have come back to my former, somewhat fatalistic attitude—to do as much as I can, but leave the rest to chance and circumstances, and blame success or failure on them too! And more than that: though I cannot believe in fate, I do believe with Goethe in a benign providence, benign if we make it that way. Thus whatever happens, can—and ought to—be incorporated into the pattern of one's life and woven into it meaningfully, to become a real asset, however difficult or useless a task it may seem at the time. For in the end, even if no clear perfect pattern can be seen, a completed work will become the highest possible achievement against all odds.

And thus this summer has, so I hope, become a major peak in my life, at once an end and a beginning, a beginning finally toward what is, or ought to become, my own life.

3.

My dear Liesl! October 4, 1954

I have kept you waiting a long time, please don't be angry with me, but today I want to send off a detailed letter. First—to be sure a bit early—my best wishes for your birthday! Stay as healthy (believe me, that is the most important thing) and cheerful as before; also I wish you much pleasure and joy and professional success.

Perhaps you will soon have an opportunity to tell me about your summer—perhaps you are already in a different place, and I know nothing about it.

Now let me report what has meanwhile been happening here. My health is very good, I have almost never felt better. The only thing I find difficult (and actually cannot do) is go for walks. Then I get such pain (presumably through blood accumulating in the liver) that I can't walk on. At the moment that is naturally very depressing, but if one arranges one's life in such a way that one never has to walk more than 1 km, it can be handled.

With the construction we have had a few problems. Besides predictably not having enough money, we were left in the lurch by our builder at the last moment. The site has been excavated since June, and he kept stalling. Then he came with untenable demands, so that we withdrew from the contract. It is of course extremely difficult during this booming economy to find a builder, and we definitely wanted to start this year, since it gets more expensive every month. In the worst case (that is, if we should run out of money), we will stop halfway.

Professionally, things have improved for me financially: I received credit for my studies, as well as a step-increase. To be sure, I don't earn millions, but twice as much as in the beginning, and it is good to know that the years of studying were not wasted.

Mutti is fine and sends greetings. She can hardly wait to live in the country and dig in the soil. Enough for this time. Once again our best birthday wishes.

Your Trude.

Write soon—even if in telegram style—whatever is new!

* * *

My dear Liesl, December 15, 1954

Your dear, long wished-for letter has just arrived and I am hurrying to answer immediately—are you speechless? Under normal circumstances this could hardly have been expected, but since I have a slight cold and am in bed, I have time. I am more than delighted that you plan to come to Europe this summer, what a marvelous idea. Since you will already arrive on June 15, you will still be able to take in the last part of the Vienna Festival—it is well worth it.

We will probably be spending the entire summer in Vienna, since in July our house will presumably be finished and we want to reserve our vacation for the move etc. Were you to come one year later, we could have already received you in a cozy home, and shown off a nice garden. This way you will see it in the raw, with all the dirt the bricklayers will have left behind—but I am very happy that you will see it. Perhaps you can come again in a year or two and then relax in a well-groomed garden.

Now to your observations re child. You are probably totally correct: from the standpoint of reason there is only one solution—no child, or an adopted child. Unfortunately, I am a very different type from you. For me, my own child would mean very, very much, and since I was doing well health-wise (and all safety measures would be observed, like, e.g., the Caesarean), we decided to try. Fortunately we did not succeed. It was fortunate because this summer new problems surfaced—I think I mentioned them in my last letter—namely back pain after ten minutes' walking, which keeps getting worse, and makes me feel sick and nauseous so that this year any walking has become impossible. As has now become clear, this is caused by fluid collecting in the abdomen and liver (a result of weak pumping by the heart), and it can therefore not be remedied.

At first this depressed me very much, but Kurt consoles me so sweetly and so effectively that I have overcome that too by now. As you know, it is not my way to let my life be ruined by things which cannot be changed. My baby plans have of course—at least for the moment—been placed *ad acta*, and Kurt is trying his best to talk me out of them. He is of course right, I admit it: once I have reached the canonical age, I will undoubtedly no longer mourn; but as long as I am physically able to have a child, I won't bury the last spark of hope. My intention to quit my job was primarily oriented toward the child, for otherwise, what would I do all day long in the small apartment? Once we are in the house, I may begin to think of quitting, but it is not clear when that will be. I like going to the office. Right now, I have rather interesting work, and it is not stressful. During the times when I am supposed to remain quiet (as during those past weeks because of draining the fluid), I get up from my desk as little as possible. All my colleagues show great understanding, and they help as much as they can. Naturally, there are days and weeks when the rush is on, but so far they always happened when my health was good. Of course, I can't leave the care of the house entirely to *Mutti* (+ cleaning lady). Therefore, I plan to stay at home about a year from now. The exact timing will also depend on our finances—you have no conception how much such a project consumes. But by now it is a real pleasure to visit the site on weekends and see by how much the house has grown. Also, one can already walk inside the future rooms—an uplifting feeling!

I still want to thank you for your nice photo. If I should have a halfway decent snapshot of us, I'll send it to you.

Have a happy and cheerful Christmas, and all the very best for the new year when we will see each other!

* * *

The previous diary entry and my plans for a European trip seem to indicate that I was finally embarking on a firm, future-oriented path. But then I found a letter to Prof. Kahler, which seems to have been written in November or December of 1954 but not mailed.

[*translated*]

Dear Herr Professor,   Saturday

Your good letter was my best Christmas present. I know that I have no right whatsoever to be so concerned about your health, but somehow I feel closer to you than to almost my entire family, as if you had now taken the place of my grandmother, who loved me more than anybody, so that I now regret greatly not having shown my love to her before it was too late.

I don't have much to report, or at least little that is new. As always, I am well outwardly, have nice housemates, no overly great worries of any kind, good friends, time for my studies—ergo no reason to complain. And yet inwardly it doesn't seem to get better. No memory, no joy in my work, only now and then a sudden, almost feverish wakeup, a few inspired hours when I hardly seem myself and yet know that this is me, or could be me; then it is over again, and my thoughts stay on top of surfaces and can't penetrate them, however much I try to force them. And finally everything is nothing but struggle and forcing, and seems more and more hopeless, as if this were the decisive failure, never to be remedied.

That must sound awfully melodramatic, and I may have talked and thought myself into all of it, and yet I cannot find the way out nor, if something looks like a way, the willpower. And somehow it all still seems to go back to that winter at Cornell when you helped me save what was still salvageable.

You know that then, after years of fairly secure, even if often hesitant progress, I came to a total impasse. But you don't know the details. I had for the first time been really sure of a spiritual union that would last, and I thought I was moving toward it totally certain and secure. And suddenly I learned that that was not so. At first with disbelief, when my companion said to me that everything was very, very beautiful but not entirely what he wanted, though he was unable to define that precisely. At that point, instead of breaking off immediately (why don't I ever seem able to do that!), I felt that it was up to me to set things right, that everything was up to me. The less I succeeded, the more appalled I became because it was I, always I, who was destroying my happiness.

Those were awful months. I had accepted his proposal to remain "good friends," just so I would not have to break off completely. Eventually, the break came about nonetheless, somehow even through me, if unintentionally. The pain and helplessness had become too strong—and thereby, strangely, weaker: my friend's existence receded into a mechanical surface sphere in which there were only soundless words and forced smiles, in which nothing was real except for an inner throbbing, and the strong will not to cry in front of others, not to reveal my lack of balance. An oddly powerful drive to act as if everything were normal—just like Gogol's Mr. Golyadkin: be just like the others, and things will be all right. And then the new shock when this disguise seemed to succeed so utterly: I was complimented on my cheerful, serene nature, on my scholarly achievements, when all I could do was think and evaluate for barely five minutes out of fifty. This uncanny self-preservation drive did it, it fooled the witnesses while I was sinking more and more deeply. To keep going became harder and harder, and I grew terribly weary. Not even the walk along Dryden to the hills, the trees, and the wide view helped. Everything was ugly and unformed or overly formed; around me were only two-dimensional masks, empty phrases, glances which did not mean me. Nothing at all meant me. Everything had become totally meaningless, and my powers to affirm weaker and weaker. They still existed, but I could barely push through even to you, and not for long enough to gather strength. And my resistance kept waning.

Just then I was reading (for your course) *The Death of Ivan Ilyich*, and *Death in Venice*, and Schnitzler. That, of course, made it worse. It was almost like a series of road signs, a link, but that did not emerge clearly enough, or I might perhaps have rallied, in the knowledge that these connections were artificial. All of it just sank into me, into soft flesh. I recall a dream, probably under the influence of Thomas Mann. On the beach, among a crowd of people, searching and running away, was one whom I wanted and feared, both of it with a physical voluptuousness. Then my flight into the water and sudden panic, an enormous wave approaching, my flight back, behind me the screams of the drowning stifled, and on the beach a laughing face, NOT the familiar face (my friend was already far away), but a highly desired and feared face, and I, half dead, move toward that grinning face, and in excruciating relief into his arms.

I no longer recall if I knew during my dream that that was death, or only after waking. On the next day, which, I remember, was sunny and full of snow, I came to your office, exhausted, and wanted to ask if you had time for a cup of coffee—but you had a conference and could not stay. I went out into the fresh air, to the lake and around it, then went back to Morrill Hall—hoping that someone might be there. Anyone. I knew that I did not want to do *it* but had no more strength to postpone it, unless someone could hold me back. The world was so empty that it seemed hopeless. Morrill was empty too. I wanted to leave again, then it occurred to me that I could read the story you had assigned for tomorrow ... and gain another fifteen minutes. I knew I could not go back to my small, narrow room with the blue bedspread and the polished brown furniture, and the yellow flower pot by the wall. But at least I could wait a little longer, do something. I couldn't simply wait—that made me too impatient to be finished with it.

The story was "The Woman who Rode Away" ... (but all that is by no means a criticism of your assignments, it just so happened! And possibly I am only stressing it to find at least some excuse for my own weakness. And of course one does not forget a coincidence like that.)

I was halfway through, when I realized where it was taking me, but I wanted to finish reading: the story could no longer do anything for or to me. Just then Alexandra Lettauer walked into the room. She began to talk, and I excused myself because of my assignment. She seemed to notice something. She asked if I had found a better room. (I had mentioned to her that my landlady and her—adopted—daughter, both extremely neurotic, could not get along with one another, and that I had to listen through the wall to the hysterical outbursts, weeping fits, and accusations, and that Linda, after an attempt to get away from her mother by accepting a position in a private clinic the previous summer, had returned in November pregnant and married, but without a husband. The marriage was being annulled just then, and the two women, irritable and probably both deeply unhappy, made life even more miserable for each other. I also must admit that by then I barely felt compassion since I could not help, since they would not even let me try to help ...)

I only responded that I had not found anything, and had given up looking. Alexandra looked at me again, then she said:

"Nonsense, finish reading your story, I'll wait for you. Then we'll go to my place, have a cup of tea, and look through the ads in the paper. Something is bound to turn up."

That was at five, and I did just what she said. She took me home in her car, we studied the paper, and immediately went to look.

And that was all. As you know, I found a nice apartment downtown, whose owner, a young woman of twenty-five, had just separated from her husband. She was self-assured as well as considerate, and we got along well.

The following summer I spent in Middlebury, VT, met a few nice people, and began to have a bit of fun, though all of it was still somewhat forced. I found it difficult, to study and did not enjoy it. Even so, I had no problem finishing my course work, though I forgot almost everything the moment school was over. To my surprise, my Russian improved even so. In August I was back in Ithaca, cramming Latin for Yale. Thanks to Connie's absence—he had received his doctorate and accepted a position at his alma mater—and to the presence of a few friends, I was able to relax and study.

Last year was actually very stimulating. Since there were no final exams, only reports and written work, I was able to work intensively for short periods and hide my complete lack of memory; all went well, honors et al. This past summer, a ride across the continent, with an elderly couple who parented me, was not quite the right thing, but their kindness felt good. There was even a bright moment in San Jose, without which I might not be as hopeful as I am. I spent many hours in the library, took long walks under the warm sun and blue sky, and for the first time in a long while found studying again a pleasure. My memory seemed better, even though I often had to force it, and much information was absorbed mechanically—yet life seemed good. That was when I decided that I still had a chance. If I was able to pull myself together now, train my memory through drills to repeat everything I had written down and work it in, perhaps I could save the last few years, and face the comprehensive examination in January knowing at least a few things.

However, since September I have been again struggling, both with the material and with myself, with my quick discouragement, my difficulty at concentrating. I have the feeling that I cannot handle things, and will approach the exam like a game of chance. Perhaps even win, but without justification or satisfaction. And that would be the definitive failure. Not that I was again thinking of suicide—no fear! Something like that one lives through only once; after that one is fortified for life. But it is that awful feeling that I have lost myself irretrievably, dispersed and wasted myself, and that Time whom I had ignored with such thoughtlessness—in November I turned 30!—is taking his revenge and calling out to me that it is too late: you have wasted your youth, and now there is a fissure, and even if you can throw bridges, the void cannot be filled; one can only erect a temporary structure that will bypass the gap.

And thus I sit over my books, do little else, am probably absorbing quite a lot but, stupidly, am more dissatisfied every day for not doing better. But even if it is too late, should one not be able to accept that? Am I once again trying to tear myself apart by misjudging the situation?

Will you still be in Princeton and available on the first? I might be able to talk a colleague into driving me down if the weather is not too bad, and if that is a convenient time for you.

I have a bad conscience for coming to you with my aches and worries, and at that with reheated ones, and only because I have not digested them, and at a time when you have enough of your own problems. Perhaps I'll hold the letter till Monday and decide then whether to send it.

* * *

Dearest Liesl!   June 15, 1955

    Since I am in the hospital for a change, I am ready to answer your dear letter immediately. First of all, many thanks for your wishes. Whether we will see each other in the summer is now not entirely certain. Please phone Kurt in any case as soon as you are in Vienna (57-85-85), because by then we will probably have moved, and you can no longer reach me at my old phone number. One week in Vienna is very meager—especially in August when the city is deserted—and also because there are so many people you know, and last not least your father. I hope we will be able to have at least one long chat.

    There is much that one would like to say and that can only be hinted at in a letter, or not even that. Especially on the subject "child," which you touched on in your last letter. Surely you are right that many people are driven to multiplying only from the hope that their children may achieve what they couldn't. But as you quite correctly surmise, it is largely a matter of feelings, and not to be buttressed by logical arguments. As for counter-arguments in general (aside from medical ones), I find that life has never been much better than it is today, and that exactly those children who were born in the most peaceful times suffer the worst during wars. To be sure, so far there have not been any atom bombs, and who knows if they will even be used during the next decades; and if so, if a sudden death by such a mass extermination tool is not more pleasant than years of suffering. I will certainly not be unhappy without a child, first because I am not the type to yearn for the impossible, and secondly because a truly good marriage in my view is much more important, and brings far more happiness than children, whom one enjoys for fifteen to twenty years at most.

    Now about me. Since June 7th I have been in the hospital (this time at the university clinic to which Kurt's cousin who worked there for a long time took me) for a thorough examination. Dr. Scharff couldn't manage the pain. But here I have presumably the best heart specialist of Austria, and at the clinic he has the best diagnostic tools available. At the end of this week the tests will be concluded, and they will decide whether to operate. The operation would have to take place in Sweden or Germany, since my case is so complicated that heart and aorta would have to be operated on at the same time. (The heart alone could be done in Vienna.) Since the operation would mean a five-week stay abroad for me (I don't yet know when, since one would first need to inquire from the foreign clinic when they could take me), it is not 100% sure whether I will be in Vienna between the 12th and 20th of August. But when you come, you can find out everything in Kurt's office.

Let me wish you a good trip and—should we not be able to see each other in Vienna, though this is not likely—have a pleasant stay in Europe! I greet you most affectionately,

Your Trude

P.S. Please forgive me if my handwriting is not always legible. I am writing in bed and am trying hard but can't manage any better.

4.

Hello Liz,   Sunday, June 17, 1955

Twice now I've called upon you and twice you've gone to bat for me...and I'm very grateful....'Tisn't often we find friends along the line who'll stand up for us when we need them...and these past two occasions have been sorely needed...believe you me.

All right, all right, I'll get on with the story since you have been most patient. Shall I be straight to the point and save all the details for another time? Perhaps it would be best that way. To go on in detail would take too many pages. First things first then...I know you'd have gone to bat for me no matter whom I might have come with...no questions asked and have taken it in your stride and possibly tossed a shrug of the shoulder my way. This is the real thing...so much so that I blush with mortification when I remember other times and other years and other people about whom I may have been confused and well nigh contaminated. But not now. I am as sure of this new friendship, relationship and love as I am of my name. Suffice it to say that I've never in all my life felt the way I do now. Perhaps if one added moment after moment of a lifetime—it might add up to the general feeling I now possess constantly.

But it is hard—rugged is a better word—on the two of us. Things at home are none too brisk...F is aware of the situation in the sense that my hours away and my hours coming have been decried and belabored...Mail has been opened, or if left around read...therein was I hanged—She states that I was at New Haven that weekend but swears that I didn't come alone—As for this last time I called—well, there has been no proof to the contrary.

As you've known—the conditions here have never been bright or brisk to make the home fires burn true and warm. But the words of Bacon—(need I quote them) "He who hath wife and children hath given hostages to fortune." are constant reminders that things can not be easy now or for some time. Yet, as I've said, the pressure grows constantly—and unless one makes allowances for a safety valve that is controllable here at home—there is no telling when the explosion (the big one) may take place—There have been several simmerings and minor explosions—but still one has an address here—

On the other hand things aren't easy at the other end of the line....Strange phone calls have been made, reporting the two of us—reporting us to all sorts of people who might do us harm—strange notes both in school, at home and at places that could (and no doubt have) hurt her. It is apparent that there is definite mischief with malice aforethought stalking us—and the pattern seems an alarming one....not each step in itself—but the insidious weave of the pattern and one can't point the finger at any particular person—. All the more to move a man to say the hell with a life that isn't what it was supposed to have been—and to throw the finger of scorn and malice back into the faces of those s.o.b's who might be concerned in the poison pen and tattle-tale business.

With Cynthia I've broken, completely and irrevocably.

The bickerings in that corner have gone from bad to worse to outrageous and so a month or so ago—the lid lifted a bit there and the vindictiveness and spite that spewed forth from that cauldron made it indeed a witches brew.....Incidentally, you'll never know—or perhaps you may have surmised it by yourself—how bitter was the animosity against you—and how one almost had to apologize to her for having known you through the years....Perhaps it stemmed from the first time you two met—but I doubt it—The animosity on C's part was directed against anyone and everyone with whom I might share a thought or a moment....and I know the damage done by her and by Fran—years ago when the episode of Lore almost scuttled my ship...So though for a time I felt badly that Cynthia would hold the bonds of whatever friendship we had so tenuously—I was amazed by some of her actions and antics...Yet—it is incredible to think that she might be at one end of the pattern I've spoken about on the preceding page.

On the other hand, there may be people in Pat's life—equally small-equally vindictive who might be involved...It would be a most grievous coincidence that people on both sides—hers and mine—should be involved in these calls, these notes, aye, these handwritings on the wall so to speak.

Withal, Pat and I have been able to weather the storm. She's a rare blend indeed. But, sundry other details will have to wait until I do see you to complete the entire picture...

The summer—my work at the beach during the day—and my work at night school throughout the long evenings (provided I am not fired or my contract revoked—again as a result of malicious tongues) will allow little chance for the two of us to see each other. She doesn't live in New York and the travel time is almost formidable.. Likewise, there are one or two other factors involved in the situation at her end, which again make it difficult to share even the modicum of free time that one may have....

It is a tough kettle of fish...Ten years ago upon my return from the Pacific when I told Fran I wasn't in love with her—I was told to pack my bags and git....These past months—in our talks—the same thing has come up...but this time—the fact that there is a youngster involved stems any overt action... Jamie is still definitely in need of a firm hand—and my firm hand must remain here fore a time...So one lives and operates in a world that is seething—tries to keep the lid on fairly tight—and is grateful time and again that Pat is genuinely sensible, realistic and understanding.

Thus—you know the reason I didn't stay any longer...although one wanted to tell you the whole story then....

And now—if you write as write you will I hope—speak of anything but the things I've told you here—simply because I do not consider this a safe mailing address for packets containing dynamite....But you still can tell me all the things about yourself that I do want to know—and how cockeyed all your plans have become because of a fractured kneecap........

Love,

R.

This is Robert's last letter from that period, nor did I find any letters I had written to him, or diary entries mentioning him. I did not respond. There seemed no need to keep complaining to him about my ruined Europe plans. I recall, however, that his odd letter left me strangely exhilarated: this man whom I had so admired and resented, turned out to be less mature than I, more confused than I, was chasing rainbows which I at least saw clearly as rainbows. I hon-

estly wished him well, and for his sake hoped the liaison with "Pat" would last and would, even if not sustainable at that level of bliss, at least assuage his restlessness. That it did not, I learned only some twenty years later when we met again and resumed our correspondence for a brief period—from December 1973 to February 1976.

I was living and teaching in California at the time. While attending a conference in New York City, on an impulse I checked the telephone directory. Yes, he was listed, though not at the old address. We dined together at the Waldorf where I was staying. He called it a celebration of our reunion.

"Remember—I was at your wedding?" he said. I tried to hide my shock: I had forgotten. "That was a lifetime ago," he continued. "I didn't hear from you after that." And he quickly added: "It is all the more wonderful to see you again, and see you look so unchanged."

I smiled in disbelief, but then it came to me: it was he who had remained the same, at least inwardly.

He began to write again, his wonderful, long letters. Whereas mine spoke of books, work and family, his were full of his adventures, of romantic flashbacks and—of compliments for the special human being I was. With an entire continent between us, I basked in the pleasure of his seductive, flattering visions, though by now they evoked neither longing nor curiosity.

Long before that he had left his wife (or been turned out by her?), and begun to spend his summers traveling on freighters around the globe—Europe, the Greek Islands and, primarily, the Far East: Bangkok, Taiwan, Manila, you name it. Hong Kong was his favorite hangout. Perhaps it was nostalgia for his wartime memories of the Pacific. He was no recluse on these trips, and I can't resist the temptation of quoting from one of his letters:

Does it boil down to a listing of a kind of hagiography—the women in my life since we once parted so long ago—Polly, Margaret, Pat, Terry, Claire, Jean, Alice, Rory, Lina, Cynthia, another Cynthia—the list seems endless…Affairs all—not in a kind of amorous litany but in a search for minds rather than bodies—and all I found were entrancing, charming, enticing, long, tall, thin, hefty, sexual athletes—some could climb mountains with me, some fly with me, one or two to travel with me, many to listen to music, some to discuss this and that…some possessive, some demanding, a few with heart—nary one with the combination devoutly to be wished.…the kind a man could say: with such a comrade, such a friend I feign would walk to journey's end. And so we lechered and we lusted and the years went by…..and we discussed the shows, and enjoyed the concerts and the ballet and the museums…..but there was little of the real thing I wanted and want…..A drinking companion, a mistress, a computer mind…..Twas a puzzlement…..As another poet put it…the time I've lost in wooing, in watching and pursuing—the light that lies in women's eyes has been my heart's undoing.....

An overly long paragraph to say—I needed and I wanted someone to talk to—who would listen and try to understand what I was saying and feeling and be forgiving and tolerant and kind and gentle....How we need gentleness and understanding along with love....

What are the virtues I've attributed to you.....? Have I fantasized? Conjured up a whole rainbow of dreams after one telephone call and a double martini?

Not on your life. You're all the things I've wanted...needed...search for—Above all you CAN listen—and how delightful to hear the things you say and the way you do.

Hoping you'll write soon....please write soon....

Much love
R

In 1971, he married Cynthia and, a year later, felt very hurt by her walking out on him, saying that he "would never change." However, when she had a heart attack a year later, he faithfully nursed her, and when he too had one, she reciprocated, as well as after his cancer surgery.

That my relationship with Cynthia has matured and ripened into a deep friendship with her—is remarkable in itself. It's a remarkable relationship....Most marriages should grow into that sort of thing and few do. Few divorces reach the point of ripeness and maturity we have. However, the most — the biggest thing that is lacking is what I call communication. Of course we talk, of her children, of my kid, of my friends and her friends, but of our intimate feelings—that is verboten and anything that is verboten doesn't make for true communication no matter how inextricably people's lives may be involved one with the other.

That's why it was so good to talk to you the other day—to hear your voice—to feel the nearness of you though a world away.

Don't tell me ever that kind of thing happens to everybody all the time. I'll not believe it. That evening of February 12th, 1950 is still—as I've told you on a number of occasions—a moment crystallized in time—....Perhaps—during the years that followed—we may-each in our own way missed the same train on which we were supposed to be riding together—but at long last, I know we're bound in the same direction.

My metaphors may be mixed, my imagery all askew, my feelings are not.

I am so rich in the knowledge of you, the thought of you. I am so proud to know you. I don't know if either of us is livable but I do know you are lovable.

And that's the understatement of the year.

I know you for a warm, emphatic, sensitive, compassionate and delightful human being—charming, gracious, vibrant.

I know you for a worry wart, a hard-working idiot, a confused bag at times-

But overall, it took me from February 12, 1950 through all these years—to realize what a glorious spirit you are.

Happy anniversary. Thanks so much for all these years.

Here is, finally, are excerpts from the last letter I was able to find. It is dated February 23, 1976.

My trip to the Orient is all set. At the moment, I'm booked aboard the Washington from San Francisco to Bangkok scheduled to leave on March 30th...give or take certain conditions.

Accordingly, I had planned to fly out to the Coast a few days earlier. If you are free evenings—I could rent a car and drive down to Monterey—perhaps on the 24th or 25—stay at your house for a few days (if convenient) and then drive back to San Francisco on Sunday the 28th...to await the departure of the Washington at a friend's house in that city.

[There follows a detailed itinerary: Bangkok, with stopovers at Taiwan, Hong Kong and Manila; another freighter to Japan; then Honolulu, to rest up there..]

I still haven't resigned from the school system—as I must have mentioned, I'm taking full advantage of my sick leave which affords me full pay through May 1 or May 7th. And since my departure from the hospital-I haven't found my time hanging heavily about me.

Need I tell you that much of the excitement about the trip comes from the chance of seeing you and being with you.

If you've written—I haven't received any letters recently.

                                            Much love

                                                  R

[*A hand-written note of mine, on plain paper, provides a postscript to that letter.*]

July 28, 1976, 3:40 p.m.

Robert just left and I am drained. It was a very bad visit and yet not bad at all. It was finally real, the reality I had known all along deep down, yet again and again let him talk me out of, again and again talked myself out of because it was comforting to receive all those ardent letters, to be told again and again how wonderful I was, and how wonderful I would continue to be. I kept saying that I did not believe him, that this was not me, that he was seeing a dream figure but not the real me, and he kept assuring me that it was, that I just didn't have enough belief in myself. Perhaps not but I did know that whatever I was or wasn't, it was not his image of me, that whatever he was saying or writing about "us" wasn't possible, wasn't us at all, and that it was dishonest to let him continue to dream.

I wanted to return to him all of his letters, but he refused them. They were mine, for better or worse, he said with a smile that was almost a smirk, ironic, perhaps even sarcastic. Then he left.

I did not hear from him again and recent inquiries remained fruitless. As I now think back of that long, strange relationship, which was both intensely personal and quite unreal, his memory continues to haunt me. What a restless, lost soul and yet, what a powerful yeah-sayer to life, to both its heights and its depths, what forcefulness in seizing, transforming and romanticizing what had never been but needed to be. With all the anguish and frustrations our relationship had brought me, I would not have missed knowing him for anything. Robert was undoubtedly the most amazing human being I ever met.

5.

July 21, 1955

Almost a year has passed since my last entry, and as I am rereading it, things falls into focus. Though I have had to postpone my Austria trip and was for six weeks hobbling around with a big cast on my left leg, it was not a bad year, in spite of a few ups and downs. Of course, now and then I again fell into my old mistake—not enough breathtaking, looking, listening and reflecting, and thus not incorporating the year into my positive "memory-hoard" as I should have done.

The ups and downs were social, scholastic and emotional, but their deviation was not unduly large. Socially the year was as satisfactory for me as any. My coop worked out well and gave me that certain satisfaction of achievement and independence I needed. Not that I made any special conquests—but I felt secure enough not to miss them.

This is a very minimal appraisal of what was an unusual and rewarding year. Rochdale provided me with an insight into a life I had not known. The co-operative was a friendly, comfortable yet rather odd place—especially if you came from the orderly Bozeman household, from impersonal rented rooms, or the sedate International House. The three-story Victorian was quite rundown, with small, dusty rooms and alcoves everywhere, with people who looked familiar but didn't live there going in and out. In the large dining room whoever was around would assemble for dinner, which we prepared jointly. Ormond Brody, our "kitchen-tsar" and treasurer, laid down the law, i.e., he assigned the chores and collected the fees. He was a post-graduate research fellow in chemistry who, though probably in his late thirties, had decided to embark on medical studies. With him were his wife and four-year old son. And that was the most unusual aspect of Rochdale for me: not its Bohemian, laissez-faire atmosphere, but the fact that among us were couples, even two families with small children, who at times seemed to belong to and be fed by whoever was around at the moment. Perhaps all this added to the general commotion and confusion, but that did not seem to matter: this was life, real life!

Kitty, a free-lance artist, and her husband Paul, who was enrolled in Yale's art department, had an infant who was casually dumped on anyone within reach, and neither he nor they seemed to mind. Lola, who was visibly expecting, always looked serene and lovely like a Madonna, with her blue hair band and loose gowns, even though, at least according to rumor, Dick, her husband, was sweet on someone else in the house. Darlene and John, neither of them at Yale, lived at Rochdale because they had been unable to find housing anywhere else in New Haven: she was snow-white, or rather white-blond, and truly beautiful, a young Marilyn Monroe; he, quite good-looking and always full of jokes, was very black. Darlene had run away from home to marry John and was now finishing her high school degree; John was working on the railroad. According to Jane, who visited me recently and provided some information on our co-Rochdalians of that year, Darlene and John had three children, but when he became abusive she left him and raised the kids on her own. She made it, too, worked as a medical assistant for many years. When she was let go for being too old, she obtained a degree in osteopathy at age sixty, and resumed working.

Jane and Susi shared a room. Jane was studying sociology, Susi was at the Gesell Institute. I should have asked her if she had known Stella. Now I no longer can, for Susi died in a car crash some ten years later, leaving behind two young children.

In the evening, anyone who did not want to be alone could sit by the fireplace and read, or chat with whoever happened to be around. That felt just right—being left to yourself when you felt like it, join others when you were in the mood for company.

Ormond saw to it that the shoppers, dishwashers, house-cleaners and cooks did their job properly. I chose setting the table, obviously the easiest job, but to my surprise not much in demand. John Kennedy had volunteered to prepare the Sunday dinners, even though he didn't live at Rochdale. I still remember his legendary creampuffs. John already had his law degree by the time I joined Rochdale. He was working somewhere in Rockland County, and spent only his weekends with us. He was interested in Barbara, who would in turn come up from New York to visit her good friend and former roommate Susi. Barbara and John married the same year I did, and we have kept in touch. After many years in Suffern, New York, they moved to Ithaca to be near their children, but I have yet to visit them there.

I recall Halloween, the night when all the witches and goblins are supposed to be out—a kind of Walpurgis Night, but on October 31. A few of us were sitting around the fire, and took turns reading Henry James' The Turn of the Screw. *It was just right for the occasion; quite spooky, but basically about the struggle between good and evil; except that evil wins. Perhaps it always does? A frightening thought.*

John's nutty but brilliant friend Larry, who would also drop in regularly, was a physician. The two owned a sailboat jointly, and I once went sailing with them in the Long Island Sound. It did not go too well. I should have known that Larry could not be relied on. We had a wild ride, and as he was mooring the boat, it promptly scraped another boat. Larry got into a shouting match with its owner, and Barbara and I quickly climbed out and into John's car. I never found out how the affair was settled, but I decided that I could live without sailboats.

I had another friend at Rochdale, though friend is perhaps the wrong word. Ernie was—the best word I can come up with—a playmate. We had a relationship, but it never became complicated or serious. This time I did not confess it to Robert, remembering the long lecture he had given me on my half-hour stand with José.

Ernie was a graduate student in chemistry and a funny guy, both fun and funny. He did not live at Rochdale but often ate with us and, as so many others, hung around. We played ping pong together, and though he kept beating me badly—usually 21 to 1 or 2, and never better than 21 to 5—I liked playing with him. After the game, he would put his arm around me, grin and claim that I was definitely improving. One time when no one was around, he kissed me, and I liked that too. On his next visit, he followed me into my room. Since it was the weekend, my roommate was gone. Once inside, he pulled me down on the bed. He was short and muscular and smelled of cigarettes, and it all felt new and different, and simple and enjoyable. And it remained a game, played off and on, just like ping pong. I could tell that he enjoyed our being together and knew that I did as well, but both of us remained casual about our relationship, and uncommunicative about our lives.

That relationship was ever so much more relaxed than any I had had before, whether with John, Robert or Connie. More like my very first romance, over ten years earlier, the puppy love during three wartime months. Now too, I knew that it would not lead to anything permanent, nor did I expect or want it to. I was grateful that there were no complications, especially now that I was preparing for my comprehensives.

Mercifully, the exam was to be oral and, as I was told by old-timers, it usually did not last longer than an hour. Even so, one of the members of the committee almost tripped me up, though he barely knew me, and his field was not even the nineteenth century. He mentioned a fifth "Untimely Meditation" by Nietzsche, when I knew of only four. Luckily, Wellek came to my rescue. "He never published that one," followed by his favorite phrase, "isn't it?" Prof. B. had to agree, and I received "distinction." If they had only known how many holes there were in my background! Either they were not looking very hard, or I had fooled them.

A week before the exam, I had run into a fellow graduate student in our seminar room. I barely knew her but was in awe of her because she was tall, slim and blond, and always so sexily dressed that she did not seem to belong in graduate school. When Charlotte von Wimmertal heard that my comps were coming up the following week, she offered startling advice: "Just pretend that you know much more than they imagine. And you probably do; so just keep reminding yourself of that. But even more important, dress as well as you can"—her eyes stripped my plain skirt and white blouse off me with one glance, and I blushed. "Have your hair done the day before, wear long earrings, and put on lipstick."

I didn't have my hair done, nor did I own dangling earrings, but I put on lipstick and a necklace, and felt like a cheat. My faithful friend Kriton was outside the room waiting for and then with me, assuring me that I would pass. But when Mr. Wellek appeared in the door and said with his sweet smile that I had passed with distinction, I was not merely pleased but as proud as if I had deserved it. Had my background been a lot more solid, the main difference would have been a feeling of disappointment that I had not been able to show all I knew; this way I really knew what I had shown, with only a little bit of faking. Or did the faking do it, was it just the way Charlotte had said, and success was a communicable conviction, even if not based on achievement? I quickly dismissed the thought and hugged Kriton—the only time in our relationship.

Kriton was Greek, a gentle, slight boy, dark-haired and pale, with glasses and a low voice, pleasant but not really good-looking, perhaps because one of his eyes was out of focus and, I believe, not functioning. I found his quiet presence soothing and reassuring. He wrote poetry, and I sensed that his soul bruised easily, and he had to be treated very gently. He may have had the same feeling toward me. We never kissed or even touched but were often together, studied side by side for the comprehensives, went to lectures and concerts together, and during that summer nursed each other: Kriton had glaucoma surgery, and I was putting drops in his unfocussed bloodshot eye, calmly after the first shock. He, in turn, would be at my place whenever he could to help with cooking, shopping and whatever chores I could not handle on crutches.

We had met at the Edelmuths, where we were regularly invited for Sunday dinner, on the assumption that we must be starving all week. But that was not why I was always looking forward to those Sundays. The Edelmuths' simple but attractive house was such a cozy, homey place that just being there felt like being wrapped in a soft, warm blanket. Kriton, I know, felt the same way.

Despite decades in this country, both Edelmuths had strong, though not jarring German accents, and both exuded warmth, concern and hospitality. Mr. Edelmuth had lost a leg in the first world war, but except for stiffness when sitting down or getting up, and his use of a cane, you wouldn't have known. He was a sales representative for a medical supply concern, and traveled a lot. But he was no Willy Loman. Well-educated and extremely knowledgeable on a great range of subjects, he was a big man—in every sense. He anchored any conversation in a quiet but firm way, and his wit added spice to our meals.

His wife was short and modest, the typical German-Jewish solicitous and acquiescent housewife. But she was more than that. She audited several German literature courses—that was where I met her—and also worked as a "native informant" in Yale's German department. I am sure she was very good at it because she was patient and full of empathy, though probably too permissive and kind. Remembering how tough I sometimes had to be at Cornell to keep the students in line (once they let a mouse loose in the classroom, and were very disappointed when I refused to let that derail me from testing their recitations), I wondered how she would have handled such a situation. But she had other problems at Yale, perhaps worse ones, though she never complained. She was not treated well by the regular faculty and even by her more assertive co-informants, the former because she lacked a degree, the latter because she was too nice and obliging, and chose not to fight for her rights when it came to scheduling or preparing exams. Even her husband treated her with a little condescension; for that reason alone Kriton and I endeavored to be doubly nice to her.

My visits to the Edelmuths did not merely provide me with a good meal. The couple's concern for others, and their awareness of the human suffering inflicted all over the world, animated their attempts to help wherever they could—at least by contributions, donations of clothing, volunteer work. They did not seem religious, but Mrs. Edelmuth, who had been an ardent Zionist in her youth, was a firm supporter of Israel, and unhappy every time it committed another lapse from democratic principles. The example of the Edelmuths made me more attuned to my human environment; it also restored my long-ignored Jewish heritage to me, and led to my openly professed avowal of an at least secular Judaism.

Coming to terms with my wartime experience and the phenomenon of the Holocaust in general was more difficult. Only when, after retiring from teaching, I sat down to lay the ghosts of those years by forcing them into a book, did the burden begin to lift. By now there are just small traces of it left, such as the discomfort at the sight of a uniform—any uniform but especially a policeman's—hearing an airplane pass overhead at low altitude or a fire engine's siren pierce the air. I still get uneasy when I see a public display of large, undulating flags, even though I am well aware that they are neither solid red nor have a black swastika in the center. I gravitate toward restaurant chairs where my back is protected by a wall, and will finish everything on my plate, no matter how full I may be. I am also still a hoarder—not only of canned food, but of string, rubber bands, paper bags, candle stumps, soap ends. I find it difficult to throw out or give away sheets and towels that are still usable, and I continue to relish a soft-boiled egg, or a slice of buttered bread, with a sliced tomato, radish or chopped chives on it, as much as a fancy dinner. But that is a minimal price to pay for accidental survival.

Once, Kriton took me along to a séance he had been invited to. We rang the doorbell of what from the outside seemed a totally average, nondescript private home, and were motioned into a large, dimly lit living room. I made out a circle of chairs, most of them already occupied. Everyone was holding hands, and we joined in. A middle-aged woman with red hair and a huge, garish kerchief draped gypsy-fashion around her shoulders was quite obviously the pivotal figure, the medium. All lights were extinguished, the candles in front of her blown out, and we sat in total darkness. Kriton had admonished me earlier not to talk. I became quite nervous and had to suppress first a giggle, then annoyance at my wasting precious time on what seemed an obvious fraud.

Just as I began to consider making my way out of there without being heard, something did happen. The room began to reverberate as if an army of soldiers were marching close by or right through it. Their heavy, rhythmic tread shook the floor. I remembered reading that armies are not supposed to cross bridges in lockstep, and I wondered if the floor, perhaps the entire house, might collapse. Kriton must have sensed my anxiety because he pressed my hand. Then the motion stopped, and our hostess began to moan, mumble, and speak in different voices.

We left the moment the lights went on, without talking to anyone. I would not have known what to say, and Kriton seemed to feel the same way. Nor did I discuss it with him, since I did not know if I might hurt his feelings by suggesting that the medium could easily have been putting on a show, especially if she knew the audience. But what about those marching hordes? That had not been my imagination; he, too, had felt their heavy step. I remained puzzled and somewhat uneasy, and Kriton only said: "There are things in this world we cannot understand."

He was also my guardian angel when I had to have two wisdom teeth pulled. It was shortly before the comprehensives and so I could not afford to baby myself. I lay down for one afternoon with ice packs, which Kriton faithfully renewed. The next day I was back in my carrel in the library stacks, cramming.

That last year at Yale I led a very monastic existence, especially after Kriton left for Greece. I missed his companionship very much, but told myself that at least nothing would now distract me from my dissertation. His farewell present was a slim, antiquarian book of Yeats' poetry. In the enclosed note he wrote:

> "Be not unkind or proud,
> but think about old friends the most:
> Time's bitter flood ... etc. etc ... (cf. p. 40)"

and added his best wishes. I still have the book and the note, and I remember his birthday every year: it was on Valentine's Day.

Irony and pain are often teammates. Though I thought of him often and kept writing, he never answered the letters I sent to his Greek address. Finally, I gave up. When I was in Athens in the summer of 1992, and the phone number which the concierge at my hotel had located for me remained unanswered, I wrote to him, giving my local as well as my home address. On September 12 I received a long letter from a clearly close friend of his, with my letter of July 9 enclosed. Kriton had suffered an aneurism in May, been in a coma for two months and had died on July 2, seven days before I tried to contact him ...

I took up smoking. I never viewed the act of smoking as a symbol of social sophistication, as so many of the students around me seemed to. I had tried it once or twice before, just to know that I could handle it, but found it neither pleasurable nor meaningful. However, now I needed something other than chewing nails to keep my library days on an even keel, and smoking was obviously less harmful than overeating. I did not inhale, and stopped the moment I left Yale.

Once the comps were behind me, I began to search for a dissertation topic, and soon found a truly inspiring one: "The literary representations of the Iphigenia myth through the centuries." I proudly announced my choice to Prof. Kahler, my mentor and fatherly friend, whom I visited in Princeton whenever I could. Mr. Kahler threw his hands up in horror. "Um Gottes Willen!" he exclaimed, "don't even think of it!"—"But why not?" I was totally perplexed. "Isn't it a great topic?"—"Sure," he confirmed, "it is such a great topic that you will still be working at it twenty years from now. Choose something limited and clearly defined, so you can get it done in a year. And pick something Wellek will like, so you won't run into too much trouble. You can write your ambitious books later."

I was both shocked and disappointed by his practicality, and it took me most of the year to come to terms with it. He, of all people, was asking me to compromise, to sell out, and at one of the most prestigious institutions of higher learning! Now I know that it was the best advice I was ever given. It made for an uninspired year, to be sure, but a productive one. Moreover, the choice I made, though under duress, turned out very beneficial, and not only in terms of deadlines.

I had been intrigued, if somewhat uneasily, by Nietzsche's Zarathustra, which seemed to echo Demian—or the other way round—and Demian was still occupying a warm niche in my heart, despite the book's disappointing ending. So I proposed to Mr. Wellek to write about "Nietzsche's literary criticism in its European setting." Predictably, he was delighted.

The complete edition of Nietzsche's works encompasses 23 large volumes which I began to plow through, in addition to consulting the older 20-volume edition, and the four volumes of works and five of letters contained in the Critical Edition. To be sure, the topic was clearly defined, and searching for references to art and artists or esthetics in general could and needed to be done methodically and systematically. But was it limited? That was a matter of interpretation. I quickly realized that, unless I put in eight- to ten-hour workdays, my self-allotted year, probably the last one for which I could get full fellowship support, would be far too short. So I threw myself into the task, did not even think of parties, romances, even just reading for pleasure, and spent little time in our communal living room, which was usually empty anyway. My only social activity was the occasional Sunday dinner, to which I—now alone—was invited by Mrs. Edelmuth. I think she missed Kriton almost as much as I did.

Smoking helped. Having a carrel neighbor, who would invariably lean out of his library stall and look at his watch disapprovingly, no matter how quietly I tiptoed in at nine-fifteen or nine-thirty in the morning, was an even greater incentive. Thus my project progressed. And strangely, though my loyalty did not switch from literature to philosophy, and I found only Nietzsche's poems truly exciting, reading his works cover to cover provided me with a great education, perhaps more so than any course I had taken. His odyssey from juvenile romantic excess to the wonderfully terse and wise epigrams, which reflected a Goethean appreciation of European culture and the "Renaissance Man"; his indefatigable search for meaning; his *amazing visions of cosmic patterns; finally, his ominous return to* Zarathustra, *now not the poet or seeker but the false prophet, who lured him into megalomania and eventually brought on his total mental collapse—didn't all this show me the dangers of "letting go" which I had indulged in, of allowing myself to drift, lacerate my soul and shut out the world around me? Didn't it clearly point to the need for clear and balanced thought instead of losing myself in the chaotic turbulence of feelings? This was the right will to power, power over myself, and over the arrogance of seeing myself as the center of the universe. It was high time I became a citizen of the world, and did so by looking, learning and serving, rather than by indulging in fantasies of how to become a great writer and create a great self.*

Perhaps all this was still immature, even slightly crazy, but it made me feel as if I were finally climbing the ladder out of the chaos toward the light, from juvenility to maturity.

Inspired by Nietzsche's aphorisms and their sparkling buoyancy, and also remembering how my master's thesis had floundered because its tone had become too "Rilkean," i.e., poetic, I now used all the self-discipline I could muster to remain objective and analytical. It was not much fun, but good training for my future career.

* * *

[*undated*]

Visit to Ithaca on Feb. 14, 1956, Valentine's Day. My reconciliation. The sleepy town in the valley with its one shopping street where browsing through its three dime stores was more fun than a whole shopping day in N.H. or N.Y.; its college bus, in front of Rothschild's, always ready to take you up the hill; its friendly salesgirls; the supermarket boy carrying the packages to the cars and cab drivers carrying the suitcases to the door; the hills, the dirty snow and puddles, and glimpses of the sun against 15:1 odds. The feel of the big university on the hill, alien to the town and yet part of it, tolerated much more benevolently than Sarah Lawrence is by snobbish Bronxville or Yale by rowdyish New Haven, or Columbia by indifferent New York. And the little town, nestled between the hills and the lake, and other lakes and hills and sleepy towns nearby, each with its own slightly different outline yet all the same, and people in them happy or unhappy or indifferent, all with more and less cause than myself.

Perspective is the word. It is not a symptom of old age, which should have amassed experiences, have more rather than less perspective. It is a matter of will power and self-discipline, of basic decency and honesty. Decency toward one's own thoughts and emotions and those of others, and honesty inasmuch as not the easiest but the best way is chosen, no allowances made but also no self-punishment inflicted.

This weekend has been good. It has returned Ithaca to me and reminded me that life is rich for whoever can see its riches. Let this be my motto for the day: perspective.

6.

My final year at Yale was spent in a house leased by five of us. 22 George Street had been a physician's residence until his wife died, and he was now renting it out. The house was small and attractive, and it felt luxurious after the cozy decay of Rochdale. Also, it was right downtown, only a few minutes from Yale. Once again I was in luck. Though I barely knew my four housemates to be, we turned out a harmonious group, with just the right amount of distance and togetherness. I had my own room, even though now I didn't really need it.

Phil was studying geology. Tall, thin and laconic, he always did his chores promptly, then withdrew to his room. He was a very good cook, even if his menus consisted mainly of quiches which, despite the French name, were a locally very popular cheese-and-egg dish at the time. He seemed to know infinite variations. I never saw him angry or excited, and he was much more diplomatic than the rest of us, when Nakho had to be lectured to.

Nakho had come from Korea recently, and his English was still minimal, but you probably didn't need much English for physics. It goes without saying that he was not much of a conversationalist. When told what task he had to do or should have done, he invariably responded with a nod and a smile, though it was never clear how much of our explanations or admonishments he understood. It was obvious that at home his mother, sisters, or whoever had taken care of his laundry, his dishes and whatever else he would leave behind. Gradually he got a little better at picking up after himself, though not at doing dishes, so we did them for him and just made him put them away. His smile was so disarming, and his pitiful efforts so well-meant that we stopped scolding him, and accepted him as our clumsy child.

We—that meant Agaath, Georgina and me. Agaath was a tall, pretty and very properly brought-up girl from Holland who introduced us to Dutch cooking, though she also had Phil teach her how to prepare quiches. She vainly tried to flirt with him. Georgie came from New Mexico, which we were reminded of each time she prepared supper. Only after many remonstrations would she serve the chiles and sauces separately, and pour them only on her own food. Sometimes she ate them by the bowlful, while our throats were burning from just watching. I, who had not yet progressed much beyond my wartime Viennese cooking, which meant being as ingenious as I could at turning potatoes into soups, stews or pancakes, whenever I managed to secure an onion or an egg, now tried my best to replicate the vaguely remembered taste of paprika chicken or other delicacies which my grandmother used to prepare. Once I saw carp at the market and triumphantly brought a piece home, glowing at the recollection of my childhood's jellied Christmas Eve carp. But though I meticulously followed the recipe of my 1897 Austro-Hungarian cookbook, which had been my mother's and which I had never relinquished, the fish had a muddy taste and did not evoke the wonderful memories I had counted on. My cohorts bravely ate what I put before them, but then Phil tactfully explained:

"You know, in Europe carp are raised, but here they are scavengers, and people don't buy them much." Agaath was most sympathetic, obviously having good carp memories as well. Nakho just smiled sweetly and said: "Quite good, really." Georgie pulled a face and fetched a slice of bread and her jar of chiles. I decided to find out during my next visit to Aunt Jenny if England had fishponds, so that I could resuscitate my memory.

We were a good team, but none of us drew close to the others. I am not speaking of intimacies, just conversations that would go beyond sharing the time and menu of the day. We must have been too busy with our studies. Perhaps that was good, for it avoided unnecessary complications.

Finding a teaching position turned out to be surprisingly difficult, even with a degree from Yale—another disillusioning discovery! I knew I couldn't earn a living as a writer, but as a teacher not either? There was nothing else I was good at. What would I do?

Yale had a connection to the University of Kansas, and several Yale graduates had found positions there. Kansas did not tempt me, but I applied. A position was also advertised at Ohio Wesleyan, and though I knew nothing about the school except the name, that fact indicated a good reputation. I did not hear from either school for quite a while. Spring was progressing, and I had booked passage for Europe on the Holland-America Line; actually, a colleague of mine, Frank Hirschbach, had offered to include me among the faculty members accompanying his students. This would enable me to get a reduced ticket. All I would have to do was talk German to the students at mealtimes. Wouldn't he be mad if I bowed out at the last minute!

When I shared my worries with Ulo Goldsmith, another colleague, he offered help. "I think the German-Russian Department at the University of Massachusetts needs someone. I'll be up there this weekend. Let me check with Fritz." Fritz Ellert was the chairman and apparently a good friend of Ulo's. Sure enough, when he came back, he suggested I apply. So that's how jobs were found, through connections, even here in the United States, the country of self-made men? Just like in Austria—and I had always hated that practice, the ubiquitous open hand not just in taxis but also from every one of the waiters who served you, one the drinks or water, another your meal, a third took your money. And all this, even though a ser-

vice charge had already been added to the bill! Not to forget the coat-check person if you wanted your coat waiting for you on the counter after the play, and even the elevator operator at the opera; finally, the "token of appreciation" to be handed in advance to the official whom you wanted to provide a document or some information for you. Another illusion gone.

I applied to UMass, as everyone was referring to it then (now locals simply call it "The University"), and was invited for an interview. Fritz picked me up at the train station himself, which impressed me until I realized that the department consisted of only four people. He was cordial and casual, and quickly put me at my ease by pointing out the "sights" along the road, large, covered tobacco barns: wrapping-tobacco was the area's main industry. Though the road was lined with gas stations and small houses between the sheds, and the university consisted of several very uncoordinated buildings, some tall and new, others low and long, and a few looking like private homes of red brick or white clapboard, they all sat in a landscape of fields and woods framed by hills. It was almost like the vacation country of my childhood. I was hoping the department would like me.

I thought it did. Two more men, one German, one American, looked me over discreetly; the one woman in the department, Viennese and of Jewish background, was outgoing and enthusiastic. In fact, she offered to show me around the area after the interview, and I knew immediately that I would like her, and she would help me adjust. All vibes were good, all the more so since I would also be able to teach Russian as needed. But then several weeks passed, and I did not get an offer.

Meanwhile Ohio Wesleyan had sent me an invitation to come for an interview. They explained in a detailed letter the Christian principles and precepts of the school. The letter rubbed me the wrong way and, naïve as I was, I expounded at length that I was Jewish, and though I shared many of the values they were stressing, I did not consider them a Christian monopoly, and was therefore withdrawing my application.

Kansas made me an offer. Their deadline was approaching, and I still had not heard from UMass. When I ran into Ulo again and complained to him, he was greatly surprised. "I thought they had made you an offer," he said. "Let me phone Fritz and check into it." That same evening he called me up: "You have the job! They lost their secretary and haven't got around to writing to you." The procedure seemed a bit strange, but in line with the informality which I associated with the area, and so I shrugged it off.. I was jubilant to be able to concentrate fully on my thesis defense, and on packing for Europe. All was well now—or so I thought.

When I handed my dissertation in for Wellek's final approval, he seemed pleased with it, except for the conclusion. That was weak. I should rewrite it during the summer, then he could schedule the thesis defense as soon as I was ready, and I would still get my degree before the new term started.

Off I went to Europe, this time not only to England but also to Austria—with a briefcase full of papers, notes, and the thesis draft.

The SS-Maasdam was comfortable, the weather good, and I did not get seasick. My mealtime responsibilities as a German prompter turned out pleasant and minimal, and so Lucy, one of my three cabin mates, and I volunteered to give free German lessons. We were immediately enlisted—to work with a group of young Mormons who were heading to Germany for their year of missionary work! Lucy—likewise Jewish—and I looked at each other in mute dismay, but how could we decline?

To our relief, those young Mormons turned out surprisingly nice, even though they were walking around the decks in white shirts, jackets and ties, no matter how hot it was, and usually with bible in hand. As Lucy and I began to work with them, we discovered a very human side of theirs. One morning a young man confessed that he had not done his homework because he had overslept, after a sleepless night. How come, and in German, please! I pieced together that someone had sewn shut the sleeves and pant legs of his pajamas and, with the lights out, it had taken him forever to figure out what was wrong, to remedy it, and take revenge. Revenge? Oh, it was only a pillow fight.

Or the morning when, after raving about the gorgeous sunrises, they promised to wake Lucy and me by pulling from outside our room on a long string which, at their suggestion, we had tied around my pillow. The sunrise wasn't very impressive that day, but it was good to know that these were regular boys, even though they had to give a year of their lives to converting people in another country to polygamy.

My arrival in Guildford was not ideal. A septic foot kept me indoors for four days, and Jenny's worrying irritated me. Then we had it out and hugged, and I was ashamed of my impatience. But reading the newspapers and listening to the radio for four days opened my eyes to England as well as to America. Or so it seemed to me:

[undated]

Seven years ago I had been here, and had loved England, but with the love for an exquisite gem at which one looks once in a while with a faint and unreal desire to possess it. Only America, I had thought, was reality, as it had to be and as it could be lived. Now I suddenly realize how much I had forgotten about deeper life, about culture and esthetic values. As I was submerged into this treasure house of tradition, and saw how meaningful it was and how much of a backbone it gave, I have again become aware of the hard struggle one wages in America against the spirit of novelty, crudeness and ugliness. The best one can do there is transform one's own life into something less average and less meaningless than the surroundings, but it still is a rootless existence based on the nostalgic sense of loss of tradition rather than its presence, on defiance from want, as Nietzsche would say, rather than the carelessness of abundance. And unless the struggle is waged constantly, furiously, it is lost beforehand.

As for England, I now am not sure either whether it is living—though it is definitely alive—too much in the past, clinging to it with the tenacity of despair, or whether it is going through a transitional stage more positively, incorporating the values of the past into a new future. The empire seems to be creaking in all its hinges, little doubt about it. People live painful, hard lives, already more dependent on nature than culture, for the latter has become difficult to afford financially. But perhaps this is a positive phenomenon—provided that the elite that has access to cultural values, is still a truly creative elite. That I of course don't know. But as long as among the rest the zest and desire for art and theater and music persists, the organic link in the cultural structure might be sound and valuable.

That actor I met at the little luncheon place on the Haymarket (assigning other people to your table like they do here can actually be quite nice, though at first I resented it; contrary to the proverbial English reserve, they will usually start a conversation with you), that actor still seemed of the old school, was not giving himself airs but was human and personable. He deplored the going down of the theater because of TV, and was wondering whether the English were going somewhere or just wandering about…It would take much more observing and experiencing to say anything more about this, except that England is undoubtedly in a cultural crisis. Does that mean that what I admire so much here is a phenomenon of the past which cannot be saved into the future? That my complaint is not against a country but against an era?

There had also been IRA bomb explosions in London, and Jenny tried hard to dissuade me from going into the city, even for an afternoon. By the time I got back, she was such a nervous wreck that I stopped going. Luckily, she did not object as strenuously to my day tours on public busses, and I saw some marvelous manor houses—Warwick, with an exhibit of the costumes used for the Masterpiece Theatre show on Henry VIII; Loseley, not far from Guildford; and Petworth House where the deer stood outside the glassed-in verandah and watched us as we were listening to a concert. One weekend Jenny and I took the train to the Isle of Wight for a day's outing. We became so intrigued by its thatched cottages and garden that we spent our last pennies (we counted our resources in a public bathroom!) on a "bed-and-

breakfast," and surreptitiously pocketed a few rolls to sustain us until our return home the next day. Our other weekend together, we took the train to Brighton and inspected the Prince Regent's onion-domed pleasure palace. Jenny was entranced, I found its frivolous exoticism distasteful. Was I becoming a prudish old maid? Or was royalty too alien to me? Jenny, to be sure, was a fervent admirer of the Queen, and did not even seem to resent that she was still only "British" and not "English," after close to twenty years in the country. "Come to America," I offered, "we don't discriminate like that." She would not hear of it.

She did, however, take a two-week vacation, and we traveled together to Austria, first to Vienna—she had not seen her brother, my father, in years—then to Salzburg, the ancient archbishopric and world-famous city of music, finally to Seefeld, an idyllic little village nestling against the Alps. Though I was anxious to see Trude, I was also apprehensive about returning to Vienna, of which I had such bad memories, and about the reunion with my father. On the latter score I did better than Jenny. When he heard that she had almost left her passport on the train, he lectured her on her carelessness, and even though he called her "Janderl," I could see how hurt she was. I, on the other hand, found him so much older than remembered, so much shorter and wearier, that my old resentment evaporated. I merely felt sad and, when Angela kept saying that she would go to America the moment her mother died, truly sorry for him. Trude commented that aging seemed to have done much for him. She was probably right, yet somehow his new mildness and warmth pained me as if it were the warmth of loneliness and the mildness of resignation. It put a lump in my throat. When he took me and Jenny to "his" café at the Hotel Regina, and introduced me to several people as "my daughter, Frau Doktor," I did not correct him, though I had not yet received my degree.

Being in Vienna for the first time since 1947 was even stranger. Most of the burnt-out buildings and rubble heaps were gone, and Father's apartment looked far more comfortable than it did when I left. Though the city had until very recently been occupied by the Allied Powers (the "Staatsvertrag," which restored Austria's independence, had only been signed the year before—incidentally, at the Belvedere Palace!), life in Vienna seemed very much back to normal or, rather, it was as if it had always been normal. But what was normal in this country? The Austrians still saw themselves as "victims," first of Hitler, then of the occupying forces, and they seemed as hypocritical and anti-Semitic as ever. The grocery store around the corner was now of course no longer sporting a sign saying "Juden unerwünscht" [Jews not welcome], but I could barely face its fat owner, when she complimented me on my "for an American" excellent German.

And yet, this city, which I had really never known nor liked, seemed almost breathtakingly beautiful and enticing. In a diary entry, I speak of the "masochistic, painful delight" with which I took in as many of Vienna's sights as I could—

... the *Victoria regia* blooming in violet on its third and last day, the incredible rooms in Schönbrunn, especially the *Millionenzimmer* with old Persian and Indian miniatures on the walls, the urns with all the Habsburg hearts in the little room in the Augustiner church, the *Prunksaal [Great Hall]* of the library in reddish marble with hundreds of gold-and-leather bound books as the background for a Mozart exhibit, the Belvedere gardens, the entrance vestibule of the Upper Belvedere palace with four giants carrying the pillars, the Hall of Grotesques, the huge round hall in the Lower Belvedere which seems to be glorifying war, the Last Judgment with two chained, agonized men enthroned above all others, the Gothic paintings with the guide talking about the trash the Catholic church was teaching, and that other guide in the *Kunsthist. [the main art museum]* who was so proud of the Raphael Madonna as if he had painted it...and the Gloriette and the many gardens, and the hills around Vienna with their old churches and ruined castles, and the public swimming pools in the woods with their view over the entire city, and the people jumping on and off streetcars and hanging onto the steps and getting free rides, and the "Espressos" which have become Viennese—and the magazines on racks in the streetcar — yes, all this is Vienna, all this is a City that lives and conquers. No wonder I got lost in it while I was still thinking I was gaining it...

During my sightseeing frenzy Jenny was playing bridge with Father at his café, and Angela was at home catering to her mother.

Trude and Kurt came to our apartment for afternoon coffee, which to my disappointment was all they had time for. I found Kurt immensely appealing, but was frustrated because there was so little chance for intimacy with Trude. However, seeing her, and seeing her radiant meant a great deal to me.

And then, with Jenny on the train to Seefeld, I was suddenly depressed and melancholy, wondering what I was doing here, though I tried hard to fake excitement since this was Jenny's first real vacation in years. To be sure, Seefeld was lovely—

... the hotel with its sun porch overlooking the sunken meadow and the Baroque chapel with its onion dome, and the trail over the creek where the cars barely made it but never stopped risking, and the slope to the left with trees on top and a few benches and the promise of the view across the lake, and the hidden dusty road on the right with a few roofs giving it away, and the gentle wooded slope of the G'schwandkopf with its chairlift on the far left and another hill on the far right, and straight back the harsh rocky peaks of a high range. And the moon above it, and hundreds of stars. Or clouds and wet grass which gave way under the shoe and squeaked. And Joseph from the Zillertal with his green apron and shiny gold tooth, his good dancing and his need to beat me at ping pong, and our walks together, and few words, only bashful hints that I should stay here and marry him. And the Stubaital with the little train winding its way up and round and round from Innsbruck until it has drilled itself high into the valley, and there has to stop, surrounded by such frightening guards as the Habicht who looks so innocent but then you see the people in little clusters and whispers, and the jeep of the rescue team is all covered, and the young man inside at the police station telling how it happened and how he could not hold her back when she slipped in the sudden snow, and telegrams to the parents in Germany, and the next day a brief notice about the accident in the paper, all because of improper shoes, it was not the mountain's fault, not Tirol's and we want tourists…

Yes, all that was part of it—was Austria which I had almost been tempted to call "home," but which was actually totally alien.

When I almost missed the boat for home, I should have known that trouble was looming ahead. I had arrived in Paris by train the day before, and stored my suitcase at the station to indulge in a bit of sightseeing. When I arrived there the next morning, I found a long line waiting in front of the baggage counter. Another member of my group turned up, and we waited together. The line progressed at a snail's pace so that we got more and more nervous, especially when the two men behind the counter began to argue and ignored the passengers for what seemed an eternity. Sure enough, when we finally had our bags and raced to the platform gate, they closed it in our faces: the boat train had just left!

What now? A kind information officer steered us to another platform, where we could take the regular train an hour later. It would get us to the train station in Le Havre, and if we took a cab, we might just, just catch the boat. She also promised to phone and alert the ship to our mishap.

It was not a relaxed train ride, though the elderly woman in our compartment, whom my minimal French had apparently informed adequately of our predicament, offered her help. Indeed, we had barely pulled into the station when she leaned dangerously far out of the window and shouted for a porter. I don't know what she told or promised him, but he had my companion lower our suitcases out of the window, then we pushed our way to the exit door, and followed him at a trot. He knew how to avoid the crowds, and got us and our bags into a cab.

We emptied our wallets into his hand and raced to the pier, this time pulling out a few dollars for the driver who was quite obviously taking his life—and ours—into his hands.

The boat was still there, the gangplank, totally empty, still lowered, with a steward standing next to it and waving at us to hurry. We had barely set foot on board when the gangplank was raised, and we were moving. Phew!

The voyage was calm and sunlit until the morning when, right after breakfast, the familiar hum of the engines stopped. Suddenly, it was dead quiet. We looked at one another, then tried to corner the nearest uniform to find out what had happened. "What should have happened? Nothing has happened," was the response. "But we are not moving!"—"Of course we are moving, don't worry, everything is fine." Just a few weeks earlier the Andrea Doria had sunk, right outside New York City, and here we were being told that everything was fine!

After endless minutes the engines started up again. Everybody heaved a sigh of relief, until someone shouted: "We have changed direction, we are no longer heading west but south!"

Again no information was forthcoming, only blank faces treating us like idiots. Finally the captain's public announcement: "We are having minor engine trouble and will stop at the Azores for repairs."

I was both relieved and newly anxious. I had rewritten my thesis conclusion at Aunt Jenny's, and thought it now much better. But it had to be typed and approved, then copies of the entire dissertation made, bound and handed in by deadline—and the deadline was three days after my expected return.

We spent two nights in the harbor of Horta on the island of Faial. Every morning and early afternoon we were ferried over to terra firma for a few hours' sightseeing. The island was enchanting, balmy, green and volcanic, with each of the few sidewalks of Horta inlaid with a different mosaic pattern of white, gray and black pebbles; many of the façades of the modest one-story buildings were covered with green tiles.

I walked into a liquor store, though the term "store" hardly applied. A one-room adobe, with door and window openings, a dirt floor, a long counter, behind it shelves with bottles lining the back wall. I didn't really know what to look for. "Brandy?" I asked. He took down a bottle and, when I looked dubious, uncorked it and offered me a sample. It burned my throat, but how could I now say no? I noticed a policeman standing in the door arch and watching, probably to make sure I was treated fairly. The bottle, the man figured out laboriously, would come to four dollars. The next day every shop had a handwritten piece of paper on the counter, giving dollar equivalents for the local escudos. Most of our group stocked up on wine, since you could bring back four bottles, but I was satisfied with my treasure. Much later, a knowledgeable colleague, who was the first to be offered a drink from it, proclaimed it magnificent.

Saturday, Sept. 8, 1956

Four hours ago we raised anchor and left the Azores. Good-bye Fayal with your four palm trees on the main square, your big red blossoms, banana leaves and bamboo stalks, pastel houses, whitewashed houses and green tile houses with shutters and balconies, your lovely sidewalks with their never repeated mosaic patterns, your innumerable shoemakers and wine dealers, your Arabic style churches, all white and black and slim and shiny but closed, your cobblestone or red sand alleys winding and climbing, marred by a few madly racing and honking cars, your windmills against the sky, your many green cultivated cones with their sunken meadow craters, and in the background The Crater, always with a bank of dark clouds above it, almost as dark as those above Pico across the bay, Pico, the master of the Azores, 2800 m high. And the men with wide straw hats and donkeys and bamboo sticks, and men and women with heavy baskets balanced on their heads, covered with sheets and probably holding mackerels and other fish, and women with long black capes with huge, stiff hoods like enormous blinkers, and barefooted skinny children pulling your arm and asking for "mony". And donkeys tied to a landing off main street like in an American Western, and the one canal coming from the sea or perhaps carrying water from the mountains in the rainy season, and the good red sandy road winding its way into the hills and to the villages between corn and bamboo and a few banana gardens, and houses hidden behind big rough stone walls, and cows, calves and flies, and watermelons and fish, and the wine store in the village with the kind old woman whose daughter is "professor" in town and probably teaches nursery school, and the mixture of wine and lemonade which they all drink out of dirty glasses, and a water container probably filled with rainwater which has to last all through the dry season, and incredibly dirty looking liquids and cucumbers, anis and other leaves on dirty shelves in dirty bottles probably turning into magic potions, and old men thrashing with hand flails and asking for a cigarette, and the blue sky with our white ship a little beyond the pier, and small boats busily plying back and forth, and half the town at the pier selling fish, bananas, straw hats, bags and barrels or just watching and talking in their language that sounds so Slav and is Romance.

It was all part of a dream, or perhaps a complete dream, lifted into a sphere totally different from the unpleasant reality of bad weather, a failing screw, a late arrival and therefore an expected mess in New Haven. Instead, a group of islands incredibly simple and pure, heartbreaking in their poverty yet glorified by their aura of beauty and contentment, into which our big white ship—and it was big and white!—broke as both an exciting but also dangerous messenger of a different world which immediately introduced a response of bargaining, begging, perhaps envy. But for us, it was nothing but beauty or, for some, "fun," wild revelry, carousing with all that cheap wine, though even those two words may be too lofty for the crude and styleless doings that would take place not from malice or meanness or morbidity, but from an incredibly naïve and helpless desire to let your hair down, to do the town, to make the most of it all… and, in almost all cases, ended on a note of exhausted satisfaction. Had I ever been like that too?

And then back on board, tired and apathetic, sitting in deckchairs and waiting to travel on, and doubting we would ever leave, and small boats around our big white one, and baskets raised and lowered with goods and money, and some last minute bargaining, more bags and barrels and hats, and big straw casks of cheap wine to get sick on, and the ship loading watermelons and grapes and bananas and fish, and custom and port officials getting off and on again, and a booing reception for three students who arrived almost three hours late, and more boats coming and going, and then, when everyone had stopped, we were suddenly moving past the sunny shoreline with its pastel houses and its onion-roofed churches, and the island's three small peaks began to recede into the distance. We were on our long weary track back to "civilization."

Of course I missed my deadline, even though I talked to the dean till I was blue in the face, about force majeure and grace periods, and my teaching commitment. The best I could get out of him was that I would not have to pay full tuition, but could simply register for another year, and get the degree at the end of that year.

And so I saw Yale once more, in May 1957, coming down from Amherst, which had by then become a real home to me. I found teaching truly fulfilling, and was engaged to a colleague. That there were no classmates in the Commencement line did not seem to matter. I was elated and, as it were, confirmed by the knowledge that I had made it, had received the highest degree available, and from one of the most prestigious institutions of this, my new home country. Of course, there was still much I didn't know, there always would be, but I was striving, and was determined to continue to strive as much as my complicated and quirky self would permit, and I would accept every success most gratefully, and every failure as a lesson to learn from.

Mrs. Edelmuth was at the Commencement ceremony and, thanks to her, I now own a photograph of me in full regalia being embraced by Professor Weigand who is, perhaps for the first time in years, almost smiling.

7.

My dear Liesl, Sept. 8, 1956

    Many thanks for your beautiful postcard from Seefeld, which hasnow arrived. I hope you and your aunt had a few lovely days both there and in Salzburg. Here it has again become very hot; the heat probably reached you only in Paris (among the lakes it would have been easier to bear). Even so, I am glad that you were still able to get hold of a few festival tickets and could breathe in at least some of Salzburg's festival aura. For me that city always has a very special magic, especially at festival time. If the operation goes well and nothing else interferes, we plan to spend part of next year's vacation again in Salzburg.

    How was the trip back? I hope all went well, and you didn't arrive at home too exhausted. There is still so much I would have liked to chat with you about if our time together had not been so short. If the picture you took of me turns out well, be sure to send me a copy!

    Here nothing much has happened since your departure. I have meanwhile received a prospectus about the clinic, and am very pleased to be housed in such an attractive and modern hospital. It was only built three years ago, is excellently equipped, mostly 2- or 3-bed rooms, at most 6 beds. It is pleasant to know that one will be housed attractively—it will ease the naturally extensive recovery period.

    At home I spend my time sewing nice pajamas and nightgowns since they will be my only outfits for several weeks.

    The construction of our house is, to be sure, progressing nicely, but the move will hardly be possible before my surgery. We are counting on completion in two weeks. Then we can spend the remaining two weeks till my departure with successively moving in books, dishes, clothing and linens, and slowly set up things. Unfortunately, I will not be able to participate in the great moment of the real move, but health-wise it is probably better for me that way.

    That's all I can report at this time. My next letter will reach you from Düsseldorf. Write for a change!

        With my best wishes to you—your Trude

* * *

On October 31, a black-rimmed envelope arrived, with Trude's mother as the sender. It contained the following announcement:

[translated]

My dearly beloved wife, my beloved daughter

DR. GERTRUDE MAYER BORN ZECHMEISTER

passed gently away and joined our Lord on 19. October 1956.
Interment will take place on Thursday, 26. October 1956, at 14:15 hours at Ober-St.Veit cemetery after a solemn blessing.

The holy mass will be read on Saturday, the 28. October 1956, at 7:30 in the parish church of the Holy Trinity in Lainz.

Vienna, the 23. October 1956
In deep sorrow

Dr. Ernst Kurt Mayer	Paula Zechmeister
Spouse	mother

in the name of all relatives

* * *

[*The following letter from Trude's mother arrived several months later:*]
[translated]

Dear Frau Dr!

Please forgive me for responding only today to your heartfelt words with regard to the most difficult loss of my life, and to thank you for your genuine sympathy.

I fully understand that you, too, first had to try to cope with the shock which my daughter's passing, unexpected despite everything, inflicted on all of us who were close to her. I therefore also hope that you will understand why I haven't responded to your dear letter sooner—I had to answer stacks of condolence letters, while incapable of a quiet thought—every letter was a new rending of painful wounds. I did want to write to you in greater detail, and to do that I needed to be a little calmer. Kurt had even more letters to respond to, in addition many worries with which he now has to cope by himself since his closest companion is no longer with him. I don't know which of us misses her more.

One thing must console us. The physicians, including the surgeon, were unanimous in their view that Trude, even if the operation had succeeded, could at best have expected one to two years of painful suffering, without any hope for improvement and with an excruciating end. Then it was God's great mercy that he took her to Him without pain and fear of death. According to the doctor's report, she went to sleep with a smile, certain that she would now receive help, and never woke again.

She was spared much suffering, especially the disappointment that, despite the surgery, she could not have recovered since all other organs (lungs, liver etc.) were affected by then.

Yesterday I received the two lovely photos, which gave me great joy. Kurt is at the moment in Klosterneuburg but visits me frequently; he will also be very pleased to get this truly good photo of her. I immediately put mine in a frame, and so Trude is with me again. We do have pictures of her, but none is as good nor in color. I don't know how to thank you for this great joy. Words cannot express it. I also want to transmit Kurt's sincere thanks.

He is very good to me and won't leave me alone in my old age since I have no more relatives here.

The house will most likely be habitable by the end of April or in May; then the road has to be built, and that is supposed to start at the end of this month. Then I will be near Trude's grave and can visit it daily. I hope to be soon with her entirely and for all time, in the Beyond where there are no more tears.

I hope that you, dear Frau Dr., are well, and I will always think of you with love as a truly faithful friend of my beloved daughter.

I am consoled by my faith in God, to whom I found my way in all those worries about Trude. I don't belong to a church, but to the Holy Scriptures and our Messiah Jesus Christ sent by the Lord. Since Trude was likewise reading the Bible during the last weeks and found her way to Him, I am certain that we will see each other again.

With the warmest remembrance be greeted by your

Paula Zechmeister

P.S. I am taking the liberty of sending you a package containing your letters to

Trude, which she kept over the years and was reading over and over. I thought that you might like to have them.

Perhaps I should have kept a copy of the letter I had written to Trude's mother—perhaps it would have consoled me too, at least a little. How I wish I could share their belief in a Beyond, with or without a God, but I can't. My throat still begins to burn every time I read those last two letters. But though I have learned that there is no justice, just as Ivan Karamazov had said, at least not in the situations that matter most—life and death, and innocent suffering—deeply rooted inside me is still the belief, call it superstition if you will, that one must be willing to pay for one's happiness, and can only hope that the payment will not exceed the scope of the happiness, and that the good memories will at least balance the cost.